IMMIGRANT DAUGHTER

stories you never told me

CATHERINE KAPPHAHN

"Sundays" appeared in a slightly different form in The Feminist Press anthology: *This Is the Way We Say Goodbye.*

Typesetting and Cover Design: Kerry Ellis

A CIP record for this book is available from the Library of Congress Cataloging-in-Publication Data.

ISBN: 978-0-578-54502-8

In memory of my parents.

For my boys, Rafael Milan and Radek David,
here is a story about your grandparents—two
ordinary people who led extraordinary lives.

Croatian Pronunciation Key

C, c: ts *ts*ar or ba*ts* (Oriovac)

Ć, ć: ch *ch*eers (Smolčić)

Č, č: ch *ch*ore (Jelačić)

Đ, đ: j *Geo*rgia (Đurđa)

J, j: y *y*awn (Kanjer)

Lj, lj: mi*lli*on (Ljubavi)

Nj, nj: ca*ny*on (Gornji Grad)

Š, š: sh *sh*allow (Anuša)

Ž, ž: zh garage (Ružica)

Contents

IMMIGRANT DAUGHTER

stories you never told me

Marijana Kanjer

1
ORIOVAC

In the back of my journal, I'd written down her address: *Kujnik 5.* I wondered if the house still existed. By now it would have been over a hundred years old. Since Oriovac was so close to the border of Bosnia, it was possible that it had been destroyed during the Croatian War for Independence. Strangely I felt unafraid, as if I were going somewhere familiar. I stared out the train window at the Slavonian landscape in Eastern Croatia; the fields, hills, and church steeples flew past. I was an American woman traveling alone, unable to speak the language, trying to find pieces of my mother.

Kutina, Ilova, Banova Jaruga; each time the train stopped at a station, I read the sign, and then searched my map for the village. With my fingertip, I traced the line from Zagreb to Oriovac, which I had encircled in blue ink. For years, I had been inching toward this elusive village, the place where my mother was born between two World Wars, the place where she spent the first five years of her life, the place I had written about but never actually seen.

Before I'd left New York City, I explained to my friends

that I had to go on this journey before I did anything else in my life. There was something driving me as I scraped the money together for my month-long Croatian odyssey. In 1993, after my mom died, I'd visited Croatia with my father, but it had been too dangerous to travel to her village because of the Croatian and Bosnian wars for independence. Before I left on this trip, Vedran, my unexpected research advisor, a doctor in his fifties with a peppery beard and a wise face, peered over the rim of his glasses and told me with great certainty, "Going to Croatia this time will change you for the rest of your life."

My dad encouraged me to go. "It will help your writing." My husband René, the son of Czech immigrants, a struggling writer, told me, "I know this is a journey you have to make alone." The truth was none of us could afford to travel.

From the window, I gazed at the villages. Goats raised their heads as the train lurched to a stop. I wondered how my grandparents met. Did Katica Smolčić notice the thin man with intense dark eyes at a local dance? Did Anton Kanjer pass her on a dusty road? I assumed that his family moved from Mrkopalj, a village nestled in a valley surrounded by hills in Gorski Kotar, all the way to Slavonia because of the rich farmland. My work, it turned out, was a lot about guessing, imagining, searching for the most likely answers since there was no one left to tell me my mom's story. My mother, only a child when her parents both died of tuberculosis during WWII, may have never known how her parents met. At any rate, by the time Anton and Katica reached their late twenties, on Sunday the 28th of July 1935, they had their first and only child, Marija Kanjer. As soon as she was old enough, she insisted on being called Marijana, and that was the name she went by for the rest of her life.

A warm wind whistled loudly through the open windows. The sound of the engine filled the compartment. Still, I could hear chickens clucking behind me; a few rows back a woman was traveling with them. There was rustling, fluttering, and an occasional squawk. I felt a shift in myself. I experienced calm exhilaration, the sensation of knowing that I was exactly where I was supposed to be, on this train, on this August day. I breathed in the dry air. A sudden faith filled my being. No matter what happened today, I was completing a circle that my mother started long ago.

Lipovljani, Nova Gradiška, Staro Petrovo Selo. I glanced at my map. I was closer than I had ever been. I had to be careful so that I didn't miss it. It could be the next village, or the one after that. Nova Kapela-Batrina. At each station, I kept my eyes fixed on the hanging sign, the name of the village. Sometimes I craned my neck because my compartment didn't stop in a place where I could see it. Most of the people traveling were Slavonians returning to their villages. I watched them get off or climb aboard the train. Clearly I was the only American, and even though I felt different than all of them, I also felt a surprising belonging. I was part of the history of this place even if only one woman connected us.

I felt the movement of the train and waited anxiously. After a while, the train began to slow down; I saw multiple signs saying Oriolik on the wall of several small buildings. It was similar, but it wasn't her village. Then I leaned back and held onto the strap of my backpack. The train picked up speed, and as we passed the tiny station I saw the sign—*Oriovac*—flash by me.

"Oh my God! I missed it!" I said to myself in astonishment. I grabbed my backpack and rushed up the aisle as if I had the power to stop the train. I stammered in English to the conductor, "I, I, I was supposed to get off there. I didn't know. I was supposed to—"

He said something in Croatian to two young women. One

stood up. "Please, may I help?" she asked, separating each word, in a British-Croatian accent.

I nodded frantically. "I missed my stop."

She spoke with the conductor for a moment. I heard the word *vlak*, train, repeated a few times, then she told me I would have to get off at the next stop, wait about 20 minutes, and then another train would come to take me back to Oriovac.

When the train stopped, I climbed down. The young woman followed after me. "Once we leave, you cross to other side," she pointed over the train, "and wait for next train, yes?"

"Yes, yes, thank you, *hvala ljepa*." I nodded obediently. She hopped back on the train and waved. The train left. Behind me there was a tiny abandoned station. The sign said Kuti. I stared down the endless train tracks. A rooster crowed. In less than half an hour, I was supposed to meet my translator, Ivana, in Oriovac. I sighed and walked across to the other side. Unbelievably I had missed my mother's village.

In my mind, I could hear the voice of my Croatian-American friend Courtney telling me, "Don't go walking off any roads or through any fields, there are still mines."

I'd laughed, and then she'd narrowed her eyes in worry.

"No, I'm serious, Catherine, promise me."

Now I looked across the innocently tilled fields beyond the track. The sun was bright and it was too hot to sit on the platform. A man drove by in a tractor. An old woman carried a pail of water from a well to her house. Swallows swooped and chattered. I was the only one waiting. I placed my hand on the top of my brown hair; it was burning hot. Far off in the distance, I saw a train. I squinted and shaded my eyes with my hand. Quickly I slipped on my backpack and bravely stepped forward. The horn blew; the train didn't slow down. Was it going to stop? The horn blared again; clearly it was not stopping. I took a step back as the train roared past; the force sent me tumbling backward into the ditch behind me. I got up and dusted myself off, my heart pounding. "Don't get yourself killed," I told myself.

When the next train came, it approached slowly and sighed to a stop right in front of me. I climbed on with relief. The conductor asked for my ticket. In English, with many hand gestures, I attempted to explain that I missed my stop and needed to go back. He chuckled. I pulled out my wallet, hoping I'd exchanged enough money to pay him and my translator. He shook his hands, "*Ne, ne, ne.*" I paused and looked at him quizzically. And he shook his hands again. I smiled gratefully.

Five or ten minutes later, the train stopped. I got off and stared at the sign in front of the station: Oriovac. Finally.

"Katerine?" asked a petite young woman in her early twenties, in a long bright blue dress.

"Ivana?" I asked back. From a payphone in a Zagreb post office, I had called a Slavonski Brod tourist agency and gotten in contact with Ivana; she had offered to be my translator today.

"Yes! I thought it was you, when the train stopped before," Ivana said happily, in a slightly nasal voice.

"I missed my stop." I smiled sheepishly.

A man with a Clark Gable moustache appeared. He greeted us warmly, and then quickly led us to his car as if he sensed our urgency. Ivana explained to me that she arranged for Zdravko, who had lived in the village all his life, to help us search for the house. In the car, I pulled out my small black photo album with pictures of my mother's family and her house. Ivana and Zdravko scrutinized the black-and-white photograph of the house. They spoke quickly in Croatian. Zdravko shook his head worriedly. We passed a street sign that said Kujnik. My mother's street! Adrenaline rushed through me. Excitedly Zdravko explained in Croatian, while Ivana translated, that since my mom lived here all the numbers on the houses had changed. We would have to ask around. I learned that Oriovac now had three thousand people and twenty-two streets.

We drove past a visibly old house. Paint chipped off the walls. Half of it was a light blue; the other half was light green. I shrugged and told Ivana, "Even if we don't find it, at least I'll know it looked something like that one."

We pulled into someone's dirt driveway along Kujnik Street. Zdravko spoke in rapid-fire Croatian to someone fixing a car. A spry elderly woman pushed open a door and we were led into a kitchen. Her two adult daughters stood quietly in the background, listening intently. I pulled out my small album. At the table, everyone huddled around it, and the old woman held it carefully. She looked at every picture, even the ones that weren't taken in Oriovac. I became familiar with little phrases like, *moja mama, moja baka, moj dido*, my mother, my grandmother, my grandfather, because they repeated them in Croatian, after I said them in English.

The elderly woman shook her head unhappily. She didn't remember ever hearing about my grandparents; she didn't know which house could have been my mother's. Zdravko responded quickly as if he were determined to not let this setback stop us.

Soon he drove us to another house on Kujnik Street. We stepped into the garden by the side of the house. An old woman sat on a stool outside beneath the shade of a tree. She wore a black knee-length skirt, a black blouse, and her hair was covered with a black scarf. She heaved her body up. Wrinkles lined every inch of her face. Her lips sank in; she had no teeth. Her middle-aged daughter stepped from the house with a curious expression in her eyes. While Ivana and Zdravko explained who I was in Croatian, I started to understand bits and pieces, *mama rođena u Slavoniji*—mother was born in Slavonia, *mama je umrla*—mother is dead. I heard my grandparents' last names, Kanjer and Smolčić every few words. As I was growing up, my mom rarely mentioned her parents; before her death, I couldn't have pointed out where Oriovac was located on a map. I didn't even realize that when my mom called me "Katie," it was an echo of her mother's name, Katica. Now that I was actually in my mom's birth village, I realized these names belonged to me; I was the only one who remained to care for their memories. The middle-aged woman smiled; her lips pressed together; her eyes softened as she looked at me. The old woman reached her hands for the photograph album. Standing, she turned each page slowly, studying each picture as if it were meaningful to her. I felt an ache in my chest.

The old woman raised her watery eyes, and told Ivana in Croatian that she was sorry. She wished I had come three years ago when there were a few *really* old people still alive, ones who might have remembered my grandparents. She glanced at the photo of the house again. She asked if I had any brothers and sisters? Any Croatian relatives? No one? She was the first Smolčić that I had ever met.

It was my maternal grandmother's maiden name. Because my grandparents left this village around 1940 to move to Zagreb, and they both died there, Katica in 1943 and Anton in 1945, I would never know if I were somehow related to this woman. "Ivana, thank her for trying." Before any of my words were translated, the old woman took two steps toward me. Her withered hands stretched out; she firmly cupped my cheeks, leaned forward, and kissed me with her dry lips.

Zdravko bustled us off into the car again. We drove a few houses down, back to the half-blue and half-green painted house. We entered the neighbor's dining room. A husband, wife, and their little boy were eating lunch. They stood up. They discussed something with Zdravko and kept repeating *Kanjer*.

A few moments later we were outside, walking in front of the half-blue, half-green house. Zdravko turned and looked carefully at the photograph then back at the house. He motioned me over. We stood in the shade beside the road. A small car roared by. I stared at the black-and-white photograph that I'd looked at so many times in my New York City apartment. I saw Anton, my grandfather, standing in front of the white-paned window. My mom's grandma, Baka stood in the open doorway. I had imagined being here in this village; I had imagined knocking on doors, hoping someone would help me.

"Katarina, *gledaj*," Zdravko said and pointed at one chimney in the photo, and then pointed to the chimney on the roof in front of us. He pointed at another chimney farther back in the photo, and then pointed to the next one on the roof in front of us. He pointed at each window in the photo and matched them to the house in front of us. He pointed to the door in the photo, and then at the one in front of us. He matched each house detail to the photo and then he grinned.

I blinked. "Is this it? My mom's house?"

He nodded, happily.

I stared at the photo and then at the house. They were one and the same. The hairs on my arms rose. Ivana came up behind us; she threw her arms around me and said, "This is your mother's house! We found it! I can't believe we found it. I was worried we wouldn't find anything."

We wandered through the house, which Zdravko had discovered had two owners, each owning half. No one lived here anymore. One half was used for storage; containers full of grain were organized in neat stacks. Ivana and I climbed a ladder and peered into the attic. We went outside and entered the other half of the house. Paint was chipping from the walls. It was filled with old unwanted things: a scythe hanging on the wall, a broken dresser in a corner, a bicycle lying on its side on the floor, a tapestry of the crucifixion on another wall. "My granny has one just like that," Ivana told me.

I stood there in silence for a moment, remembering. I could imagine my mom sleeping on piles of blankets, on the ceramic-tiled, flat-topped brick oven. "The warmest place in the house," my mom had told me. The bricks retained heat deep into the night. My mom, little Marijana, would rest her head on a pillow, nestling beneath a goose-down comforter, rubbing her stocking feet against each other. Katica would kiss her forehead, tickle her daughter's belly, shake her head slowly from side to side, saying in a sing-song voice, "*Ti si mala, mala, mala. Ti si mala, mala, mala.*" My little, little, little one. My little, little, little one. The same words Marijana would one day say to her own baby.

I scanned the walls and floor. Something caught my eye, a sled with metal runners lying on the ground. A sled like the one Anton once lovingly made his daughter Marijana. It couldn't possibly be the one her father made her, yet it felt as if she were giving me a sign, as if she were whispering, *Catherine, my darling, this is the house.*

Ivana, Zdravko, and I stood outside, marveling at our discovery. Two neighborhood women crossed the street in order to ask us questions. One of them was tall and slender, she spoke a little English. "I knew this was the one you were looking for!" News traveled fast. She clapped her hands together. She lived across the street with her family. Quickly she invited us in her home to escape the heat. A wooden cross hung on the white wall of her kitchen. She gave me a glass of *sok*, fruit juice, and I watched Ivana, Zdravko, and the woman speak Croatian in raised voices, gesturing their arms in the air. So Croatian, I thought to myself, smiling.

The woman's two tall, graceful, teenage daughters appeared. They led me outside and introduced me to their goats and new litter of kittens. We sat on the ground, and as the kittens pounced on our toes, the sisters told me how they hid in the basement during the war, and how they covered their ears during the bombings. "I was afraid. It was so loud," one of them said to me. They had experienced the brutality of war as my mother did in her childhood.

Before I left, the entire family came out onto the porch. They discussed how the priest was away so I would be unable to go through the town records, to look through the pages of births, marriages, and deaths. They promised to look for me. And months after I arrive home, when they go through the church records themselves, they would write to me that their grandmother Anka Lalić was my mother's godmother.

Ivana and Zdravko drove me to the cemetery on the hillside, and we searched the headstones for names. There weren't any Kanjers or Smolčićes. We drove to Zdravko's house beside the village's school. His three children, eight, ten, and eleven, one boy and two girls, hid from me. I caught sight of them, peeking behind the couch, peering through a crack in the doorway. Soon Zdravko's wife served freshly baked pastries as Ivana and I watched videos of them dancing in the traditional costumes in Slavonian festivals. Their son climbed up the doorframe like Spiderman, showing off for me.

All the grown-ups piled into the car, and we headed to the church. I stood across the street and wondered if this was the place where my grandparents married. I imagined my great-grandmother Marija Jakovac, Baka, walking through the doors for mass. A small elderly nun, dressed in a black robe and a habit, unlocked the gates and we followed her in. Right hand, I reminded myself as I dipped my fingertips in the holy water and crossed myself. I had not grown up Roman Catholic like my mom. Zdravko's wife, who spoke no English, communicated with me by repeating certain Croatian words, using sign language, pointing, gesturing, this was where people confessed their sins; she held her hands together in prayer and bowed her head.

Before we left, I tugged on Ivana's sleeve and whispered, "Do you think we'll still have time to go to the Sava River before my train leaves?"

"Yes, that's where we will go next."

We drove across the train tracks, through another village. After we parked, we walked past a bombed-out stone church and a wandering cow. Then, for the first time in my life, I saw the Sava River. I felt pain and beauty circle my chest. The only childhood memory that my mom had shared with me took place here. The Sava was much wider than I had imagined, and on this particular day it was smooth and calm. Ivana informed me that the Sava could rise quickly and had a strong current. The four of us scrambled down the bank and sat on a small wooden pier. Instinctively, I began to pull off my sandals and then hesitated. "Is it okay?" I asked, slightly embarrassed.

"Why not?" she waved her hand at me as if I were being silly. Ivana squatted beside me, her dress hung over her knees. I sat on the edge of the wooden dock and slipped my bare feet into the water. I'd been waiting for this. The temperature of the water was perfect. I had the impulse to jump in and swim. I sighed contentedly, swinging my legs back and forth through the water, laughing. It felt as if I were being baptized by history.

Zdravko grinned at me. I noticed that he'd already kicked off his sandals. He sat beside me, dipping his feet in the water. Zdravko's wife chatted with us, while Ivana translated. Across the river was Bosnia. Serbs stood on the banks fishing. Behind them was a village; I could see the spire of a mosque. The Bosnian hills became cobalt as the sun set. Ivana explained that the Serbs lived in the village across the river, and that the Croatians from this side used to have vineyards over there. I asked if they were ever able to go back to their vineyards. Zdravko and his wife shook their heads, *Ne*.

A lanky boy, about twelve, stood beside us on the pier. He dove into the river. We watched him swim, his feet kicking, splashing, his arms crawling forward, freestyle. When he got to the middle of the river, he stood up. The placid water reached his rib cage. He turned around and swam back to the Croatian shore.

Zdravko said a few words in Croatian; his eyes grew bright. Ivana translated. She said he had imagined what it must have been like for me to have traveled all this way to my mother's village to find her house. His wife patted his arm tenderly. I gazed downward, moving my feet back and forth through the still waters of the Sava.

2

THE SAVA

Swallows darted and dipped beneath the eaves of the red-tiled roof as Marijana scampered out the doorway. She slipped her small hand into her father's as they walked down Kujnik Street through the village of Oriovac. As they passed by the village church, she gazed at the high steeple. Here she went to mass with her family each week. Even at five, she was accustomed to the stillness inside. She learned to daydream, letting the priest's voice carry her to different places as she stared at the hanging chandelier or the statues of saints perched along the walls. She remembered to repeat after the priest, *Gospodine, smiluj se. Lord have mercy. Kriste, smiluj se. Christ have mercy. Gospodine, smiluj se. Lord, have mercy.*

She skipped ahead of her father on the empty road as they passed cornfields, plum orchards, and grazing cows. Wildflowers fluttered in the wind. They walked away from the hills behind their village and headed toward the Sava River. Dogs barked in the distance. Marijana gripped her father's hand as she looked up at the wide-horned ox lumbering past, pulling a cart. Slowly, peasants made their way across golden fields, rhythmically swinging scythes. Beside a whitewashed house, a woman with a red scarf hung up her laundry to dry, and a granny shuffled around, flinging grain into the air as the hens scrambled about her feet.

Marijana daydreamed about her own kitchen. Sometimes a stray hen wandered into the house, and she was delighted to discover a warm egg by the stove. Her Bakica, her grandmother, would shoo, shoo, shoo the hen out the door, then she'd lift Marijana up onto a chair. Soon a plate with a piece of crusty bread and slices of *pršut* appeared in front of her. "Eat, eat, my little one or you'll become a sparrow," her Bakica would say.

A wagon rattled past; empty milk cans clinked against each other. Marijana smiled at the sound, glancing up at her Tata. "Look, Marijana," he said pointing to an enormous pig in a stone enclosure. Her grandmother had told her that Slavonia had the fattest pigs in all the land. Now she asked, "Tata, is it true?"

"Yes, of course it is. My little Marijana, your Baka has never told a lie," her father said.

She thought of Christmas time when she watched her grandmother, a small robust woman, carry a bucket of fresh blood from the slaughtered pig into the house. Her mother tenderly held the fragile intestine as she rinsed it with water from the well. The wood shifted and crackled in the stove. Marijana's mouth watered as she thought of the salty smell of *krvavice*, blood sausages, sizzling in a skillet.

Once they reached the Sava River, she wandered down to the bank. Bees buzzed around flowers. Black birds perched on the branches of oak trees. She stared at the placid river. A silvery fish flung itself upward, arching through the air until it splashed back down into the water; she clapped her hands together in delight. On the opposite side of the wide river there was another village, and behind that village lay the mountains of Bosnia. Men fished on the opposite bank; women washed clothes over wet stones. She heard the faint murmur of their voices, but she could not hear their words.

She cupped her hands and dipped them into the river. The water was surprisingly warm. She smiled and glanced up to see Tata speaking to another man. They leaned against the stone wall. She sat down, slipped off her shoes, and set them carefully, side by side, on the bank. Mama had taught her to always take off her shoes, when she entered the house. She brushed the tips of her toes over the surface of the water and then allowed her bare feet to sink in, so that she could feel the tug of the current. She gazed at the blueness of the mountains on the other side. Laughing, she lifted her skirt, reached her legs down, and felt the muddy bank with her toes. She leaned in until the water hit above her knees, until the edge of her skirt grew wet. The shadow of a bird glided across the river. She caught her breath as she saw a black stork overhead. Its long scarlet legs extended backwards; its enormous black wings were outstretched.

His daughter, playing beside him a moment ago, was nowhere to be seen. He walked alongside the river, his dark eyes scanning the banks. Peasant women washed clothes in the distance; men fished across the river. He could hear one man laughing at another's jokes.

She couldn't have gone far. "Marijana?" he called; his voice sounded unfamiliar. Surely she was just out of sight. He stepped forward, nearly tripping upon the small shoes. They were placed together, facing the Sava River. He couldn't move as he stared at them, bewildered. His daughter's small shoes. He scooped them up and held them, pressing them against his racing heart. The water was completely still. Deceivingly smooth, he thought. Everyone knew there was a strong undercurrent. Villagers joked that she was a moody river. In a moment's time she could rise or fall. He took a few abrupt steps forward, splashing into the water. He felt the current. "Marijana!" he shouted, "Marijana!"

She smoothed a wisp of hair, which had slipped out from her braids, behind her ear. She scratched her eyebrow and took small steady steps. Her dust-covered feet were now scratched, but she didn't feel them. She only felt the need to move forward, to see what was ahead. The Slavonian sun was still bright when Marijana past an apricot tree with ripe fruit dangling from its branches. This made her think of her Mama's apricot preserves, which she had on warm bread each morning.

With every step, Marijana saw something unexpected, something she hadn't noticed before. A kitten ran across the road, pausing to stare at her; its black paw raised. Marijana squatted and rubbed her fingertips together. "*Mic, mic, mic*," she sing-songed to the kitty, who took a few cautious steps toward her, before scampering off into a field.

Katica was surprised to see the silhouette of her daughter standing in the doorway. For an instant, she admired Marijana. It had taken a long time. For some reason, the pregnancy wouldn't come. The women in the village tried giving advice, old wives' tales that she didn't believe. But finally, by the time she was twenty-nine, she had given birth on the kitchen table like all the other women in the village. She sensed that Marijana would be her only child, though she wished there would be more, God willing. She stared gratefully at Marijana in the doorway.

She admired her daughter's green eyes and thick braids. Daylight rested on her shoulders as she stepped into the cool darkness of the house. She was barefoot, and dusty; there was a streak of mud across her cheek. She pushed the heavy wooden door shut with her grandmother's help, and explained that she'd forgotten her shoes by the river. She'd seen a stork, its wings spread, coasting over the water. She stretched out her arms to show her mother. She boasted how she'd walked home all by herself. "Mama, I may be little, but I know the way!"

Katica asked about Tata. Was he following her? Had he stopped to check on the animals? Confusion flew over Marijana's face, and then she lowered her chin with shame and said, "Mama, I forgot him by the river." Her grandmother slipped her shawl over her shoulders and headed outside to search for him.

As the sun began to set, Katica lit the petroleum lamp in the kitchen. A mirror behind the lamp reflected the light into the room. The flame flickered; shadows danced on the white walls. She unbraided Marijana's hair, smoothing out the waves with her hands. Marijana climbed on her mother's lap and rested the side of her head against her chest. From time to time Marijana raised her head to glance at her mother's long face. Katica stared at the closed door. A breeze lifted the thin lace curtains.

Anton entered the house calling his wife's name, "Katica, Katica..." wanting to explain. He was frantic and white-faced. Then he caught sight of his daughter. He couldn't speak. Her bare feet. "Your shoes," his voice broke. The shoes tumbled onto the floorboards, scattering in different directions. He knelt down and crossed himself quickly as though he were in church. Marijana rushed to him and threw her arms around his neck. He lifted her and embraced her tightly. Relief swept over him only after he felt the full weight of her small body, as he felt her breathe.

3

LIMA

"Catherine, are you ready for more?" my mom called out from the kitchen.

"Yeah," I yelled from the bathtub.

With both hands, she carried a large metal pot of just-boiled water around the corner and through the hallway of their rented San Isidro apartment. I placed the international edition of *Time Magazine* on the ledge of the tub. "Thanks, Mom," I said as I bent my knees toward my chest. Slowly, she tipped the pot and hot water poured into the opposite end of the tub. "Okay?" she checked, looking at me, pausing. I nodded as the warm water drifted around my naked body.

It was a relief to be home, even though this was an unfamiliar one. In the late 1980s, my parents and I had been living on separate continents, communicating through letters, when there wasn't a postal strike, or the occasional phone call, when I would stand in a red London phone booth and wait for the operator to put through my call to Lima on a crackly line. After a year at a Midwestern college, I'd quit. In the library, I'd discovered that I could get a temporary work visa for England, so I sold my used car and paid for a plane ticket. For the past eight months, I'd been living and working as a waitress in London. While I was overseas, my dad had finally found another job, and they'd moved from Colorado to Peru, where we had lived years ago when I was a little girl.

In Peru there were blackouts and sometimes no water. Today there wasn't any hot water. The Maoist *Sendero Luminoso* (Shining Path) guerrillas often bombed the pylons that brought power from the Andes to Lima. "Everything is so complicated here," my mom said, sitting on the toilet seat beside the tub, talking with me.

"Everything is complicated everywhere," I said, splashing the water with my hands like my mom sometimes would do. For me, at the age of nineteen, this was an adventure. For my mom it was traumatic. She had lived without running water and electricity, but I was unaware of that then.

Peru had changed drastically since we last lived here. It was too dangerous to leave the city and travel to the Andes like we once did when I was five. During my final month in London I was desperate to make travel plans to see my parents again, but my mom attempted to dissuade me from coming to Lima. She described how the terrorists were throwing bombs through open car windows, kidnapping and killing tourists in the Andes, and killing innocent peasants in the countryside.

I told her fiercely that I was coming whether she wanted me to or not.

Now as I lounged in the bathtub, she finally confessed that she'd been living for the day I arrived. "You know how much we love you. It's only I worried so much about the situation here. So, you think you're getting used to it?" she asked.

She was recalling my second night here. My parents had taken their now-grown-up daughter for a drink at a hotel in Miraflores; they wanted to celebrate my arrival. In the elevator,

I stood between them. My European mom in her chic navy-striped blouse, sleek black pants and high-heeled shoes. She was slim with shapely hips. Her thick short, brown-layered hair curled about her round face. She wore red lipstick, and I could smell a hint of her Estee Lauder Aliage cologne. She looked slightly pale, a little tired, but otherwise happy. My slender father looked down at us. At six-foot-five, he was my beacon in crowded places. He leaned against his stronger leg. Before I was born, when he was in his early thirties, he had contracted polio and now he walked with a limp. I looked at my dad's long boyish face. His easygoing manner always made him seem hopeful. He was our family's optimist.

A waiter, with a black bow tie, placed three Pisco Sours on the white tablecloth in front of us. Pisco brandy, sugar, crushed ice with lime juice topped with whipped egg whites went down smooth, but then, my dad told me smiling, his dimples appearing, "It really hits you when you stand up." The three of us laughed.

As we sat at the round table beside a window that overlooked the lights of Lima, a thousand thoughts hit me; I was trying to absorb the newness of everything; I was struggling to express how my London experiences had transformed me, what it felt like to be alone in another country, the wonder of it and the despair of having to build a life from scratch, of trying to support yourself with no family nearby. I'd hoped to study acting, but it took all my energy to support myself. I only managed to waitress and travel a little. My parents had started over in a new country so many times, and now I understood how painful it could be.

While I was living in London, my parents had moved. After being out of work for two years during the big drop in oil prices, my father, a geophysicist, was finally offered a consulting job for the Peruvian national oil company. They sold our Colorado house; they sold and gave away all our furniture, our plates, our beds, our books, our records, and then they packed ten suitcases, and boarded a plane for South America.

My mom reassured my dad, "I don't get attached to places." But suddenly, it felt as if they were starting over again. When they sat on the edge of their hotel bed together, staring at all their earthly belongings, she lowered her face into her hands and wept.

As I sat sipping my Pisco Sour, I thought about how most Americans my age were attending college, and now I had lost the stability of school. Because my dad had been out of work for a while, I quickly grasped that we simply could not afford college. Since I felt the strong pull to go out into the world, I moved to London to work, travel and experience *real life*.

There I worked full time at a vegetarian restaurant behind Oxford Circus, on Marshall Street, the birthplace of William Blake. One afternoon, I sat on a long wooden bench in an empty St. Paul's Cathedral, reading my parents' letter. The dry, sweet, woody incense floated into the cavernous space. It had been three weeks since I last heard from them. I was worried. Their letter had been confiscated by the British mail service perhaps because it was from Peru; it was checked for drugs, I imagined. Now my fingertips touched the delicate onion-skinned paper; I held onto their familiar handwriting. My father's was nearly a straight line with tiny bumps for letters; in contrast, mother's elegant curves appeared artistic and emotional. She wrote, "*Katie, I wonder how you are. You never complained much but it must not have been too easy to do all those things on your own, look for work, places to live. We are very proud of you. I am also glad you like it there. I wonder if the kids there like to go to the States. Sweetheart, keep in touch even if you write just a few words. We will keep writing.*"

I had never been so far away from them. Of course, I'd been eager to escape the United States, to try things in a different country, but imagining one's life *alone* is quite different from actually living *alone*. After my work visa expired, I wanted to go home to my parents, wherever that might be.

At the hotel bar in Lima, sitting between my mom and dad, I wondered how long they would live here and I wondered how long I would stay. I wondered about my life. My mom put her arm around me. She said, "You'll learn some Spanish again, you'll go to ballet class with me...."

I nodded.

My dad gently patted my shoulder, and said, "Katie, don't worry. Things will work out. Things take time. You just got here."

On the outskirts of the city, we drove around until we found the street where we had once lived, *Calle Jacarandá* in Camacho de Monterrico. When I was a child, we had rented a white, flat-topped, ranch-style house with a green lawn, bordered with red geraniums on this street. My dad pulled the car over and the three of us sat there, staring at the place where we had lived over thirteen years ago.

"You lost your first tooth here," my dad reminded me, smiling.

From the back seat, the past flashed before me: I was four years old, and my mom lifted me up; my arms wrapped tightly around her neck; my legs wrapped tightly around her waist. I was not going to let go. She and my father were going to a work dinner party. They were saying goodbye to me in front of the house. My first separation. The babysitter tugged me away; I screamed and clung onto my mom until I could hold on no more.

Later that night my mom called to check on me. The

babysitter told her that I had gone straight to my room, slammed the door, and stayed there for the rest of the night, without speaking a word.

One day at that same house the earth rumbled beneath my bare feet. I bounced in my mom's arms as she ran outside. Wide-eyed, I watched as the front yard rolled like ocean waves; our car slid up and down the driveway. From our front door, my mom desperately screamed out, "Dave!" When the shaking finally stopped, we rushed in, climbing over fallen books and furniture. We found my dad, white faced, leaning in the kitchen doorway. "I couldn't get out in time," he told us. The earthquake had registered a magnitude of 8.1.

One afternoon in that same Lima house, a hummingbird flew into the glass of the bedroom window. Bang. We ran to see what happened. My mom took care of him until his royal-blue chest became steady with breath. He took refuge in the safety of our enclosed courtyard. My dad constructed a feeder for him. The three of us took great pleasure in watching him. His tiny iridescent head and long dainty beak moved from flower to flower. His blurry wings suspended his tiny body in stillness.

When I lived in London, my mom had written me, *Katie, I miss you awfully and I wish you were here. I know you could cheer me up. Sometimes I get depressed. Your letters mean so much to us. You are the most important person in this world.*

After I arrived in Lima, my mom's depression lifted. My dad took our only car to work. While he mapped the layers of Peruvian earth, searching for oil, we walked, sometimes all the way to Miraflores, over an hour away, where we had avocado salads at Vivaldi's, and bought a loaf of bread at the bakery on the way home. We stuck our hands in the paper bag and broke off pieces. My mom ate the heel of the loaf, and I let the warm dough melt in my mouth. She told me how her grandmother would send her to buy bread when she was a girl in Zagreb, and by the time she got home, the bread was half gone. "It smelled so good, I couldn't resist," she said grinning. She'd rarely spoken of her family with me; I was intrigued.

"You remind me of her sometimes," she said wistfully.

"Your grandmother?"

She nodded, and added, "Sometimes, the expression in your eyes. She was strong like you, Katie, and had common sense just like you." She reached out and gently poked at my stomach, tickling me. I laughed and threw one arm over her shoulder.

A nearby Catholic college offered adult Spanish classes, and I enrolled there. I started mid-semester and felt shy. My fellow students were from China and Israel; they were young wives who had moved to Lima with their professional husbands. Each night, I sat at the dining room table with my blue-photocopied textbook and studied, making my dad quiz me when he got home from work. It had always been a struggle for me to learn new things. Throughout school, I had attempted to learn and relearn Spanish a couple times, and French once, but couldn't keep up after the teacher moved beyond the basics. I couldn't understand how my parents picked up languages easily and I struggled so much. Here in this new place, I tried again. As a little girl, I'd spoken Spanish fluently, but when we moved to another country, I'd forgotten everything. Both my parents were fluent Spanish speakers. They had met and married in Caracas, Venezuela, and lived in Spain for years before I was born. The first year of their marriage, they spoke only Spanish.

Expressions quickly slipped into my head: *¡Qué horror!* How horrible! *¡Qué frío!* It's cold! *¡No te creo!* I don't believe you! Then words like *apagón*, blackout after the *Sendero Luminoso* blew up electricity towers. I repeated Peruvian jokes, "*No hay luz, no hay agua, no hay nada.*" There's no light, there's no water, there's nothing.

As my mom and I walked to ballet class, my brown hair pinned in a bun, I practiced rolling my Rs. "Do it again," I urged my mom, listening carefully, watching her tongue.

"*¡Qué rrrrrrico!*" she said, tilting her head back when she finished. Her green eyes flashed, then she added, "It's just at the top of your mouth."

"*¡Qué arico! ar, ar, ar, ar….*" I made weak attempts, my tongue refused to flutter.

"Daddy can't do it either," my mom said, shrugging.

"*ar, ar, ar, ar*…. You can do it just because you speak Croatian," I protested.

"Try rrrrruffles have rrrridges," my mom teased, rolling her r's perfectly.

I laughed and tried again, "Ruffles have aridges."

As we approached the judge's house, we grew silent. Military trucks were parked in front. Young men in black boots and camouflaged army uniforms had machine guns slung casually over their shoulders. They leaned against the trucks; they smoked and played cards. As we passed, they whistled low; they cat-called and laughed. My heart beat harder. My mother ignored them. She held her head up high and kept walking.

In Lima, for the first time I began to see that my mother wasn't just my mother. She was a woman separate from me with a history that I didn't know at all. Perhaps I saw her differently because I had spent the last seven months without her, or at nineteen, I was becoming a woman myself.

From early childhood, I understood that my mother's biggest fear in life was to lose me. She once told a close friend, "If your daughter died, at least you have your other children, but if I lost Catherine, I would lose everything. I would die."

I was her last blood relative; she was the last woman in my family. My mother's history was faintly drawn in my mind. I knew no details other than she had suffered during her childhood. I understood a few basic facts: as a little girl, she lost her mother and her father, and then her grandmother died when she was a young woman. When I was a little girl, her aunt and uncle, her last relatives, also died. My mom was completely alone except for us.

My mom had survived war, illness, communism, and immigration, but what did I know of it? As a girl, I'd discovered *The Diary of Anne Frank* on my own, and more recently, I had traveled from London to Amsterdam and climbed up the steep wooden stairs to see where Anne and her family had hidden. Judith Kerr's autobiographical novel *When Hitler Stole Pink Rabbit* had also found its way into my Colorado girlhood hands, showing me what it meant to escape a country on the brink of war, what it meant to leave everything you know and love behind, to continually reinvent yourself in new places in new languages.

As a family, we were also captivated by a television series where British officers defused unexploded bombs in 1940s England. At the time though, strangely, I never connected these stories with my mom or her family. She never once spoke about wartime Zagreb to me. When I graduated from high school, a British film called *Hope and Glory* crossed our paths. My mom and I were both drawn to the story of a boy and his family's experiences during the London Blitz. During one scene, the boy and his friends climb over the rubble after a recent bombing. And at that moment, my mom turned to me and said, "That's how I used to play."

Many years after her death, I realized that we spoke to each other in half-truths in order to protect each other. I wanted my independence. I wanted her to stop worrying about me, and she made certain to keep her history beyond my reach.

Once while crossing a busy street in San Isidro, I lagged ten steps behind my mom, daydreaming. Brakes screeched. I glanced up to see a black SUV less than an inch away from my body. I held my breath. Frozen. The driver stared at me. I stared back until I heard a loud metal whack. My shoulders shot up. I saw my mom's fist on the hood of the car. In Spanish, she shouted furiously at the driver. He stayed inside his car, his eyes wide with fear. She took my hand and led me away, declaring that Peruvian drivers were crazy. Suddenly I felt admiration for her fierce protectiveness of me.

When we visited other families, I noticed that adult Peruvian children were physically affectionate with their parents, leaning against them, holding their hands, hooking arms in a way that I hadn't experienced in the States. Here a strong physical language connected people. My mom had always been that way with me, and suddenly it felt natural to throw my arms around her whenever I wanted, to take her hand in mine, to lean against her. In South America, I liberated the part of myself that might have felt self-conscious in the States. This was part of my mom's Croatian character and part of my own character, and it was something that made us not-quite American.

I began to regret how, during my teenage years, I had pushed my mom away with a certain degree of coldness. I couldn't wait to leave home and go to an out-of-state college, where I soon flooded my parents with letters and phone calls. I felt miserable without them. After I left, my mom couldn't bear to enter my bedroom. When she finally did open the door, she sat on the edge of my bed and cried.

I always understood that my mom was different than American mothers in my neighborhood. In Colorado, my mother's friends would tell me with admiration, "Your mom… she's so real." And I understood what they meant, she had dignity, but there was also an underlying rawness to her.

My friends also noticed her accent. "It's so exotic!" But I didn't hear it really. She wasn't a foreigner to me. When she would answer the phone and speak to a stranger, only then would I hear her Croatian accent emerge.

My mom was an artist who spent months on a portrait, only to give it away. When she took a hot bath in the evening, she'd have a glass of red wine on the ledge beside her. She could hold a grudge for a really long time. When we were in an argument, sometimes she'd bring up something I'd done to upset her years ago. She didn't like to share her clothes. At the same time, she would do anything to help me. When schoolwork was crashing down upon me, she'd let me stay home. We'd spend the day on her bed, with my papers sprawled out, as she helped me catch up. She knew how to stop time for me. And strangely she wasn't disappointed when I brought home below-average grades.

She was a woman who was intensely private. She preferred the company of her husband and daughter to anyone else. "Your mother isn't one for small talk," my dad reminded me. She avoided parties and didn't join any groups or clubs. She wasn't a social person or a traditional mom, at least not in a PTA, suburban-backyard-barbecue sort of way. And there were times, I suppose, when I wished she were. Yet my rebellious nature appreciated the fact that she didn't have the ability to conform. It was impossible for my mom to pretend to be someone she was not.

One afternoon, after she had left to do errands, my mom rushed back into the apartment. "Katie, do you have any clothes you want to give away?" she asked, her voice rising in panic. A woman from the Andes, carrying her baby, approached my mom in the park. "*Señora, por favor*," she begged, trying to push her baby into my mom's arms. The woman didn't have money for clothes or food. "I can't, I can't," my mom tried to explain to her. My mom told her to wait there and promised to come back.

I went through my drawers, and we quickly filled a bag with clothes; my mom went to the kitchen to find food to give her. My mom kept saying to me, "I don't know how you could give away your own child."

"Maybe she feels like she doesn't have a choice, like that's the way for her baby to survive..." I told her.

My mom picked up the large bag and went to the front door. She paused for a moment and turned to look at me; her eyes filled with despair. She could not conceive of abandoning her family, yet she understood something about the desperation that woman felt.

"Go, go, before she disappears," I urged, nudging her forward.

"Thank you, Katie," she said, and I closed the door behind her.

In Lima, I spent some afternoons sprawled on my bed or the couch, or stretched on the floor, or sitting at the kitchen table, reading. There weren't distractions or interruptions. Hours could be spent within the world of a novel. My mother encouraged me to read Chekhov, Dostoyevsky, and Tolstoy, whom she had read in Russian when she lived in Zagreb. She wanted me to read Austen, Dickens, and the Brontë sisters, authors she had read in her youth and stories she had watched on the big screen. She was unable to communicate to me how these stories had helped her survive, but early on in my life I understood one thing: when I grew up, I would somehow bring stories to people.

As a little girl at an American school in Lima, I found it impossible to learn to read and write, so my mom taught me at home. It didn't matter that English was not her first language. As I grew up, in the mornings and the evenings, it was not uncommon for me to hear my parents' voices, reading novels to each other. They journeyed through entire books together. Now as my mom and I walked home from the fruit stand carrying a straw basket filled with grapes, mangoes, papayas, and chirimoyas, we spoke of *Wuthering Heights, David Copperfield*, and *Anna Karenina* as if the characters were real, as if they were my mom's old friends.

The longer I spent in Peru, the more my teenage self-consciousness disappeared, at least momentarily. I had no real friends here; there was no one watching me, no one judging the way I lived or learned. My mom could be playful and sometimes we ran wild through the apartment, yelling at the tops of our lungs, imitating the man who walked the streets, collecting bottles and selling tamales, calling out in his low, gravely, frog voice: "*Taamaalee Tamale, Tamale, Tamaaalee, … Boteeellaa, Botella, Botella, Boteeellaa…*"

We made each other laugh, collapsing on the polished wooden floors, until I started hiccupping every few seconds. My mom pointed to a place beside me, "Look, a spider," she said. I glanced down, startled, only to see nothing there. She believed the best remedy for hiccups was scaring a person. "That's ridiculous. That never works," I told her, shaking my head, breaking down into peals of laughter again. "By your foot," she tried again, unconvincingly. I clutched my belly as I laughed and hiccupped some more.

During these intimate moments, I felt free with my mom. Being in a different country made us more vulnerable to each other, more dependent and more open.

Wherever we had lived in the world, my mom always found a place to go walking. In San Isidro, there was a large country club with a swimming pool and golf course, enclosed by a high cement wall. Outside of the wall was a dusty trail, where Peruvians and my mom walked the five-mile circular path. It was one of the first things she wanted to show me. She said hello, nodding her head, to the people passing by, "*Buenas.*"

"*Buenas,*" they replied, nodding back, smiling at us.

"*Mi hija,*" she proudly introduced me.

"*Encantada,*" I responded politely, when they greeted me.

After a few weeks of walking around "the golf" as she called it, I noticed her slight impatience; I had too many questions and a part of her wanted to return to her walking solitude. Walking was her meditation, it was her time to recover from the Peruvian life that was wearing her down. One afternoon when I saw her pick up her little radio and headphones before we left, I protested, "Mom, I came all this way so that we could talk, so that you could tell me things. Why are you bringing your radio? Don't you want to talk to me?"

"Oh Katie, you can bring your Walkman if you want," she suggested.

I frowned, then grabbed my Walkman.

Sometimes we did listen to our music as we walked around, but usually we ended up talking to each other. "*¡Ay, qué calor!*" I said dramatically as we began making our loop. The air was dense. "You're really picking up the expressions," my mom said amused. She picked up our walking pace.

"Mom, guess what?"

"What?"

"*Rrrrrrrrrrrr.*"

"Katie, you did it! You can roll your Rs."

I smiled proudly. "*Rrrrrrrrrrrrrrrrrr.*"

She rolled her Rs back at me, "*Rrrrrrrrrrrr.*"

We laughed.

"Mama, why didn't you ever teach me Croatian?" I asked suddenly.

"Oh Katie, what will you ever need Croatian for? When would you use it?" she said, shrugging her shoulders.

"You can teach me now," I commanded.

She rolled her eyes and stared into space thoughtfully.

"Do you know any Croatian songs?" I suggested.

My mom loved singing; she had a strong voice, but wasn't always on key. She would often break into song at home. She loved musicals like: *Oklahoma! Carousel, The Sound of Music,* and *My Fair Lady*. She was particularly fond of American country music: Patsy Cline, Johnny Cash, Marty Robbins, and Merle Haggard. She liked to tease me by singing "I'm proud to be an Okie from Muskogee," because I had been born in Oklahoma and spent the first three months of my life there.

I listened to our footsteps, the gravel crunching beneath our shoes. "Come on, Mom. Teach me one."

She started singing a little folk song with a quick rhythm:

"*Sve ptičice iz gore, sve ptičice iz gore,*
sve ptičice iz gore, spustile se na more…
sve ptičice iz gore, spustile se na more.
Samo jedna ostala, samo jedna ostala,
samo jedna ostala, koja mi je pjevala…
Samo jedna ostala, koja mi je pjevala.

She hummed and then finished with "*ljubavi.* "

We both laughed.

"Okay, okay, okay," I said excitedly. "Do it again, slowly."

She said a verse in Croatian and I repeated it, struggling

to get my mouth around the soft unfamiliar sounds, making her repeat the verse many times, so that I could feel her language. Soon we were singing the first verse together, over and over. Finally, I asked what it was about. She said the Croatian to herself, then paused, glancing up at the hazy sky before explaining in English: "All the little birds fly to the sea, and only one stays behind to sing to me. I tell him, '*zbogom*' go with God, my darling, my only love."

I placed both my hands on my heart and was quiet.

"Oh Katie," she said, running her hand along my cheek.

Heading back through our neighborhood, we passed fancy, square, flat-roofed houses with elaborate gardens enclosed by white walls, where embassy families lived. Many had night watchmen, or twenty-four-hour security guards standing in front. With suits and ties, they looked like Secret Service agents.

I walked beside my mom, daydreaming, holding my Walkman with my left hand. I didn't hear the running footsteps, instead I felt myself being shoved hard from behind. My head flung forward. My hands reached for the ground. There was the blur of an arm, a hand. I felt something being ripped from me. I heard my mom screaming. For a moment, I thought someone had tried to grab my thigh, but then I looked down and realized that my hand was empty, my Walkman was gone.

A skinny young man ran full force, arms swinging, chest thrust forward, down the street. My mom was no longer by my side, she was shouting with her fist raised high in the air, running after him.

"Oh my God," I said, wide-eyed, and took off after her. "Mom! Mom! Wait!"

A yellow Volkswagen bug zipped by me. It was crammed with four young men, their windows open, their arms hanging out. They pulled up next to my mother, who wouldn't stop chasing our assailant. They shouted to each other in Spanish as she kept running. She waved her hands. The car brakes made a high-pitched wail, and they came to a screeching halt. Car doors slammed shut, and the men followed my mom in pursuit of the thief. Shoes pounded on the pavement.

My mom's muscular legs and her strong will for justice carried her. The four guys and I ran after her. My heart felt like it was going to explode out of my chest. She turned into *Parque Roosevelt*. The four guys ripped around the corner, energized by the chase, calling out to each other as they ran. I lost sight of them for a moment, until finally I came around the corner.

I saw them standing in the middle of the park. The four guys and a man in a dark suit, a watchman from a nearby house, held the young man, while my mom screamed at him in Spanish, pointing her finger at him, "Why! Why did you do this?"

He looked about sixteen. He had oily black hair, worn pants, and a short-sleeved striped shirt. He stared at the grass, shaken.

"Mom, mom, it's okay. I'm okay," I pleaded with her. I tried to catch my breath.

"It's not okay!" she said, visibly upset.

They discussed what to do with the boy. The watchman had seen us running from the other street and gone the opposite direction through the park, so that he could intercept the boy. I saw my Walkman lying in the grass; beside it was a screwdriver and a knife.

The watchman pulled my mother aside and they spoke in low voices. He did his best to reason with her, so that she wouldn't call the police. He told her it wasn't worth it to press charges; the police were corrupt. She might end up in jail instead of the boy. This was Lima, he reminded her. We both knew that he was right. Finally she relented, telling the boy that if he ever showed up here again, she wouldn't think twice about calling the police. He looked terrified. No one wanted to end up in a Peruvian prison. The watchman and the four guys released him. We all stared at him as he jogged away, relieved. The four guys waved goodbye as they strolled back to their Volkswagen. The watchman strongly advised my mother not to chase after anyone else who tried to rob us. Palms to the sky, he gestured as he said, "You never know what they have in their pockets. It's not worth it."

My mom nodded, disillusioned.

I picked my Walkman up off the ground.

"Come on, let's go home," I said, tugging at her arm.

As we stood on the tile floor in the entrance of our building, waiting for the elevator, she looked at me intensely and said, "No matter how hungry I was, I never stole from anyone. Never."

We went to buy fresh needles, sterilized syringes. We had to get our yellow fever shots, and my dad had heard that some clinics were reusing needles. I had been in Lima for two and a half months, when my mom decided that we both should leave. "It's so hard on my nerves here," she told me. I was surprised only because I knew my mom didn't like to be apart from my dad; she would do anything not to be separated from him. However, it was clear that she was becoming more fragile and physically unwell as the situation in Peru was becoming more unstable. It was excruciating for her to witness so much poverty and suffering. Her Peruvian friends told her that she should just accept the way things were, but she couldn't.

My parents were thinking of retiring after my father finished this job. My mom was constantly searching for a place that would feel like a real home. She dreamed of renting an apartment in Europe close to the country where she had grown up, maybe near a lake in Slovenia or northern Italy. My father dreamed of somewhere with mountains like Washington State, where he had grown up. He had almost a year before he finished his contract. They decided that my mom and I would go to Mexico, at least temporarily. My dad would take a vacation from work, so that the three of us could travel to Acapulco and search for an apartment to rent while he finished out his contract.

As we drove to the clinic on the other side of Lima, I asked my dad why we had to get yellow fever shots. He told me it was because Mexico required it. "It's silly really because you can only get it in the jungle, and we haven't been in the jungle. Still they make everyone who comes from Peru get one," he said and swerved around a car that pulled in front of us, missing it by an inch. I grabbed onto the edge of my seat and gasped. "Dad!"

"It's not my fault," he protested.

"Your father has turned into a Peruvian driver," my mom said, turning to look at me.

"Everyone drives so crazy here!" I was constantly catching my breath as cars almost careened into us. In the backseat of the car, I started feeling like I was getting sick.

In the clinic, the nurses took us all to an examination room with pink walls. They unwrapped our needles, and began putting together the syringes with the vaccine. My dad went first, looking away from the needle. Then it was my mom's turn; she looked at the floor. Then me. I closed my eyes and felt the prick, the dive into the muscle, and then it was finished. Lightheadedness swooshed over me as I stood up, and my mom took hold of my arm.

That night, I couldn't eat dinner. "*No tengo hambre,*" I joked with my mom. I lay on the couch. As we were watching our favorite Venezuelan *telenovela Cristal*, I grew feverish. I was cold, teeth-chattering cold; I kept asking for more alpaca blankets. Every centimeter of my skin felt prickly. The hair on my arms ached. With each small movement, I could feel every bone and joint. And then I was hot, flushed-face, burning-forehead hot. I told my parents not to worry. I pushed away the blanket. My mom smoothed my hair away from my face, then folded a cool damp washcloth and placed it gently on my forehead. My dad called Dr. Naranjo, a family friend and he informed my father that you should never get vaccinated if you are feeling run down, or have a cold. "Didn't they tell you that? Keep a close eye on her through the night."

They helped me climb into bed. "Katie, I'm so sorry you're not feeling well," my dad said, holding a glass of water and some aspirin.

I looked at him weakly, pushed myself up, took the aspirin and a sip of water, then let myself sink back down.

"Thank you," I said hoarsely. I closed my eyes.

"I always know when she's sick because she becomes such an angel," my mom said to my dad.

I smiled.

As I lay in the darkness of my room, I knew in their bedroom my mom would be getting upset. She would blame herself that we had gotten the vaccination, that everything turned out to be so difficult here. "Why did I let her come here?" she would ask my dad.

Images flew through my mind as I drifted asleep.

I saw my mom's fist on the hood of the car, then I saw myself in Colorado, in our two-story yellow house. I was running to the bathroom. I was a teenager; I slammed the door so hard that the walls shook. I locked it. "I hate you!" I shouted.

"If I adopted someone they would love me more than you do," my mom cried back at me from the other side of the door.

"Fine! Adopt them!" I shouted.

I saw myself sitting in my old Datsun 810, listening to Depeche Mode, driving to visit a friend in downtown Denver just because my mom told me that I couldn't go.

I saw the night that I came home at three in the morning. I had forgotten to call to say I'd be late. I quietly slipped through the front door. The light was on in the kitchen. I could hear my mom ironing. The iron hit the board hard, the steam whooshed. She saw me peer around the corner of the wall, the iron hit the board again. Her eyes looked frantic, she shook her hands at me, "Where? Where? Where have you been?"

I saw myself sitting on the edge of our front porch, the cement scraping against the backs of my thighs. The sun was bright. She wouldn't let me leave. When I was a teen, she had this rule that when we were in a fight, I couldn't leave the house if I was still angry with her. If something happened to her, she didn't want me to feel guilty for the rest of my life.

I awoke with a start, catching my breath, almost sitting up. My mom was beside me on the bed. Her hand was on my forehead, seeing if I still had a temperature. I lay back down, and curled onto my side.

"I think it's going down," she said, then added, "When you were a baby, I would keep getting up all night to make sure you were still breathing. I was so worried something would happen to you. We waited so long for you to come."

I put my hand on her arm. They had tried to get pregnant for ten years; I was their miracle.

"Are you okay?" she asked.

I nodded.

"Do you want me to get you anything?"

I shook my head.

She kissed my forehead.

"Mama?"

"What?"

"How do you say goodnight in Croatian?"

She smiled, then said, "*Laku noć.*"

"*Laku noć,*" I said softly.

A foamy wave curled and broke over my bare feet and then drew back. Another wave crashed against my bare calves. The cold water made me laugh. It was our last weekend in Peru. After a few days, I'd recovered from the vaccine. Now I felt a breeze against my arms and legs; strands of my long brown hair flew up into my face. I pushed them away and glanced behind me. My dad lay on his side on a blanket; he was propped up on his elbow, reading a mystery. Behind him, the desert coast was lined with treeless mountains. The brown barren landscape looked like another planet.

Along the beach, I saw my mom walking in the distance beside the weaving line of wet sand. Her hips swung slightly from side to side. There were only a few people out that day, all Peruvians, lying on towels. I looked out at the Pacific Ocean and dug my toes into the sand. The children were swimming and splashing. Beyond them surfers were paddling out, turning their boards around, waiting, until the moment before the wave surged, then they pushed themselves up, their toes gripping the board, their knees bent, their arms outstretched for balance, and suddenly they were gliding on a wave. I watched one surfer as he pushed himself onto his board, suspended and moving, leaning and lurching, catching himself before he fell into the water. I saw a dorsal fin. There was more than one, circling around the surfers. A dolphin's head popped up, he pushed the water with his nose.

"Oh my God," I whispered to myself. "Wow!" I said more loudly. It was the first time I'd seen one in real life. I looked around. I wanted to call to my mom, but she was too far away. My dad was engrossed in his book; he hadn't seen anything at all.

With wonder I watched the dolphins play beside the surfers, their dorsal fins circling, their grayish blue snouts peering curiously above the water for a while before diving down, their flukes appearing and disappearing beneath the water. They were so close. I felt elated as I stood there, my feet sinking deeper and deeper into the wet sand with each wave.

I'd been certain that I would have to travel far away to find my independence, to find out who I was without my small family. But in that moment, I felt grateful to be in another country with them. I wondered if people sometimes spent their entire lives looking for a place where they could be themselves. Strangely, here, for a brief period of time, I had found that place.

4

WHERE WE DIE

Hospice Nurse's note: *Patient smiling, pleasant, daughter to come home this eve.*

Their apartment bedroom was dark, only yellow lamplight slipped into their room. "Mom?" I called out softly as I stood in the doorway. She was curled on her side in a hospital bed that had been crammed into the far side of their bedroom. She looked frail, so I was surprised to hear her strong voice beckoning me closer. "Katie, come here." She reached out to me, her twenty-two-year-old daughter. I moved to her. As soon as I was close enough, she took my hand and folded it into hers. Dry and warm. If I were blindfolded I would have recognized it.

Plastic oxygen tubes ran from her nose across her cheeks and wrapped around the back of her ears. I bent down so that I could be near her. As I traveled by plane from New York City to Colorado, I'd kept calling out to her in my mind, *Wait, wait for me.*

Since I finished high school in Colorado, our lives had become transitory. After I stayed with my parents in Lima, I returned to Colorado with my mom, where we rented an inexpensive apartment outside of Denver and I worked for minimum wage at an independent bookstore. After finishing his contract in Lima, my dad returned to Colorado, and I moved to New York City to start anew. At twenty, I wanted to be an actor or dancer or a photographer. I rented, and shared, a tiny room at the 92nd Street Y. Five months later, I stood at a payphone in the hallway and was stunned to learn that my mom had been diagnosed with ovarian cancer and already had undergone major surgery removing a melon-sized tumor.

When I walked through their bedroom door that first night, it had been a year and eight months since her surgery. She'd struggled through rounds of chemotherapy, one almost killing her because the dosage was too high. And then, just as she was finishing her treatments, my mom decided that she'd had enough. No more doctors, no more hospitals. She stopped seeking medical care; she tried homeopathic alternatives.

When her health worsened and she could barely leave the bed, I convinced her to go to the doctor. In New York City, I sat on the edge of my mattress on the floor of my bedroom, in an apartment I rented with four other people. Anxiously, I waited to hear the news. In Colorado, my mom did her best to try to stop my dad from calling me when they returned home from the doctor. "Don't tell her. Don't tell her because then she'll want to come. I don't want her to come here; I don't want her to wait for me to die." She didn't want to be a burden.

The cancer had spread.

After I hung up, I couldn't move or speak.

Now my mom ran her hand over my long brown hair. "I'm

so glad you're here to help Dad." She smiled as if everything would be all right because the three of us were together. She leaned her head forward and unlatched the gold *Tumi* necklace that she always wore, an Inca god with an emerald center. It was an anniversary gift my dad had gotten her on a business trip to Colombia. She set it in the palm of my hand and said, "I want you to have this, Katie." It felt symbolic, a final gift. My dad helped me latch the clasp, squinting through the darkness.

"It looks good," he said, smiling, and then lowered himself down on their bed across from my mom. His long face looked thin and pale, and his white hair, usually perfectly combed, looked windblown. "We're so happy you're here," he sighed. My mom informed me that she was going to have them take away the hospital bed tomorrow. She didn't like it; she wanted to be back in her own bed beside my dad. She asked about my flight, my dance classes, my boyfriend (who I was now living with, much to her shock), the restaurant where I worked. "Can you start college again when you get back?"

I understood that she meant after her death. I wondered how long did I have left. Suddenly this New-York-City life that I had fought so hard for, seemed meaningless. It was composed of dance classes, visiting museums, and exploring the city when I wasn't waitressing at an Upper East Side, *Cheers*-like restaurant. As I struggled each month to pay my rent, I hoped I was creating an artist's life.

Questions spun through me. Why hadn't I realized that she was dying sooner? Why hadn't my dad told me when she was diagnosed that she wouldn't have long? I should have dropped everything and moved home as soon as I found out she was sick. That evening continued with my parents as though this reunion were like any other that we'd had in the past, with the awareness that we would never have another with the three of us.

My mom asked me to sleep on the couch in the family room; it was right outside their bedroom. I pulled off the big couch pillows and stacked them on the carpet, and then I unfolded the soft flannel sheets that my mom had bought especially for my visits and made up the couch. This became my evening ritual. Only a thin wall separated me from my parents' bedroom. Their door was cracked open. I listened to their murmuring voices, their evening conversations that I had been listening to since I was a child. After I finished making up the couch, I fell onto it gently and stared up at the white ceiling.

My mom used to ask us, "When am I going to rest?" And she meant *rest* from all the things that happened in her life. She wanted a peaceful life. She wanted to feel rooted somewhere.

When my mom found out that she had cancer, they had been in the midst of searching for a permanent home, but whenever they came close to finding one, my mom became disillusioned, wondering if people who had lived in so many places could ever find a real home.

Once, while I was in high school, I'd driven her to get a mammogram. As we sat in the waiting room, she flipped through pages of medical forms to fill out. Usually my dad did it for her, but he wasn't able to come that day. She glanced at me nervously and picked up the pen attached to the clipboard. After her eyes scanned the questions several times, she said, "I don't know."

"It's okay, I'll help you," I said.

"I'm a foreigner," she said, as if that explained it.

"Mom, what are you talking about? You've been here forever." I rolled my eyes like a typical teenager.

In fact, she had lived in ten countries, and within those countries she had moved countless times. This was the fourth time my parents had moved back to Colorado. "I just want to have a home for you," she'd often say.

"Wherever you and Daddy are—that'll be my home, even if it's in Australia."

She'd laugh.

When my dad asked if she ever wanted to move back to Croatia, she'd shake her head and say, "No—too many memories." Croatia was the place she'd been born, the place she lived for nineteen years—but since she had fled Communist Yugoslavia at the age of nineteen, she had only returned twice, and time had distanced her from the place that she once might have considered home.

On her two visits back to Croatia, her friends teased her, saying that she spoke Croatian with an American accent. Of course, she spoke English with a Croatian accent. Occasionally my mom would get upset and say to us, "I have an accent in every language!"

My mom was certain that when you found a place that felt like home, you would know. But I'd known for a long time that my mom would never find a home in one place. Instead, home would be memories of the places she'd lived: Croatia, Italy, Argentina, Venezuela, California, Washington State, Spain, the Canary Islands, Egypt, New Jersey, Oklahoma, Alaska, Peru, Singapore, and Indonesia. Colorado, a place where none of us had been born, would be the place where she would die, in a rented-third-floor apartment, in an unfamiliar Denver neighborhood, in a temporary home that had no history other than the one we carried within ourselves.

Nurse's note: *Daughter Catherine here from New York, very supportive of mother and father.*

The following morning two men came and carried away the hospital bed; my mom was cheerful about its departure. My dad filled the humidifier with water while I helped place pillows behind my mom, so that she could sit up. Her abdomen stuck out now, full of fluid caused by the tumor, and she felt the pressure, but not pain, at least not yet. Her body's cells were reproducing too quickly, pushing against the organs she needed to live. Cancer had spread to her left breast and made another home in her left lung. Since lungs don't have nerves, my dad had told me, it wasn't causing pain. But the tumors were making her uncomfortable and making it difficult to breathe.

There was an oxygen machine in the corner of their bedroom. My dad worried about power failures even though the hospice had given us an emergency generator. He wished that he could do a test run to make sure the generator really worked. He threw all his energy into the logistics of caregiving.

My mom couldn't wait to show me off to the hospice nurse and nurse's aide. When my dad answered the door, a small middle-aged woman with intense blue eyes and curly gray hair entered. Janice greeted me lightheartedly. She came three times a week to check on my mom and make sure that she had everything she needed. We could call her any time of the day or night. She was the middle person between the unseen doctor and the dying patient.

She also had a daughter who had moved to New York and was teaching at a public school in Brooklyn. My mom proudly announced, "Catherine is going to Hunter College in New York City!" This wasn't exactly true. The day I flew home to take care of her was the same day that I was supposed to start college again. Still, I didn't correct her. My mom beamed at me from the bed.

When we were alone, my dad confessed to me that the last doctor, who spoke to my mom, didn't seem sympathetic. No bedside manner. Coldly, he offered more chemo, but added it wouldn't prolong her life.

"You're dying," the doctor had said unfeelingly.

"It must be so hard on you, to tell people they are dying," my mom responded with compassion, looking at him directly in the eye.

The doctor seemed taken aback.

Later she told me, "Katie, I've been afraid of a lot of things in my life, but I'm not afraid of this."

I noticed that a new sense of urgency raced through me. I had a certain amount of time to ask her everything that I would need to know for the rest of my life. In the beginning I would go into the bedroom and ask her things like what books should I read, what movies should I see? Quickly I realized that it was no use. I didn't know what questions that I would need to have answered in the future, I only knew the questions that a twenty-two-year-old would ask.

A few days after my arrival, I announced to my parents, "I'm going to find a job." I took the car keys from my dad. One hour later I barged back into their bedroom and said, "I got one!" My mom clapped her hands together. Her face glowed with pride. I was going to waitress at a nearby Italian restaurant. I had lied and convinced the manager that I'd moved back to Colorado permanently. Lying was so much easier now that my mom was dying.

I would make enough money waiting tables to send my roommates my share of the rent. When my parents had found out that my mom was terminally ill, my dad had been about to start another temporary job, but he gave it up in order to take care of her. For over two years, he'd been jobless. When I looked at our scant grocery list and opened our nearly empty fridge, I could feel how careful they were being with money.

When something broke, we couldn't fix or replace it. My parents were living off of their dwindling savings. My dad was still paying off medical bills from my mom's surgery and week-long hospital stay from the first stage of her illness, when they had been caught between jobs, without health insurance. They had planned to move out of this apartment because it was more than they could afford, but then my mom's health had taken a turn for the worse. We had to bear immense financial stress and simultaneously appreciate my mom's final moments of life.

As I grew up my mom often said, "It's in God's hands." And I'd get frustrated with her. "No mom, it isn't. It's in our hands. It's up to us to change things about our lives." My mom had been through enough that she believed in letting go. I believed in the power of will. During those first few weeks at home, I witnessed her surrendering to something, and that's when the real battle began to take place within me.

Each night sleep evaded me. I was desperate to find it. My days were filled with taking care of my mom, and only at night could I hide in sleep and find a way to absorb the intensity of living beside death. In the darkness, I lay on the couch and smoothed out the creases of my pillowcase; my thoughts swirled like the tornado in the *Wizard of Oz*. If I could only fall asleep, I'd suspend time; I'd force my brain to stop. Eventually sleeplessness led to one image: a soft rosy-gray color appeared inside my closed eyes. I felt myself lying in a hospital bed. Above the sheets, my arms were outstretched. The inside of my palms, wrists, and forearms faced the ceiling. Vulnerable. Exposed. Someone's hand shifted my arm so that she could see my vein better. She pressed her fingers. I didn't turn away; I kept looking. Her needle punctured my skin. Needle into vein. Sometimes there were drops of blood. She was hooking me up to an IV.

As it began to drip into me, I felt myself falling backward. My muscles relaxed, and my body sank. I was doing something. I held my arm perfectly still, facing upward. I was fighting cancer for my mom, who was dying in the next room.

Social Worker's note: *Pt. feeling weak and minimally communicating today. Pt accepting of terminal status and preparing for death. Spouse/dgtr openly discuss illness and terminal status but struggle with acceptance. Close family system. Pt. has asked a friend to see that funeral is planned. Family reluctant to plan right away.*

Every couple of weeks, a social worker from the hospice came. First she'd speak with my mother alone, then she'd come out and shut the bedroom door. This was the time my father and I would sit out in the family room and speak to her alone. She encouraged us to speak about my mother's dying. My father told her about the physical changes that were happening, like how my mom was sleeping more during the day and less at night. He asked concrete questions about what we should expect during the following days and weeks. "I just want to make sure she's not in any pain," he told her firmly.

She nodded in agreement.

"How long do you think we have?" he dared to ask.

"It's hard to say," she said gently.

He nodded sadly.

"Soon," she added.

Nurse's note: *Pt. very private person. Difficult for pt at times to talk about personal care.*

Each morning, I felt as if I were stepping back into my childhood as I entered my parents' bedroom. My dad, sitting up on the right side of the bed, held a folded *Denver Post* newspaper with one hand, while he filled out the crossword puzzle. My mom always did the first half, then handed it off to my dad to finish off the difficult ones.

My parents' bedroom had always been a stopping-off point for me, a place where I paused to look at myself in the mirror, tried on my mom's lipsticks, sprayed some of her perfume on my wrist, and chatted with them while I did an occasional *pirouette*, or tested my balance in an *arabesque*. As a teenager, after a late night out, I'd try to silently climb up the stairs, and inevitably I'd hear my mom's voice calling out from their bedroom, "Katie, are you home? Did you have fun?"

They had both stayed up, waiting for me. "I can't go to sleep until I hear the garage door close," my mom protested. So I'd tell them about my night out and edit out any parts that would worry her.

Now I sat at my usual place, at the end of their bed, with my legs crossed beneath me. My mom lowered her glasses and smiled. As soon as the nurse's aide arrived, we got to work on my mom. When my mom was too tired to get out of bed, I helped the nurse's aide roll her on her side so that the sheets could be pulled out and we could replace them with fresh ones. But that day my mom wanted to get up, so we got her into the wheelchair. My mom placed her hand on her belly. I could see that her stomach was more swollen.

I pushed the wheelchair to the family room. I brought out the things we would need: a comb, lotion, several washcloths, and towels: a hospice spa day. The nurse's aide worked on washing my mom's hair. My mom wore one of my dad's long white undershirts; it took too much energy for her to get dressed now.

I dragged the warm washcloth over my mom's thighs, knees, and calves. Although her legs were beginning to get thinner, they still looked beautiful to me. My mom closed her eyes. I massaged her legs and hands with rosewater lotion. For a moment she could forget that she was dying, and for a moment I could feel useful.

As a child in Colorado, sometimes I'd wake up in the middle of the night to the sound of my mother's voice. She was crying. That sorrowful sound that hung in the night air came from another country, from another time. It pierced me.

At the age of ten, it made me sit up in bed, startled. It was familiar, yet I couldn't pinpoint its origin. I felt her cry echoing in my body. I strained to listen to my father's comforting words. She couldn't tell him what was wrong. I padded quietly down the hallway and stood in their doorway. And then I took a breath and bravely asked, "Mama? Mama, what's wrong? Tell me."

She reached out silently, her thin arm extended from the bed.

"Tell me," I urged her as I stepped toward her.

"Oh, Katie," she finally whispered, falling into silence. The words, the memories were trapped within her body.

I wanted to fill her silence. I knew that I could save her. Instead I stood helplessly beside her bed, barefoot, in pajamas. A part of my mom left us. She was elsewhere—somewhere near the ghosts of her past. I wondered who they were, and what they wanted. She was unable to put words to her traumatic memories. No matter how hard I tried to convince her that I could handle anything, she couldn't tell me what haunted her. Instead she lay curled on her side, her face in anguish. My father stroked the side of her bare arm, murmuring her name, "Marijana, Marijana," so that she would know that we were still there.

My dad imagined that her cry arose from her childhood during the war, from the death of her parents, from the death of her grandmother.

Now that my mom was dying, I felt as if I were losing something impossible for me to grasp. I'd never go to Croatia with her again. When I was six, I'd traveled there; it was my only trip to my mother's country and my memories were fragmented.

My mom laughed as she sat at a table with her friend, Ružica, eating tiny vine-ripened green grapes. At one time, they had been teenagers fighting tuberculosis together in hospital. But during that visit, I knew nothing of that, I was happy in my peach-crocheted dress, standing beside my mom, slipping my arms over her shoulder as she held my waist. I was dark from swimming beneath the Adriatic sun; my olive skin tanned as easily as my mom's.

We drove through the Yugoslav countryside together. The car windows were rolled down; summer wind blew into the car, sending my brown hair flying wildly around my face as my mom and Ružica taught me my first Croatian nursery rhyme about a little bear who enters a shop and forgets to say good afternoon.

Doš'o Medo u dućan
Nije rek'o dobar dan
Idi Medo van
Nisi rek'o dobar dan!

In the car we chanted it over and over, my arm out the window, the wind suspending it.

During that brief holiday, my family had driven along the Dalmatian Coast. One afternoon we found a cove outside of Makarska; large rocks opened out to the Adriatic Sea. I swam in the transparent aquamarine water with my mom. She wore a bikini and kept her head above the water, swimming breaststroke. I plunged below the small waves and rose up, laughing, splashing my mom, and disappearing underwater again before she had a chance to splash me back. Tiny fish swam between the rocks. On the bottom, there were the round, black, spiny sea urchins that my mom had warned me not to step on.

Nurse's note: *Daughter and husband very caring. Many questions about prognosis and pt's care.*

Each day felt orderly. Everything happened at a certain time, the nurses came and left, we cleaned, did laundry, cooked, gave my mom her medication, took care of her physical needs, and sat and talked with her. I knew exactly when everything was supposed to happen, except I didn't know when she was going to die.

It was difficult for me to be inside for entire days, so I began to go running. One afternoon, armed with my Walkman, I made my way through carports, around townhouses, apartment buildings to a landscaped path. It ran alongside a little canal and bordered other apartment complexes and a golf course.

I ran a little too fast, my sneakers hitting the asphalt hard. I wanted to run and run until my body disappeared. When my stomach cramped, I remembered that I hated running. Then I started up again a little more slowly, and after a while I realized the physical pain eased something inside me.

I felt lightheaded; I felt slightly sick. The music from my headphones flooded my ears. Stravinsky's *Rite of Spring*. There was something unbearable about the music; there were too many different sounds at once, it was too chaotic, too full of life, the dissonance broke me. I tore off my headphones and hurled the Walkman hard on the ground. It bounced on the asphalt, sending the white tape and batteries flying across the path and off into the ditch.

I dropped to the ground, my knees slamming into the

asphalt; my hands got embedded with little stones. I shouted, "Stop, stop!"

No one could hear me. I dropped my head and bit the side of my lip hard; it started to bleed. I wished that I could physically tear myself apart. I didn't want to be here; I didn't want to exist.

I stared at my Walkman lying on the ground, half-open on its side. I wasn't going to get up. Seconds, then minutes passed. I sat there staring at the endless rows of townhouses and apartment buildings. They all looked the same, empty and lifeless. I got up, scooped up my Walkman, batteries, and tape and walked home, where my family was waiting.

One evening, my mother's friend Laura arrived. In order to see my mom, she'd driven 600 miles with a friend, all the way from Montana, where she now lived on her husband's cattle ranch. Laura stood beside the bed, her high airy Argentinean accent mixed with a Montana twang. I listened as Laura and my mom recalled their time together in their early twenties when they had lived in the same building in Alexandria, Egypt; my father and Laura's husband worked for the same oil company.

"Marijana, you remember the smallest things. Catherine, ohhhh, your mother used to make us laugh with all her stories," Laura said, shaking her head. "And remember, Marijana, how you would buy some meat and Dave would make us hamburgers?" My mom nodded and laughed; hamburgers were so *American*.

Laura and my mom gazed at each other, and I could see their Egyptian memories: horse-drawn carriages; haggling at the market; going out with their Lebanese friend Katya and Australian friend Beverly; sipping strong Turkish coffee while they chatted about Signore Bianchi, a bald-headed Italian, a former Olympic wrestler, who taught their exercises classes and did my dad's physical therapy; I could see them rushing to the government store when the frozen Polish chickens arrived; the stray cats circling around the garbage bins; Sabah with cloths wrapped around her feet, gliding across the wood floors like an ice skater as she sang in Arabic.

"Laura, do you remember this song?" my mom asked, pushing the button on the tape player on the bedside table. Nana Mouskouri started singing "Never on Sunday" a song from a Greek film with Melina Mercouri that they'd seen together long ago. The bright and tinny music sent them back into nostalgia. My mom smiled and tilted her head from side to side with the rhythm. Laura sighed and nodded her head.

It was difficult for me to look into Laura's eyes because it was clear that she understood what all this meant. Friends for thirty years, saying goodbye. I still had a little longer, but for Laura, these were the final seconds. She held my mom's hand tenderly for a moment. I heard Laura say, "Marijana," then she let go.

5
SUNDAYS

I sat at the end of my parents' bed with my legs crossed beneath me. My mom kept oxygen tubes in her nose all the time now. She didn't take breaks like she used to. She was too weak to walk, even with our help. Now she was bedridden, but she still read, listened to the radio, napped, and chatted with the hospice nurse and nurse's aide. She was still alive.

It was March, my second month at home. I'd stopped thinking about everything I was about to lose and concentrated on how to make things easier for her. I glanced at my mom and noticed that the pillows propping her up were now bunched at the top of her head. She wasn't in her usual sitting-up position. Gradually, over the afternoon, she had slid downward and no longer had the strength to lift herself back up.

"Mom, do you want me to lift you back up?" I asked.

She nodded. Her perfectly even top teeth brushed over her bottom lip, and then she gave me a tired smile.

"You do it," she sighed, raising her chin at me.

The others had tried and failed. My tall, slender father, leaning on his strong leg, could only lift her up partially. In his feeble attempts, he would lose his balance nearly tumbling on her. Throughout my life, he'd walked with a limp and I could see when he was trying to lift my mom, he became frustrated with himself; his brow furrowed, his jaw clenched. He didn't want her to suffer. The nurse and nurse's aide had their own methods, but they still couldn't lift her back up without causing pain. Our goal: avoid pain.

Each time the nurse asked my mother if she was in pain, she said, "No." *Denies pain*, they wrote into their records again and again, as if they didn't believe her. Panic, which skimmed her green eyes during their attempts to lift her, settled into relief when I accomplished the task swiftly. She told them with pride, "Let Katie do it—she does it the best."

My dad, who had been lying next to my mom reading his book, now nodded at me as if we had been called to action. He walked around to her side of the bed. I stood up on the mattress and put my hands on my hips. My dad held up his hand and said, "Wait. Let me fix the pillows." I leaned my mom forward so that she could sit up for a moment while he rearranged the pillows, patting them into place so that they would feel like the back of a soft chair. "Okay," he said and took a step back.

I climbed over my mom. I placed my left foot beside her right hip and my right foot beside her left hip. My legs were in a parallel plié as I bent toward her, reached my hands under her arms, and interlaced my fingers behind her back, making a swing. She wore one of my dad's white undershirts; she wore them every day now. I could feel her ribs through the thin cotton. She put her arms around my neck and looked straight into my eyes.

"Ready?" I asked.

She nodded and held her breath.

"One, two, three." I breathed in and straightened my legs at the same time, shifting her back into place in one swoop. She exhaled. A glow spread over her face; she was proud of my invention.

"Thank you," she said. My dad reached over her so that he could fix the pillows at her side where she kept her left arm raised. *Metastasizing*, the nurse had said. Sometimes that word echoed in my head as I looked at her swollen arm. The cancer was spreading. It would overrun her body until she died.

Three mornings a week, I drove to downtown Denver to take ballet classes with the modern dance company Cleo Parker Robinson. My mom insisted I go, and I didn't argue. When I waitressed, I worried that my mom would die before I got back home, but when I went to dance class, I knew that she wouldn't die. She loved the ballet and as an adult, she'd finally had the chance to begin taking classes.

And it was my mom who filled my childhood with the fairy tales of *Swan Lake*, *Cinderella*, *Coppélia*, and *Giselle*. As a girl, I watched her sketch a series of charcoal portraits of Natalia Makarova in an exquisite *arabesque*. When I was nine, she gave me Noel Streatfeild's 1937 British classic *Ballet Shoes: a Story of Three Children on the Stage*. When I was a teenager, she took me to see a special screening of *The Children of Theatre Street*, a documentary about the Kirov Ballet School. My mom adored Carlos Saura's flamenco version of *Carmen*. We were both captivated by the passionate rhythms and the fierceness of the women. She had her Spanish friend Margarita teach us the Sevillana in her Colorado basement.

Dance and art expressed something for mom that language could not. And now as she lay dying, my mom sketched people from the images she had cut-out from *National Geographic*. While she did her final sketches, I drove downtown and placed my hand on a wooden barre. The familiar rituals—*pliés*, *tendus*, and *frappés*—brought me into a state of clarity. Each movement felt essential. As soon as I brushed my worn ballet slipper against the black marley floor, I felt safe. As my body moved through space, I felt relief. Each time I came to the dance studio, it felt as if somehow things might be all right.

One day after class, the ballet teacher, who happened to be Croatian, asked if I would consider dancing in the opera Wagner's *Die Meistersinger* that he was choreographing at a large theater downtown. Rehearsals would be after class; the performances were in the second week of May.

From her bed, my mom was delighted. "You should do it," she said instantly, adding, "it would be a good experience!"

I felt uncertain.

"I know I won't be here, but I think you should do it," she urged me.

I accepted the offer, knowing that I would have to perform after her death.

Social Worker's note: *The Pt very prepared to die. Somewhat frustrated that "God isn't ready" for her yet. Feels all affairs are in order and all issues are resolved.*

The sound of the humidifier blended with the sound of the oxygen machine, and everything hummed. I sat in my usual place at the foot of their queen-sized bed. My dad rested his back against the wooden headboard. I had put on a tape of Dalmatian folk songs that I had copied for them. I watched my mom smile and sway to the music, and we swayed with her.

When one song finished, my mom said, "Katie, tell me once again about your favorite day of the week." And I was surprised she remembered. I said shyly, "Sunday—Sunday mornings." Six months earlier, I had called her from a pay phone on a street corner on my way to work. I often walked from my apartment on the West Side across Central Park, through baseball fields, to my Sunday brunch waitressing shift. That particular morning I was early, so I decided to call my parents. My mom answered and I told her that Sunday mornings were my favorite time in the city. I told her about the silence; how the streets were empty. I told her about my walk across the Central Park, about the joggers who stared ahead, about the hunched-over cyclists who sped by, their wheels buzzing. I described the way the leaves made a shadow of lace for me to walk over. I told her about starlings, leaning into the wind until they vanished behind the trees.

And she told me how much they missed me. How my father was making breakfast, pancakes, of course—it was Sunday. How they wished I could be there with them.

When I was growing up, I remember drifting in and out of sleep as my mom called my name from the bottom of the stairs on Sunday mornings. The sound of her voice mingled with the comforting smell of pancakes and melting butter.

"Caatheerine, breakfast." She softened the first part of my name, *Caa*, then placed an accent on the second syllable, *teh-rine*, making my name into a song.

On Sunday mornings she would take out her Dalmatian records and play them on our record player. Lively folk music filled the entire house. In songs about village life and falling in love, the voices mingled in dissonant harmonies. The *tambura bisernica* and three-string fiddle made a bright sound. Sometimes she took my hands, and we spun around and around, faster and faster, gravity pressing our feet into the ground, until I shouted, "Stop," and collapsed with laughter into my mom's arms, and we hung on to each other until the room stopped whirling.

On Sunday mornings, my father always placed three plates on the counter. He buttered the top of each pancake carefully while it was still hot. My mom sat on a wooden stool reading an article from the newspaper to him. As I was growing up I believed that my family didn't have any traditions, and I longed for them. But every Sunday morning my dad made pancakes, and my mom played her Croatian records—they were traditions we kept without knowing that we were keeping them.

Nurse's note: *Pt states: "I think I am getting closer. I am ready. I do not want to live this way." Family in the other room.*

I swept my long brown hair into a ponytail and stood across from my mom. She was sitting up, propped up by lots of pillows.

"I want to go through all my clothes today," she said matter-of-factly, as if it were nothing out of the ordinary.

"What?" I said, pretending I hadn't heard her.

"Decide what you want, and then put everything in bags so that we can give them away," she said.

"Are you sure? Everything?" I glanced at her hesitantly.

"Yes," she sighed, impatiently. "Everything. I don't need them now. Those things aren't important."

Was this my mother speaking? The woman who used to dress up in black leather pants and high-heeled boots to go to the grocery store?

"What about the shoes?" I asked.

"Keep one pair," she said and then added, "one nice pair."

I didn't say anything because I knew those shoes were for the coffin. I sighed and got some garbage bags from the kitchen, went into the walk-in closet, and began pulling her things from hangers. Her blue silk suit, her red wool jacket, her black leather jacket, her purple angora sweater, her pumps, her running shoes, she was never going to take another walk; we would never take another walk together. I held her silk blouse in my hand; she was never going to wear it again. I could still smell her perfume in the fabric. She called my name, "Catherine." She wanted me to hold the blouse up, against my chest, so she could see how it looked.

"That looks good on you," she said.

I nodded.

"You could get that altered," she said.

I nodded. I had to agree with a dying woman.

She was an inch and a half taller than me, so most of her pants were too long, but some of her shirts fit me.

"If there is anything your friends might want, you can give it to them," she said, tossing her hand through the air nonchalantly. And suddenly I wondered if it was all right to give your friends your dead mother's clothes.

I rummaged through all the drawers, pulling out her shorts, jeans, T-shirts, and socks, separating them as I went along. My mom directed me from the bed. She seemed filled with energy. I folded the clothes and placed them tenderly in the bag.

Nurse's Note: *Pt visiting with family. Pleasant and appears comfortable, always has a smile for nurse.*

The next day we went through all our family photographs. My mother lamented that she never took the time to put them into albums. The photographs had been carried from apartments to houses to apartments in large worn manila envelopes. I lay on my side, propped up on one elbow. She was sitting up in bed, her knees were bent. Her large round glasses had slipped to the middle of her nose. She held one photograph close to her eyes and stared at it for several moments. It was the only family photograph of my mother as a little girl with her parents.

She pointed to her mother's ankles and said, "Look Katie—look," raising her chin, "look, how swollen they are." We both scrutinized Katica's ankles. They seemed unnaturally round. Her hands were swollen, her knuckles bulging. My mom shook her head sadly and said, "She must have already been sick." I slipped both of my arms around her thin shoulders. It was the first time she had spoken about her mom to me.

After my mom placed that photograph back down on the bed, she picked up a large magnifying glass that she kept on the bedside table. As she was dying, her vision was deteriorating. My dad came back in the room and sat beside her. It felt peaceful, the three of us together on the bed. It was like being on a boat, drifting farther and farther away from the world. I watched with fascination as my mom systematically examined each photo. It was as if she were looking for something specific. She came across one of the three of us, which was rare since my father usually took the photographs. She smiled and glanced at my dad, tilting her head sweetly.

"Look—look at us," she said as if she wanted to convince us of something. "You know, I never realized how happy we were." She sighed, then held up the magnifying glass to the photograph again before she moved on to the next one.

As it grew dark outside, we put away all the photographs for the last time. My dad and I didn't notice that she had put aside the photograph of the three of us. She placed it on her bedside table. It had been taken on our Italian holiday when I was fourteen. We stood in front of Il Duomo in Milan. The cathedral spires twisted upward into the fog. An Italian photographer approached us and offered, in half-English and half-Italian, to take our photograph. He held onto a camera with a large flash, assuring my father that yes, he most certainly would send the photograph to us. But my dad was skeptical and said no, we didn't want our photograph taken. My dad told my mom that *he* could take our picture. She quickly persuaded him that we should have the photograph taken. He grumbled, "We'll probably never see it." He wrote down our address and paid the man.

We were given some breadcrumbs to attract the pigeons. We held out our hands, palms to the sky, waiting. All at once the pigeons flew down. Some landed in front of us; others were suspended in the air, wings blurring. It was overwhelming and wonderful, the clapping of wings, the fluttering upon our hands.

In the photograph, my mom and I are dressed alike: tight faded jeans, puffy purple ski jackets, and black suede boots that bunch at our ankles. My dad's hair isn't gray yet, but it is beginning to change. He looks tall beside my mom and me. My mom's curly light brown hair almost reaches her shoulders. My long hair is frizzy with a bad 80s perm, and I have braces. My mom is radiant. She smiles, her lips are parted slightly and she is gazing at the pigeon that has landed upon her palm.

A month after we returned home, we received a package from Italy in the mailbox. There were three copies of our first and only family photograph.

The day after she died, my father discovered that same Italian photo, hidden beneath something on her bedside table. He flipped it over and saw on the back, my mother had written something.

Dear God, Thank you for my happy family and the good time we had in Italy and Milano. We never quite know how closely and gently you watch over us. When I see the smiles on the faces of my family, I see all the times that you were there in our midst. I thank also all the people in my life who ever prayed for my soul, as I continue to pray for my daughter Catherine till I am able. All my love, Marijana.

Nurse's note: *Pt states: I am happy. I am with my family. I am comfortable and I am ready to go. I wanted you to know.*

In the apartment doorway, the nurse whispered it could happen at any time now. She prepared us by explaining that my mother might slip into a coma and then stop breathing, or she might be in a coma for a while, and that was when things could get complicated. The hospice nurse looked me straight in the eye. I bit my bottom lip; I understood. Quick, painless death. I was supposed to hope for a quick death. There was no such thing as a miracle anymore, and the truth was that my mom didn't want one.

That night, as I was sleeping on the couch outside my parents' bedroom, slipping in and out of consciousness, I was jarred awake at three in the morning by voices. Disoriented, I looked around me. The TV and radio were blasting inside my parents' bedroom. Words over words filled the apartment. I slid off the couch and almost fell to my knees. I ran to their doorway. My dad, sleeping on his side, completely exhausted, wasn't stirring. The room was cold. My mom insisted on keeping the patio door slightly open because sometimes at night she felt as though she were suffocating.

She looked at me, alarmed, as if she had gotten lost in a crowd of people. She was confused; I was confused. I rushed to her side of the bed and lunged for the television remote control. I struggled to find the volume button in the dark, fumbling with it until I managed to turn off the television. Then I ran my hand over the top of the radio until I turned it off. Instantly we were submerged in silence.

I turned on the bedroom lamp on the lowest setting. "I,

I, pushed the wrong one, I was turning it down, but…" her whisper drifted off. Her wary eyes had lost their lucidity. She took the top of the blanket and pushed it away from her angrily, then stared at me.

"It's okay, Mama," I said, then bent down beside her and stroked her hair away from her forehead. I could see her gray roots; the rest of her hair was still the same color as mine. She was afraid to die at night, and that was why she kept the radio or television on. Lately, while my dad and I slept, she tried to stay awake.

I returned to the couch, pulling the comforter over my shoulders. My head pounded and my heart raced. My mom's body and mind were deteriorating. I wondered what would happen if she lasted too long.

She was suffering now. It was selfish of me to want her dying to last forever. I wished desperately that I could just fall asleep. It felt like torture to stay awake. And then I said it, two words I knew God would hear: *Take her.*

Nurse's note: *Family coping fair, but very sad and tearful at times.*

Over the next couple days, she entered a different dimension. She spoke less and slept more. She gave up trying to eat. Sometimes she nodded at me, pressing her dry lips together, and I got the little pink sponge on a stick, dipped it into water, and put it in her mouth. I brushed her lips with the moisture. She looked at my dad and said, "I'm tired." My stomach fluttered. It was coming. I rubbed her feet because they were violet and cold.

One afternoon she surprised me with a surge of energy. While my father was doing the laundry, she asked me to open the curtains. Usually she wanted the room dark. She always liked to keep the curtains closed, and I was the one who wanted to let in the light. I would tease her, "You're like a bat." But that particular morning, for some reason, she wanted to see the sunlight.

She asked me to help her sit up. I placed my arms around her, pressed my feet into the carpet and used the strength in my legs to lift her. We sat on the edge of the bed alone, mother and daughter. My leg touched the side of her bare leg. Her legs used to be muscular, but now the muscles had softened from being in bed so long and hung limply from the bone. We leaned against one another, her shoulder against mine, her hand resting on top of my hand.

"I know this must be hard for you, Katie," she said gently.

I was silent.

"But I know it will make you stronger."

We both stared ahead. I wondered if I had said everything that I needed to say for the rest of my life. My voice wavered, "Do you forgive me? For everything?" And I meant for all the times I'd said things that I didn't mean, for all the times I'd fought with her just to start an argument, for all the times I'd pushed her away thinking that she would always be there.

"For what? I love you. You're my daughter." She patted my leg. The sun poured into the room from the window across from us. Tiny dust particles danced through the rays of light. They were suspended in constant motion until they reached the edge of the light, and then they vanished.

I swallowed and sat there, wordless. I held her hand gently, the way she used to hold mine when I was sick.

That night, while I was waitressing, she became disoriented. Her body was shutting down; less oxygen was reaching her brain. She asked my dad, "How did we get here?" He explained the different places they'd lived before they moved into that apartment. She nodded as if she understood, then looked at the wall across from the bed where there was an impressionistic oil painting of a blue vase with pink flowers. "What's that?" she asked, and he explained that was a painting we had bought on our trip to Yugoslavia many years ago.

Then she asked, "How can I die?"

"Well, it will feel like you're falling asleep," he said hoarsely.

She sighed.

I came home that night from waitressing and glanced into their room. They were both sleeping beside each other. My mom's chest was still rising and falling. She was still breathing, but often it was uneven. The lengthy pauses unnerved me; I watched until she returned to a more predictable rhythm.

The next morning, I took the flannel sheets and blanket off the couch. I folded them and placed them on the carpet. I heard the shower. I sat back on the couch groggily, waiting for my father to finish. Soon he stood in their open doorway. He paused for a second too long. Before he said anything, he leaned against the doorframe. I went to him.

"What is it?"

"I think Mama's in a coma," he said. "I tried to wake her up, but she didn't wake up." He looked stunned.

We both stood there for a moment. For one instant I felt relief, and then I felt as if I were waiting again. Wanting it, but not wanting it.

"How long?"

"I don't know, could be a while," he said, raising his eyebrows. We had never been in this place before.

She was lying on her back in the bed that they shared. I got on my tiptoes and put my arms around him, and he bent his shoulders down so I could reach. The nurses had told us it was coming. This is what we were supposed to want. My dad said that he thought he should make us breakfast. He returned to the tasks that had gotten him through each day. We didn't know how long she would be in a coma.

I entered the bedroom. I climbed up on the bed and sat across from my mom. She was motionless, but continued to breathe. Her chest barely rose. My dad had removed the oxygen from her nose just as the nurses had told us to do. I took her warm hand and placed it in mine. I stroked it, and her unconscious fingers collapsed against my own fingers. I wanted to remain there for an infinite amount of time. The slight movements of her body hypnotized me. Her eyes were barely open like those of a child sleeping. I thought she might wake up, but her body seemed too silent.

She swallowed. Her throat moved. I counted. She swallowed four times, then she was completely motionless. Gradually, a tiny amount of brown fluid slid from her lips down the left curve of her mouth until it reached her chin.

I knew she was dead. I heard my father shifting a frying pan on the stove; I could smell pancakes. It was Sunday morning.

6

ZAGREB

The first time that they walked through Jelačić Square, little Marijana gripped her mama's hand. They passed by men wearing fedora hats and women in mid-calf skirts and high-heeled shoes that clicked against the cobblestones. Marijana gazed with wonder as she watched electric trams pull in and out of the square. The wires sparked. She craned her neck to see the tall cathedral spires. Pigeons flew above them. Church bells chimed. A man in a suit rode past on his bicycle. Horse's hooves clopped alongside roaring automobiles.

Marijana felt a sudden longing for her Tata, but today he'd begun his new job at the railroad. He'd explained that a machinist fixed things that were broken and he would make certain that the trains would run on time. On the side, her Tata also found work as a locksmith. Marijana boasted to her new friends that he could open any lock. It was true that he liked to use his hands and was an accomplished carpenter; why, only last winter he'd made her a wooden sled with shiny metal runners. She smiled to herself as she recalled gliding down a snowy hill in her village.

At Dolac market, Marijana followed her mother past a row of plucked, dangling chickens. Peasant women in white skirts and puffy blouses, with red scarves tied over their heads, walked beside city dwellers. Marijana looked at the trays of shiny fish, carts piled high with tomatoes and peppers, figs and peaches. People were buying olives, cheese, and loaves of crusty bread. Before dawn, peasants from the countryside arrived at the open-air market. Women came with large baskets perched upon their heads, men pushed heavy wooden carts filled with their most recent harvest.

Katica bought fresh eggs, grapes, and tomatoes. She noticed that the woman selling to her had the same flat handmade shoes that she had once worn. Katica was overwhelmed by a desire to see her home, the family that she had left behind in Slavonia. She sighed. Her husband didn't want the village life anymore. He was finished with farming. Through friends he'd found two houses in Zagreb; one was in a better neighborhood, but across from a cemetery. Anton refused to live so close to the dead. Katica wondered why it bothered him so much. Once he made up his mind, it was impossible to get him to change it. Stubborn like his daughter, she smiled to herself. She took Marijana by the arm and helped her climb onto the tram to begin their journey home to a tiny street at the city's edge, a small house at Lupoglavska 3.

Katica stared out the tram window. She was getting accustomed to their city life. The fashions were more modern; she smoothed out the pleats on her skirt and then adjusted her small hat, which was angled on the side of her head. She put her arm around Marijana. The night before, she and Anton watched their daughter sleeping. Anton had told her, "In this beautiful city, we will watch Marijana grow up and marry, and one day hold our grandchildren." They laughed quietly. It seemed impossible that there was a time before Marijana existed. She gazed at her sleeping daughter's outstretched legs. At that moment, she wanted another child. She wondered if it were possible.

A spark from a tram wire startled Katica from her day-dreaming. Marijana giggled.

"It's the tram, Mama," she said and then asked curiously, "How long do you think we'll stay here?"

"Until you are grown, my little one."

"When will that be? When will I be grown?" she asked.

"It will be many, many years from now," Katica answered mysteriously.

"Will you, and Tata, and Baka be here with me, many years from now?" she asked, trying to grasp what a year felt like.

"Always, my little one. We will always be near you."

"But what about our chickens, back home?" Marijana asked worriedly. "What will happen to them?"

"Our neighbor is taking care of them, and when we go back to visit, you can go collect their eggs."

Marijana nodded and wondered who was living in their old house.

On quiet summer evenings Katica and Anton took Marijana for strolls in Maksimir Park. Beneath a gazebo, an orchestra played. Pensioners sat gossiping at open-air cafes. Cigarette smoke wafted through the air. Young couples held hands as they walked along the promenade. Mothers pushed prams with sleeping babies past neatly planted flowerbeds and pavilions. Marijana ran ahead of her parents on the winding paths and discovered a lake where people were rowing. She begged her Tata to take them.

As her father rowed them across the lake, they gazed into the surrounding oak forest. Marijana leaned over the ledge of the wooden boat and scooped up the water with her hand.

Katica pointed out a turtle, lounging on a rock. Marijana's eyes searched for the rounded shell.

In the rowboat, Katica felt as if anything were possible in their new life. By moving, they had changed the course of their future. Anton was right, life on the farm was physically grueling, it was too hard of a life. Her daughter would have a better education in Zagreb. In a year or two, who knew what their lives would be, and she yearned to hold this moment, a family of three, gliding peacefully over the lake in a rowboat.

Katica looked over at Anton and asked if they could have their portrait taken. "What is a portrait?" Marijana asked. They had never had a family photograph. Katica asked Anton, Could they manage to find the money? Her husband paused, thinking it over, "Why not, we will find a way," he said, smiling at her as he leaned back and pulled the oars.

In the days that followed, Katica discovered a photographer's studio on her walks through the city. They scraped together enough money so that they could go to 7 Strossmayerov trg. Marijana was growing so quickly. Better not to wait, Baka had told them as she pressed their finest clothes.

Inside the studio, the photographer pointed to the darkly painted wall and told them to stand beside an intricately carved wooden chair that looked as if it belonged in a castle. Marijana asked her mother if a king ever used it? Katica smiled and told her that once, not long ago, a princess, who looked very much like her, sat there.

"Really Mama?"

Katica nodded.

Marijana asked as politely as she could, "May I sit there? Please?"

"After the photograph," Katica said, and then bent down and pulled her daughter's white socks up to her knees. Her leather shoes were worn at the tips. She smoothed runaway strands of her daughter's light brown hair away from her forehead and placed her braids in front of her shoulders. Her daughter stood unusually still as Katica straightened the blue and white stripped dress. Anton, in his dark suit and tie, stood behind them, chatting with the photographer about the recent rain.

As she stood up, Katica felt the blood rush to her head. Dizziness swept over her. There was a swirl of black dots as she looked out. The sensation passed. The blurry image of her daughter slowly became clearer. Katica blinked. She took a breath in. With one hand, she gripped the base of her aching neck.

The photographer told them to get into position. Katica ran her hands along the sides of her dark dress, and fixed her white collar. Marijana sensed something was wrong. "Mama?" she asked. Katica pressed her dry lips together, shook her head and said nothing. Anton cast his dark eyes toward Katica. She reassured him, "I'm fine." She forced the worry from her mind and told Marijana to look at the camera. Gently Anton took Katica's hand. They stood together, their shoulders touching, behind their daughter. Their shadows were barely visible on the dark wall. The three of them looked solemnly into the camera's lens.

7

WAR

In the early morning hours of Palm Sunday in 1941, hundreds of planes filled the sky of Belgrade, the capital of the Kingdom of Yugoslavia. The Stuka dive-bombers flew low; German soldiers machine-gunned down fleeing civilians. Bombers roared, hitting vital areas of the city. Windows burst, doors were flung from their hinges, ceilings collapsed upon floors, gusts from explosions hurled people to the ground, flung sleeping children from their beds. Fires erupted, houses split open, buildings crumbled, bodies twisted, half buried in the rubble.

Each morning in Zagreb, Katica and Anton sat at their table, sipping coffee, worrying about what was happening. They felt the tension mounting. They were surrounded by countries that were part of the Axis: Austria, Hungary, Romania, Italy, and Bulgaria. The Kingdom of Yugoslavia had mounted a fruitless effort against Adolf Hitler, but was quickly defeated. Now Germany began its occupation of Belgrade, and Hitler dismembered Yugoslavia. Nazi tanks rolled into Jelačić

Square in Zagreb, the city where Marijana and her family were beginning their new life. *Nezavisna Država Hrvatska*, the NDH, the Independent State of Croatia was declared with the support of Nazi Germany and Fascist Italy.

Five-year-old Marijana and her parents went out onto the streets and watched the precise lines of Nazi soldiers marching. Their boots drummed in perfect rhythm. Zagreb was more kindly disposed to the Germans than points south and east, and people hung out of windows and trolley cars. Children waved their paper flags in the air. Katica and Anton witnessed the celebration and whispered to each other. Croats had survived centuries under other powers. The country had a Serbian monarchy and the Serbs had dominated the Yugoslav government. Now in Croatia, there was a Nazi-supported puppet government. What did this occupation or independence mean? Anton watched the armored vehicles and tanks roar by and wondered what would happen to his family.

After his work at the railway, Anton hurried home before the evening curfew. He nervously passed German soldiers smoking and chatting with ease on the streets. As he walked, Anton couldn't erase the day's images from his mind. Mussolini and Hitler helped Ante Pavelić, a Zagreb lawyer and politician living in exile in Italy, into power. Pavelić's Ustasha soldiers were loading Serbs, Jews, and Roma onto trains headed out of Zagreb. Anyone suspected of planning or committing acts against the Independent State of Croatia, including Croatians, could be arrested or sentenced to death.

Anton slipped his hands into his coat pockets and was surprised to discover a folded letter. Perhaps one of the prisoners had slipped it in. So many were being led toward the trains. At first Anton couldn't bring himself to open it. He stared at the address, and then stuffed it back into his pocket.

When he stole a moment alone, when no one could see him, he gently unfolded it.

My dearest one, they are taking us somewhere. Where, I don't know. I will write to you as soon as I'm able. Tell the children that I love them. I will find my way to you. Please take care of yourselves and do whatever you need to. I will live for the day we are all together again.

Anton refolded the letter and placed it back into his pocket. He decided that he must deliver it. His heart pounded as he wandered the streets in search of the address. Finally he located the house and slipped the letter beneath the door.

When he was a block away, two Nazi soldiers passed by him. One met his eye. Anton nodded and kept going. He held his breath until he could no longer hear their footsteps behind him.

One day Katica ran into her friend Eva. Katica glanced at Eva's coat; there was a yellow patch with the Jewish star and below it was the letter *Ž*, for *Židov*, Jew. With the patch came the loss of all rights as citizens. Together they turned down a narrow side street, so that they could be alone. Eva tearfully confessed how terrified she felt when she saw signs in shop windows saying "Jews Forbidden to Enter." In a matter of days, Eva's father had been dismissed from his job, and their family's bank account frozen. "They made him surrender his radio," Eva told Katica, "his prized possession." Katica embraced her. She felt outraged that now Eva could no longer take a stroll in the park, go to the cinema, or be out past curfew.

Eva explained that their family's flat was about to be overtaken by another family; they would have to move out. "We only have twenty-four hours to get out of our own home," Eva said. "I don't know where we will go. How we will manage?" What would happen to all their things, their books, furniture, their photographs, and her little brother's toys? "Will we ever be able to return to our home?" she asked, bewildered.

Katica told her to put some things together and she would keep them for her. "I can't, Katica. I don't want you to get into trouble," Eva said softly, shaking her head. They both knew that the legal decree of concealing Jewish property carried a prison sentence.

"What trouble? No one will know," Katica told her firmly.

Eva nodded and her gaze fell to the ground. Katica took her hand and squeezed it. Eva met her eyes again. She struggled to speak. "My family has been helping the Viennese Jewish refugees. What will happen to them? They have nowhere to go." The Austrian Jews had come to Zagreb before the occupation; they had been trying to escape Hitler, and now Hitler was here.

Eva explained to Katica that when her little brother had gone to school yesterday, his teacher called out all the Jewish children's names before the lesson began. They stood beside their desks. His teacher told them to leave immediately. Her brother timidly raised his hand and asked when they could come back. The teacher pointed to the door. He gathered his things and ran home in tears.

Katica wondered if the same scene had occurred in Marijana's classroom yesterday. Her little girl had returned home despondent and was unwilling to explain why. A feeling of dread filled Katica as Eva told her about the arrests, other Jewish families were being taken away. A transit camp had been set up on the outskirts of Zagreb. "Will we be next?" Eva asked.

"You must leave as soon as possible. There is no other way," Katica told her. Eva's father was scrambling to obtain all the travel documents that would allow them to board a train out of the city. Even a visa to escape seemed impossible now that they were surrounded by Nazi-controlled countries.

"I must return home," Eva told her.

Katica nodded. They embraced one last time.

As she walked home, Katica prayed. *Please, please let her be safe. Please God, help her family get out.*

Marijana pulled the black paper curtain aside to peek out at the empty street. "Don't look outside, my little one," Katica warned Marijana. Not a sliver of light could be seen during the blackouts, Katica explained, or there would be trouble. Marijana wondered what kind of trouble.

After dark, Anton cracked open the door and looked up and down the street for passing soldiers. After he closed and locked their door, the family huddled beside the radio. Baka kept motioning to her son to lower the volume; they strained to hear the familiar signal of the BBC weekly broadcasts in Croatian. Listening to the news broadcasts from enemy countries was banned, but still they listened.

Katica looked at her husband and felt a rush of relief that he had already served his mandatory military service. His work maintaining trains was considered important. At times the rail lines outside the city were sabotaged and had to be repaired. The trains often transported troops and equipment, so they had to be running smoothly at all times. Her husband worked on the engines and did not speak much about his days, but she was aware that he was surrounded by soldiers doing their work. He witnessed prisoners loaded onto trains being sent away from the city. Anton came home pale and tired. Sometimes he cried out in his sleep. Nightmares. Katica shivered as she watched little Marijana sitting happily beside her father.

Marijana leaned one arm on her father's knee and whispered into his ear, "Tata, did you know, if you buy a radio in a different country, it will speak a different language."

"So if you buy a radio in Spain, it will speak Spanish?" he asked.

She nodded knowingly.

"That, my little one, is an intelligent radio," he said, and patted the top of her head.

Early one morning, Marijana walked at a brisk pace alongside her Tata down a street. They were on the way to the *pekarna* to buy bread because her mother was feeling unwell. Her father's strides were longer, so she gripped his hand to keep from tripping.

"*Tata,* not so fast, not so fast," she urged.

He smiled, slowing down.

"We will get to the same place, even if you slow down," she added.

He laughed and they began to walk again. She listened to his shoes hitting the street, keeping time. Her half-steps broke his rhythm. Every so often, they turned and made their way down a tiny street or through a small square. Sometimes her shoe got caught between the rounded cobblestones, and they paused. He led and she followed, holding onto his hand.

As they turned one corner, her father stopped abruptly. Marijana's body was flung forward. Her father caught her, so she wouldn't fall, and then scooped her up into his arms. She wrapped her legs around his waist, her arms around his neck, and pressed her face against his shoulder. She could feel something was wrong. She could feel fear. She turned her head to see why he had stopped. The cast-iron lampposts lining the street looked strange to her. Men floating through the air, she thought, until she caught sight of the ropes. They were hanging, lamppost after lamppost after lamppost, all the way down the street. Their heads slumped downward, their wrists tied with wire behind their backs, their tongues swollen, hanging out from their open mouths, their legs dangling in the air.

She remembered that her father had once taken her to watch the man with a long pole light each of those lamps at dusk; they cast warm yellow flickering light onto the streets. She placed her hand on her father's cheek, turning his face toward her. "Tata, what are they doing?"

For an instant he'd forgotten her. Now he squeezed her tightly. He must take her away from here. Quickly he turned and hurried in the opposite direction. He felt horror race through his body. He didn't want to run into the soldiers responsible for this act. He wanted to erase the images from his daughter's mind.

When they got home, she ran to her mother. She had been waiting to tell her about the men. Excitedly she showed her mama what she had seen, holding her little arm extended up into the air like a rope, and dropping her head down, letting her tongue hang out of her mouth.

"Marijana!" her mother cried out and then stared at her husband. He sat down and pressed his face into his hands. Katica held her daughter closely; Marijana listened to her pounding heart.

After they put Marijana to bed that night, they spoke to each other in hushed voices. Who were those men? Serbs? Jews? Roma? Anti-Fascists? Croatian political prisoners? Katica felt a sharp unbearable pain in her chest as she imagined her husband and daughter witnessing so much death on a Zagreb street where they walked each day.

Katica thought about Eva and her family. They had managed to escape the city, but she didn't know where. She knew some Croatian Jews obtained false documents and fled to Italian-occupied Dalmatia; it was easier to hide there. Some Italian soldiers were sympathetic to their plight and protected Jews, refusing to hand them over to the Ustasha soldiers or their German allies. Or they smuggled them out of dangerous areas. There were Jews who joined the Partisans, or boarded fishing boats and sail boats and made their way across the Adriatic Sea to Italy.

Katica had heard of Serbs fleeing their burning villages for the forests and mountains. In the countryside, they could join Josip Broz, Tito's communist Partisans, or they could join Draža Mihailović's Serbian Chetniks, started by pro-royalist officers from the Yugoslav army. The Chetniks and the Partisans competed for the support of the Allies. Katica and Anton wondered who would decide their fate. The Chetniks? The Partisans? Germany? Russia? Pavelić? The Allies?

That night Katica lay in bed sleepless. Her stomach clenched with worry. There was a three-way-civil war amidst a world war in her country. Yesterday, Katica's friend had confided that when she looked out her window, she'd seen soldiers storming the square. They led a group of civilians to a nearby forest; they disappeared into the trees. A few moments later, she heard the echo of gunshots.

In the deep of night Katica remained awake. She rubbed her chest with one hand and shivered. Her entire body ached, the base of her neck, her spine, the tops of her legs. She curled her body against the warmth of her sleeping husband. Closing her eyes, she tried to sleep, but it was useless.

As Anton worked in the railyard the next day, he thought about Croatians who lost sons, brothers, and fathers to the Chetniks. What was happening in the village where he had been born? He heard of Chetniks looting Croatian villages and burning people's homes. A Ustasha soldier passed behind him. He froze. He didn't feel as if he could trust anyone now although he knew there were some soldiers who tried to help people. There were Croatian civilians who witnessed the violent treatment of the prisoners and were horrified. Some were forced, under the threat of death, to dig graves for mass executions. Some bravely spoke out or tried to protect and hide their neighbors and were arrested. Some smuggled food to prisoners. Some smuggled letters out of the prison camps. Some warned people before the soldiers arrived in their villages. Some hid people in their cellars. Some helped families escape before their fate was sealed.

Katica pressed her palms together tightly in her lap. She told herself, *listen to what he's saying*. The doctor continued speaking, but she'd already fallen into the darkest part of her mind. "Tuberculosis," he said as he looked at her sympathetically, explaining how it was inevitable because of wartime conditions. Not enough food, overcrowding. It was affecting her lungs.

She nodded and tried to summon questions. "How? What, what can I do?" she uttered. Her mouth felt dry.

He told her to rest and eat well if she could get her hands on more food. Behind the doctor, out the window, was a tree. She fixed her eyes on the yellow leaves that fluttered with the wind; some leaves fell from the branch and drifted to the ground.

"My daughter?" she asked, trying to shake herself out of the shock.

The doctor glanced down at his desk for a moment before meeting her eyes. "It's difficult now. I cannot tell you what to do. Unless, do you have friends, family she could stay with? I know with the war… Well, what you must do, is send her somewhere safe."

They were both silent.

She stood up and slipped on her coat.

She stepped onto the street. She needed to think, to figure out what they should do. How would she tell Anton?

She kept hearing her daughter's name in her mind, *Marijana, sweet little Marijana.* She could hear the distant hum of bombers. Soon they were roaring overhead. She could feel the vibration beneath her feet. Where was Marijana now, she asked herself as she began to run toward an air raid shelter. Glass shattered in the distance; she could see smoke rising. Then she remembered, Baka was walking with Marijana home from school. They would find the nearest shelter and take cover, Katica reassured herself. If she didn't make it through this illness, Baka and Anton would take care of Marijana. Her dear husband would do anything for their little Marijana.

In the days that followed, Katica sent word to her family in the countryside, pleading with them to take Marijana for a little while. She couldn't imagine being separated from Marijana for even one minute yet alone an entire day, but she was desperate not to infect her daughter with a disease that could kill her. They had no family here in Zagreb. Anton could take Marijana on the train to Slavonia. Yes, that would be the best way, the best thing for all of us. Just for a little while, until I'm well, she convinced herself.

When, weeks later, she received the letter saying that it was not possible, Katica was devastated. Her family wrote that they could not take Marijana at this time. It was better if Katica kept Marijana in Zagreb. They sent their love to little Marijana and promised to pray for Katica's health.

Katica wept. She felt utter despair. That night her face flushed with anger. She told Anton that she couldn't believe that her family wouldn't take their own blood into their house. Didn't they care about her daughter's life? Her head pounded. Anton tried to calm her. He reached across the table and put his hand on her arm, but she pulled away from him. She wanted to throw her chair, but it would wake Marijana, who slept beside her grandmother in the next room.

Anton suggested that perhaps her family was afraid Marijana had already been infected. Maybe they were afraid of getting tuberculosis themselves. Maybe the situation in the countryside was worse than they had heard. Katica felt something break inside of her. She didn't want to die. She wanted to be there for her daughter as she grew up. She wanted to help her with her school work, she wanted to teach her how to make Croatian cookies, she wanted to tell her stories from her own childhood, she wanted to see her married, she wanted to hold her own granddaughter.

She slammed her fist onto the table. Her light green eyes blazed. "I will never speak to them again." She paused, then added quietly, "None of us will."

Katica did not know about the death camps sixty miles south of Zagreb not far from her village. Serbs, Jews, and Roma, men, women and children were rounded up and sent to the five camps of Jasenovac run by the Ustasha regime. In Sisak, there was one just for children. These families left behind sheep, pigs, and cows. They left behind their wheat fields, plum trees, and barking dogs. They left behind their tables set for dinner. They left behind an open bottle of wine and empty glasses.

Along the Sava River, in concentration camps from Sisak to Nova Gradiška, prisoners starved, they were hit with typhus fevers and dysentery. They froze. They were forced into grueling labor. They slept curled on sprinkled hay, they slept on the earth, on bare stone, they slept without blankets, they slept in puddles of water, they slept shackled, they slept on bruised skin, they slept beside metal buckets filled with excrement. They woke to screams of pain, moans of hunger and thirst, and the footsteps of soldiers.

In the days to come, they would feel the force of an ax, hammer, and gun. Some of their bodies were thrown into the Sava River. Some drifted by the place where Marijana had once carefully placed her shoes together on the banks; where she had dipped her bare feet into the river and felt its steady current.

One morning in 1943 the doctor came to the house; Katica's condition had suddenly worsened. He pulled Anton aside in the dark hallway and whispered, "tuberculous meningitis." A death sentence. There was little time; the membranes that encircled her brain and spinal cord were infected. Katica was only thirty-seven years old.

That afternoon, eight-year-old Marijana stood in the doorway of her parents' bedroom. She watched her mama as she rested in bed. Her mother moaned. She was inconsolable. She held her forearm against her forehead, crying soundlessly. The headaches were excruciating. Katica tossed and turned; her swollen legs became tangled in the blankets. Her pillow fell onto the floor. Marijana waited by the doorway; her mother had forbidden her to enter the room.

Marijana's legs grew tired from standing, so she sank to the floor and pulled her skirt over her knees. She could smell her mother's sweat. She ran her fingertips over the wooden floorboards, feeling the grooves of the wood. Her *Baka* told her to go get some air. Marijana insisted on staying in the doorway, as close to her mama as she could be. When she grew tired of sitting, she stood again, peering around the corner, transfixed by her mother's unnaturally pink cheeks.

Through feverish eyes Katica glimpsed her daughter. Marijana's wool socks were bunched around her ankles. Her long brown hair was unbraided, strands falling about her face. She drifted into memories of holding her daughter when she was a newborn, when she would gently press her lips against Marijana's warm forehead and smell her soft skin.

The doctor tried to convince Anton that there was nothing to be done. Still, Anton wanted to take Katica to the hospital; he believed that somehow they could save her. The next morning he found someone to drive them. "Marijana, you stay here with Baka," he told his daughter sternly.

She pleaded, "*Tata*, please, please, let me come. I want to go with you."

He shook his head, his patience worn thin.

She grabbed his arm desperately, crying.

He pulled it away. "Marijana, stop it!" he shouted.

Her grandmother tried to hold her, tugging her back into the kitchen, but Marijana let out a high-pitched scream. Her grandmother let her stay where she was. Silently Marijana watched her father carry her mother through the house. Her grandmother shut the door behind them. Marijana ran to the window.

A black automobile waited in the street. The engine rumbled. A man jumped out and held open the door. Anton placed Katica gently into the back seat, then closed the door and ran to the other side. Marijana watched motionless. She held onto her mother as long as she possibly could, until the car disappeared, until she stared at the empty road.

Baka buttoned the black dress as Marijana stood perfectly still. She followed her grandmother and father out of the house. They did not speak to each other on the journey. It felt as though her mother was still beside them, traveling through the city, up the slope to Mirogoj. Ivy climbed the fortress-like walls that enclosed the sprawling cemetery. Marijana looked up at the light green domes before they entered. Daylight trickled through the leaves.

They passed by two men discussing Italy's recent surrender to the Allies; Germany would now occupy the Italian territory of Dalmatia. Marijana took in the world around her as they walked by pavilions and covered passageways, elaborate mausoleums and marble gravestones. They gradually made their way to the newer section of the cemetery. She looked at the ground, wondering where her mama was going, how she would find her again. She needed to hear her voice; she needed to feel her mother's arms holding her. She remembered how in Oriovac her mama would give her a cup of warm milk straight from the cow, and they would laugh together. Marijana looked up at her father; he stared ahead, his dark eyes glazed as if he couldn't see anything around him. She wanted to ask him what heaven was like.

There was no money for a gravestone, but at least Katica could rest nearby, her father explained to Marijana. We can visit her often, he promised. Marijana bent down and placed white lilies upon the grave. Anton lit one candle for Katica. He took his daughter's hand and they both stood there, staring down at the freshly turned earth.

At home, Marijana felt her father's anger. She heard him cursing God for taking Katica away from him. So young! How could He give her such a cruel death? Marijana could tell Baka was upset that her father refused to pray anymore. Her mother's death had torn away something from him. When her father began to cough, Marijana felt terrified.

Her grandmother scrubbed the floors; she scrubbed the walls. She made certain to give her son his own plate and cup, so that the disease wouldn't be passed on to her granddaughter. She tried to suppress bitter feelings for her dead daughter-in-law. She knew it wasn't Katica's fault. TB was everywhere. It could have come from anyone, a neighbor, a friend, someone at the market. The doctor had explained to her that one person coughs, another person inhales the bacteria, and then it lodges in the lungs and infiltrates the tissue. Still, she couldn't stop herself from feeling upset with Katica for bringing this cursed disease upon her family.

After school, Marijana helped her grandmother in the kitchen and waited for her father to come home from work. Beside their stove, Marijana tried to learn embroidery from her grandmother, but she didn't have much patience.

When her father opened the door, she rushed into his arms. She held onto his sleeve. She helped him take off his shoes. She watched him sink into a chair; his face flushed with fever, his eyes shiny. He gently rubbed his sore ribs. At night, while she lay in bed, she listened to the sound of him coughing. His breath sounded raspy.

One morning he sat in a chair beside the kitchen table. His shirtsleeves were rolled up, even though it was cool inside the house. He pulled his white handkerchief from his pocket and coughed until it was spotted with dark blood. "Rest, or you'll never get better. Your daughter needs you alive," Baka told him, her voice breaking. Anton felt heavy with exhaustion, but still he made certain he rose each morning and went to the railroad. The work was physically demanding; he had to lift heavy machinery in the damp cold.

If he worked, at least he could leave them a small pension, he told his mother. At least they would have something. He pushed himself up from the chair, which teetered forward. She grabbed it just before it fell to the ground. Anton stayed bent over, his hands on his knees, staring downward. It seemed as if he could no longer resist gravity. She took a step toward him, but he put his hand up to stop her. He took small shallow breaths, then stood, walked to the door, opened it, and left. As he went to work, he wondered how they would survive all by themselves: an old woman and a little girl.

On his way home, he concentrated on putting one foot in front of the other. He had a vision of himself collapsing on the street, not having the strength to get up. He swallowed. His throat felt dry; a hacking cough overtook him. He held his fist up to his mouth until finally it subsided. Anton rubbed his hands over his sallow cheeks a few times and continued on his way.

That night, he went directly to bed. The coughing fits shook his body. There were beads of sweat on his forehead. Marijana watched her grandmother come and go from the room, bringing *čaj*, which he tried to sip. He could hardly eat. He was adamant about not going to the hospital. "There's nothing they can do," he muttered. Deep down, Bakica knew her son spoke the truth.

Marijana spent much of the night sitting on his bed, talking to him. She told him stories that her grandmother had taught her. When they heard the explosions from the Allies bombing in the distance, Marijana curled forward against him, burying her face into his chest. He patted her back. When it was quiet again, she sat up and continued her story. He rested his eyes and listened to the sound of her childish voice. It was the only thing that brought him relief now.

On Christmas Eve, Baka checked on her son Anton, then she bundled up her granddaughter in her warmest coat so that they could go to midnight mass. They stepped onto the street, beneath the Zagreb moonlight. Tonight they broke curfew. The church bells chimed. Marijana inhaled the winter air and held her grandmother's hand as they walked below barren tree branches.

In the church, they dipped the tips of their fingers in holy water, and crossed themselves. Head, heart, left shoulder, right shoulder, the way her mama had taught her when she was small. Marijana watched her grandmother light candles for her mother and father; the flames flickered. They sat silently on the wooden pew. Marijana inhaled the rich incense, and she felt as if she were falling asleep, as if she were slipping into a dream. Her mind floated, yet her body felt heavy. Was her father still breathing? She wondered if her mother was calling out to him. Everyone around her rose, she felt herself standing, crossing, and repeating, *U ime oca, i sina, i duha svetoga, amen*. In the name of the Father, Son, and Holy Spirit, amen. Her voice sounded as if it belonged to someone else.

A few months before the Germans surrendered and Tito's Partisans marched through the streets of Zagreb, in February of 1945, her father's dark skin turned ashen. He could no longer leave his bed. Baka lit a candle in the bedroom while he lay curled on his side, sleeping fitfully. Baka sat in a chair beside the bed, crossed herself, and prayed for her son's soul. Anton had been so stricken by grief, he hadn't meant what he said, that he didn't believe anymore; he'd lost his faith briefly, she explained to God. Forgive him, please, please, forgive him, she pleaded.

Marijana watched her grandmother from the doorway. Without a word her grandmother stood up, brought another chair into the room, and placed it beside her own. They sat together. Night came. Shadows wavered on the white wall. Marijana kept her bright eyes pinned on her father. They were enveloped by a deep nighttime silence. Nine-year-old Marijana leaned against her grandmother's wide arm, her cheek pressed against the scratchy wool sweater. She blinked, trying to keep her eyes open, telling herself that if she could only stay awake, he would live.

Eventually her eyelids grew heavy and she surrendered.

8

CROATIA, 1993

Just as our plane was about to land in Croatia, it was diverted to Slovenia. A Serbian ground-to-ground missile had been fired at the Zagreb airport. My dad was taking me on a trip to my mother's country after her death, but we couldn't even land there.

When my mom was first diagnosed with ovarian cancer, communism collapsed and Croatia held free elections. When my mom was undergoing chemotherapy treatments in 1991, Slovenia declared independence, and after a ten-day conflict against the Serb-dominated Yugoslav People's Army, Slovenia was able to break free of Yugoslavia.

At the same time Croatia also declared independence. While my mom secretly worried that her cancer was back and invading her body, Croatia was struggling to hold onto its border territories. In certain areas along the border, Serbs were refusing to accept Croatian independence, and they were backed by the Yugoslav People's Army. The month after my mom died, Bosnia-Herzegovina declared its independence. The Federal Republic of Yugoslavia's Serbian Leader, Slobodan Milošević, refused to allow Croatia or Bosnia to separate and used the Yugoslav People's Army to exert his control over Yugoslavia and create a "Greater Serbia."

Once, when my mother was bedridden and dying, she'd received a letter from her Croatian friend Tončika. My mom held up the envelope for me to see and said, "Look, Katie, we have our own stamp!" Strangely, other than that, we never *once* spoke of the war.

In all our years together, my mom had never explained the religious differences within Yugoslavia to me. During that time, I knew nothing about the ethnic tensions between Serbs and Croats. I did not know that Serbians wrote in Cyrillic script and Croatians wrote in Latin script. I did not know that Serbs, Orthodox Christians, had survived four centuries of Ottoman Turkish occupation, and their religious identity was connected to their national identity. I did not know that Croats, Serbs, Jews, and Muslims lived for many years side by side. They even inter-married in diverse cities like Sarajevo. I did not know that Bosnian Muslims came from families who had originally been converted to Islam during the Ottoman occupation. Nor did I know that Croatians, Roman Catholics, had spent centuries under the Austro-Hungarian empire, or that Yugoslavia meant the land of South Slavs, and that Croats, Serbs and Yugoslav Muslims are all Southern Slavs with basically the same language.

Despite the war raging in her country, in the last days of her life, my mom had asked my dad to take me to see the village where she was born in eastern Croatia. Oriovac. It was her final wish, my dad would tell me later. She had one last impulse to connect me to a place that she had been so careful to keep from me.

After her death, I returned to New York and went through the motions. I waitressed at the same restaurant on the Upper

East Side and began taking one course at Hunter College, City University of New York. My father, jobless for a few years, finally found a job with an Argentinean oil company that had an office in Texas. He was now renting a small, one-bedroom apartment in Houston; it was a city where he didn't know anyone. In New York City, each morning I dragged myself out of bed in my tiny apartment. I was so stunned by my mother's death that I did not grasp the present horrors happening in the Croatian and Bosnian wars.

So much had occurred in the former Yugoslavia during my mother's last six months of life and in the year since her death, but at the time I knew very little about Serb forces shelling the city walls of Dubrovnik and the bloody siege and devastation of Vukovar, Goražde, and Sarajevo. I did not know about the artillery shelling, the exploding land mines, the rocket launchers, the mass arrests, the detention camps, the men reduced to skeletons who stood behind barbed wire. I did not know about the ethnic cleansing of Muslims and Croats. I didn't understand that the enemy could be someone you recognized, someone you went to school with, someone you played with on the street, someone you drank, sang, danced, shared a coffee with, a neighbor and friend. I did not know about Serb soldiers barging into homes and dragging women and girls away from their families, holding them in rape camps where soldiers took turns with them until some lost consciousness.

I did not know about Bosnian Muslims signing away all their property and possessions to Serbian officials for a chance to survive or possibly escape on a bus convoy. I did not know about the hospitals where patients died from infections because of the scarcity of antibiotics, pain killers, and bandages; where malnourished and overworked surgeons cut out shell fragments and bullets from their patients, some children, and amputated limbs without anesthesia, working lights, or clean water.

I did not know about Serbian soldiers shouting for families to come out of their homes only to shoot them. I did not know about families running for their lives down village streets, carrying the old on their backs, the young on their hips, clutching their infants to their chests. They crawled on the earth in the darkness of night, holding their breath as they hid, crouching behind trees in the forests, or surrendering to Serb paramilitary forces, not knowing if they would live or die.

I did not know about villages and towns where grandmothers and grandfathers, mothers and fathers, sons and daughters, children and infants were torn from each other's arms and brutally executed in front of each other. Sometimes they were barefoot. Sometimes they had slipped shoes on. They were machine-gunned down. Their throats cut. They were shot in the chest, in the back, in the head. As their bodies crumpled, they were pushed over a bridge into a river. They were mutilated by soldiers with knives. They were abandoned, sprawled on an open street. They were buried in the mass graves of Vukovar, Tomašica, Kevljani, and Srebrenica, some of whom still have not been found.

On the plane to Croatia I did not know any of those things, but I did know this: my father and I would not make it to Oriovac. The village was in Slavonia, which had endured some of the worst ethnic cleansing in Croatia at the hands of the Yugoslav National Army and Serb paramilitaries. It was also very close to the border of Bosnia. The city of Osijek, 79 miles away from my mom's village, had faced heavy bombardment. The razed city of Vukovar, 86 miles away from my mom's village, had endured a three-month siege. When the city finally fell, two hundred and sixty people were transported from the town's hospital to a nearby pig farm where they were massacred.

Snipers took aim across the Sava River at the place where my mom had spent her early childhood. Bosnian refugees were fleeing their homes and farms to the city of Slavonski Brod, only 14 miles away from my mom's birth village, which was being hit with heavy artillery fire. It was too dangerous for a father to take his twenty-four-year-old daughter. Because I was desperately trying to survive my grief, I was relieved to be traveling. For the most part, Zagreb and its surroundings were safe. I was riding on blind faith because I was sure that in my mom's country we would discover pieces of her that we couldn't seem to find in America. I had no idea that this was only the beginning of a journey that would last over twenty years.

When our plane landed in Maribor, Slovenia, we boarded a bus that would take us back to Zagreb. I tried to stay awake. I didn't want to miss anything. Fields, vineyards, haystacks, whitewashed houses, and cows flickered past before a heavy jetlag sleep overtook me.

"Katie, Katie, we're here," my dad said as he gently shook my arm. I stumbled down the bus stairs, blinking in the daylight, searching for Tončika. I saw her behind the crowd, a petite woman, dressed in matching brown jacket and skirt. Her large glasses were tinted against the sun; she suffered from cataracts. She certainly didn't look like a woman in her eighties. When she saw us, her face lit up.

Tončika bustled through the crowd, as I helped my dad down the stairs.

"*Dobar dan. Kako ste*?" I said shyly, and she threw her arms around me.

"*Dobro, dobro*, you're here," she cried happily. She looked up at my father and said, "Daave, Daave, you came, you really came," in a thick Slavic accent. He bent down so that she could kiss him, on each cheek, the Croatian way.

As soon as we arrived at her house, she rushed to the kitchen to prepare lunch for us. I tried to help, but she said, "*Ne brini, ne brini*, sit, sit," and pointed to the dining room. I wandered through the rooms on the ground floor of her two-story house, looking at her sculptures and paintings. I came across a black-and-white photograph of her grandson who had died in an accident on the Adriatic Sea a few years before. He was a handsome young man sitting at a piano.

My dad, Tončika, and I ate together—cabbage salad, chicken soup, breaded chicken and rice, exactly how my mom made it. We sipped Croatian red wine out of delicate crystal glasses. Tončika kept piling more food onto my plate. Eat, eat, she urged. I wondered if she had said those exact words to my mom. Tončika's husband had been my mom's doctor when she was a girl struggling with tuberculosis. Oftentimes, Tončika had beckoned my mom from the crowded waiting room into her kitchen. For the rest of my mom's life, they wrote to each other.

And all of a sudden I longed to hear my mom's voice, I longed to feel her arms around me. I wanted her to worry about me. Maybe grief worked like this: the more I lived, the more I would mourn what she missed. And then I began to wonder about the perpetual nature of grief. Does it ever really end, or do you just keep discovering new parts of it the longer you live?

Over the next several days Tončika's friends took us walking around the city. I tried to salvage my memories as a six-year-old of this place. I wondered about my mother's childhood during WWII, during her parents' illnesses, during Tito's time. We strolled up to Gornji Grad, the Upper

Town, and everything started to feel familiar, the tiles atop St. Mark's Church, Strossmayer Promenade, the blue funicular, the steep stairs. "I used to climb up those stairs every day to go to school," my mom once told me.

We made our way down to Jelačić Square, which was lined with outdoor cafes. Zagreb seemed unusually quiet for a city. There weren't any tourists because of the war. It seemed as though everyone was in shock from witnessing so much violence. "Why are you going now? Isn't it too dangerous?" my waitressing friends had asked me before I left.

"They're not really fighting in Zagreb. And I have to go. I have to," I said, knowing that it was impossible for them to understand. Now I watched people on the far side of the square, cramming onto a packed tram. I saw benches filled with old men, and women who wore scarves over their hair, tied at the base of their neck like my mom did whenever she vacuumed our house. The peasant women stared straight ahead. Knee-length skirts exposed their bare calves. Dark socks were bunched around their ankles. There were plastic bags filled with things beside their feet. They were war refugees. Behind them an old wall was crumbling. Bricks exposed and discolored. Above the old women, graffiti had been spray painted in wide black letters, *Fuck you, die*. It startled me to see the rage of teens above the refugee women who had lost their homes, all their possessions, and family members.

One evening my mom's friend Ružica, her husband Iv, and son Igor visited us at Tončika's house. They hadn't seen me since I was six. Each Christmas my mom and Ružica wrote to each other and exchanged photographs. Their time together in the TB sanatorium remained an unspoken history between them. We huddled in the doorway, kissing each other on the cheek, speaking in broken English and Croatian. Ružica grew tearful. I realized that I had never seen anyone, other than my dad, crying for my mom. Maybe people felt as if they had to hide their grief.

I understood that Ružica saw my mother through me. Tončika had looked at me with the exact same expression when she first saw me. I felt pain at their recognition, but I didn't turn away. I wanted to feel this pain; I wanted to understand it. I put my hand on Ružica's arm and said, "It's okay, really. It's okay." She nodded quietly.

Then she asked me in a soft voice why my mother hadn't written to tell them that she was sick, that she had cancer. Her son translated. Tončika glanced at me protectively, yet I sensed she too wanted to know. I wondered what I could say to make them feel better. It must have been such a shock to get a letter from my father, explaining that my mom had died, when they didn't even know she had had cancer for almost two years. Maybe she didn't want anyone to know. Maybe she needed to make her world smaller and smaller until she felt okay about leaving it.

I stared down at the floor, then took a deep breath and looked at them. "I really don't know," I said helplessly, and they accepted my answer.

My father and I rented a car and drove north toward the Slovenian Alps. I was relieved to finally be alone with him. No one was guiding us, or taking us on tours of the city. I didn't have to pretend to feel better. In Croatia, I kept stumbling across wonder mixed with pain. I wanted to be in my mother's country, but at the same time, I didn't. Maybe that's how she felt about her own country too.

In Bled we wandered along the banks of the lake, and then drove onward to Kranska Gora to stay the night. And it was the next day, high in the Julian Alps, that I felt temporarily freed from grief. We stopped so that I could photograph sheep wandering a serene mountain meadow. We went over the Vršič Pass and stopped in Kobarid, so that my dad could visit the museum that honored the largest mountain battle during World War I, when Austro-Hungarian soldiers fought against the Italians in the harsh winter conditions and countless soldiers died. Afterward we drove down winding roads and found ourselves beside the emerald Soča River. It was otherworldly and crystal clear, and we admired it in peaceful silence.

After crossing over the Italian border, we curved southward to Croatia and drove down the Istrian Coast. We spent our final days wandering the quiet seaside town of Rovinj. On our last night, I told my dad I wanted to go for a walk and sit by the sea. "I'll come with you," he said quickly, and so we strolled away from the town beside the Adriatic Sea, our footsteps following the curves of the coastline. I listened to my father's airy voice for a while and then we both fell into a steady silence. We watched fishermen untangle their nets beside their boats. Then we sat on stone steps and faced the water. I let my chin dip into my cupped hands and listened to the waves softly splash against the rocks.

I thought about how when my mom was driving me somewhere and we had to make a sudden stop, she would try to shield me. Her right hand would fly off the steering wheel, and she would reach her arm across my chest, trying to stop the impact of something that hadn't yet hit me. Now I understood the impulse to protect someone who's a part of yourself.

There was so much I wished that I could say to my dad at that moment. I wanted to tell him that since my mom's death I was living a life that didn't belong to me. I dreaded going back to New York, to the tiny apartment that I shared with my boyfriend. After his bartending shifts, he was coming home later and later, stopping for drinks and staying out until the early morning with his friends. Sometimes he was explosive when he drank hard liquor. He'd always come home with glassy and bloodshot eyes. He'd sit on the couch and take hits of pot from a water bong, and then get up the next day and do it all over again. We had both lost a parent in a matter of a year. He'd given up on his acting career and seemed lost. I was hanging on to each college class that I took, hoping that learning something would keep me going a little longer.

I couldn't imagine getting myself home from the airport. I couldn't imagine working another waitressing shift. Everything felt meaningless. I often heard *I can't* chanting in my head. I wanted to leave my boyfriend, leave my apartment, but where would I go? I thought maybe I could move to Houston and stay with my dad, but it would be hard to relocate to a place where I didn't know anyone, and when his job ended, my dad planned to leave. I didn't have the money to move anywhere, and I didn't have anywhere to go.

I sensed that my dad knew something was wrong. He seemed vulnerable without my mom, and so alone. I didn't want to burden him with all my troubles. I sighed. The wind picked up and my father lifted his shoulders and shivered like a little boy. We stared at the horizon; daylight faded into a rosy dusk. I breathed in the salty air and listened to the waves. I liked the repetition of the water breaking, gently pulling backward, curling and unfurling onto the shore, then drawing back once again. It was circular; it kept going.

As I stared at the waves, I thought about our time a few days earlier in Bled, Slovenia, when we had taken a *pletna*, a wooden flat-bottom boat, toward a tiny island in the middle of the lake. A white-haired man with dark sunglasses stood perfectly balanced, at the back of the boat, holding an oar. He paddled us outward toward the island. On the far side of the lake, to our right, there was a castle at the top of a limestone cliff. A breeze ruffled the surface of the water. Small waves rocked the ducks floating beside us. On the island hilltop, I could see the white steeple of a church peeking above the trees. I listened to my father speak with a German couple on the boat.

"I didn't think I'd remember that much of my high-school German from forty years ago, but I did pretty well," he told me and laughed. We gazed at the fast-approaching island and both caught our breath.

Wide-eyed, I stared at the endless stone stairway that led up to the church and instantly thought about my dad's polio, his left leg. Stairs were challenging for him. I wasn't sure if he could make it up. The man rowing the boat boasted that there were ninety-nine steps to climb. The stairs were crumbling and beyond them, I glimpsed a freshly painted white stone building. I stepped off the wobbly boat onto the island and reached out to help my dad. He gripped my hand.

Once my dad got his footing, he looked upward.

"We don't have to go up, Dad. We could just stay here and enjoy the view," I suggested.

"No, I'll be fine." He clenched his jaw, determined.

"You sure?"

"Yeah."

"Okay, I can help you."

"Okay," he said, looking again at the steep hill of stairs.

My father's left leg was skin and bone without much muscle. He placed his right foot on the next stair's edge, pressed his right hand into the low stone wall beside the stairway, and then leaned his hips back slightly in order to swing his weak leg forward and rest it on the stair, and then he straightened his strong leg to push himself up. It was a process and it worked better when there was a railing. I stood on his left side and tightly held his hand, trying to help him level his balance.

In truth, he never let anyone help him except my mom. I could see her appearing by his side, taking his hand before he even asked. She would take slow steps, keeping her hand steady so that it would be more supportive. My dad stared down at the stone steps, concentrating. I listened to his hard breathing.

"You can stop and rest," I encouraged him.

"Let's just keep going," he said breathlessly.

As we slowly tackled each stair, I thought about how hard it must be for a man who loved the outdoors and mountain climbing to have contracted polio at the age of thirty-three. Only ten days earlier, he'd gotten the Salk vaccine; some of those polio vaccines still had the live virus. In March of 1962, my dad was working in the Spanish Sahara as a seismologist, when he noticed his foot catching on the doorway of the office trailer. When he flew back to Gran Canaria to see my mom, he was unable to sleep at night. The dull ache in the middle of his back grew stronger. The following day at the doctor's office, he tripped again at the entrance. He felt run down. When he described his symptoms, the doctor prescribed pain medication.

Early the next morning, my dad attempted to get out of bed; his legs suddenly felt floppy. He leaned upon a chair to make his way to the bathroom, and it was then, that he collapsed. My mom awoke to the thud.

For three months he remained at a clinic in Las Palmas for Spanish sailors. There the doctors believed that he had Guillain-Barré Syndrome. Eventually, his doctor advised him to return to the States. As an in-patient for three months at the Kessler Institute in New Jersey, he spent time with fellow patients, who survived car, train, mining accidents, and strokes.

Through rehabilitation, they were learning to live life in new ways. And finally there, my dad's polio was diagnosed. "I was lucky," he told me. He could have been paralyzed, ended up in an iron lung, or died. For the next year, he would use a leg brace. Never again would he run, jump, ski, climb mountains, dance with his wife, or kick a ball with his daughter. For years afterwards, he did physical therapy, so he could do things like walk without a cane, drive a car, and climb stairs.

Now on an island in Lake Bled, we faced these stone steps together. My dad took each one with determination. Occasionally he'd look downward and then glance up to the top, which finally began to get closer and closer, until we reached the 99th step.

"Daddy, you did it! We made it!" I patted him on the shoulder.

He smiled triumphantly.

In that moment, it dawned on me that we had to go on whether we wanted to or not, and somehow, we would learn new ways to be in the world without my mom.

9
BAKA

"Marijana, let me tell you a story," her grandmother said as she lowered herself on the edge of their bed. Marijana rolled on her side, stretching out her legs, and then curling herself around her Baka.

Marijana's light brown hair fell over one shoulder. She seemed small and frail for a ten-year-old girl, and Baka worried constantly about her health. In the months that followed her Tata's death, Marijana would hardly eat. One afternoon a neighbor mentioned seeing Marijana standing alone in front of the house. Pigtails hung in front of her shoulders; she looked lost. The neighbor came out of her house and asked, "Marijana, what are you doing? Do you need something?"

Marijana's eyes had filled with tears. Without a word, she turned and walked back to their door.

The bed creaked as her grandmother shifted. Marijana scratched her bare leg, then glanced up. Her grandmother's thick neck, wide jaw, and double chin made her seem strong as if she could withstand anything. Her white hair was pulled back in a bun and curly wisps escaped, softening her full, round face. Marijana reached up and gently pushed a strand of Baka's hair behind her ear.

Her grandmother sighed once, rubbing her forehead with her hand. It had been a long day, but she would do anything to help her granddaughter. Baka cleared her throat, then began, "Once, there was a little Croatian girl who lived in the small village of Mrkopalj," and she lifted one finger to her thin lips, and her small eyes twinkled. Marijana smiled knowingly. She'd learned that since Tito came, people weren't allowed to use the word "Croatian" to describe things—now it was Yugoslav this and Yugoslav that. At least, that's what they taught her at school. At home, her grandmother had told her that she had to be careful. "Better to say nothing," Baka advised, then added that she should always remember that she was Croatian and Roman Catholic, even if she couldn't say so at school.

Baka continued, "Mrkopalj is in a green valley surrounded by mountains. *Mrko* means dark, my little one, and the woods around the town are dark; there are bears and sometimes in the mornings, when they are hungry, they come out of the forests to steal cherries from the village trees."

Marijana raised her eyebrows.

Bakica chuckled. "They don't bother anyone. It's the wild boars you must watch out for."

Marijana eyes widened, then she cozied up to her Bakica a little more.

Baka continued, "Most keep hens, sheep, cows, or goats, and sometimes they wander through the village. As a child, my house had its barn on the ground floor, so those goats and chickens would stay warm with us in the winters. Oh! I remember so many things now. Sometimes the men went mushroom hunting in the shady forest, sometimes they stacked the wood high against stone walls to get ready for the snowy winters. The women plucked plums from trees in their gardens."

Marijana could imagine it all.

"My little one, the main road of my village is lined with houses, with steep tiled roofs; there is a church with a spire and a cemetery. In the winter, children ski down snow-covered mountains and you can smell the smoke curling into the air from the chimneys. In the summer, the wildflowers bloom." Baka sighed. "When I was a child, long afternoons passed when not even a dog barked. Nothing moved. Doors were unlocked, windows thrown open. You could smell the wind, the spruce trees and the earth."

"What about the little girl?" Marijana reminded her, nudging Baka's wide waist with her elbow.

"Ah, yes, the little girl," her grandmother nodded. Her eyes were far away as if she could once again picture the little girl's face.

"What did she look like?"

"She had long brown hair and light green eyes," her grandmother said, then squinted as if she were examining something way back in her memory.

"Like me?" Marijana blurted out.

"Well, yes, you look very much like that little girl!" her grandmother exclaimed, smiling, touching her cheek tenderly.

"So listen, my little one, this girl was the most beautiful little girl in the village. When she passed villagers on the road, she'd greet them with such warmth that they'd feel differently for the rest of the day."

"How?"

"Well, my little bird, they would be kinder to anyone they came across."

Marijana nodded.

Her grandmother pulled out an embroidered handkerchief

and blew her nose, then crumpled it and stuffed it inside the top of her blouse into her brassiere. "Everyone in the village adored this little girl. She always went out of her way to help people. She loved every animal in the village, and every animal in the village loved her. She was constantly rescuing cats from one mishap or another. When she would see a kitten, she would squat down and rub her fingers together and say, '*mic, mic, mic.*'"

Marijana smiled because that was what she did.

"One day," her grandmother said, stopping to take a deep breath, "One day, she heard frantic meowing from the branches of a tree. Somehow a large gray cat had climbed up a cherry tree, but couldn't get down. He gripped the bark with his claws, his fur stood on end. He was very frightened. The little girl ran over to see what she could do. She reached her arms up to the cat and spoke to him in a low, steady voice. The cat looked at her and then leapt into her arms.

"She set him on the ground and as he scampered away, she noticed that his claws had scratched one of her arms. She could see the blood beginning to rise on the surface of her skin. She didn't tell anyone about her arm; she never complained when tiny red specks began to run along the inside of her arm. Her arm started to ache and she began to feel feverish and one morning, she couldn't get up from bed, so she called out to her mama.

"By the time the doctor came it was too late. 'Blood poisoning from a cat scratch,' he whispered. The villagers gathered outside the house and waited until the little girl took her last breath, until her mother shut the bedroom window.

"The men and children walked into the forest and picked every flower they could find. The women cut all the flowers from their window boxes and gardens. Soon there were no flowers left in the entire village except the ones that encircled this little girl's coffin. She wore a brilliant white dress for her journey to heaven. The summer wind blew some of her long silky hair over the edge of the wooden coffin. Everyone whispered that she looked like an angel. She had a serene expression and it seemed as if she had already been lifted up.

And now Marijana, your parents are there and watching over her, with the angels." Her grandmother paused and took out her handkerchief and dabbed the corners of her eyes.

Marijana became thoughtful. "Bakica, you were born in the village of Mrkopalj."

"I was."

"Did you know that little girl?"

Bakica lifted one hand to her heart. "It was a long time ago."

Marijana sat up on her knees and wrapped her arms around her Bakica.

"Marijanica, she was your age when she left me. And now she's an angel watching over you, keeping you safe. She'll make sure nothing happens to you."

"Bakica, do you think that when you go to heaven, you stay the same age you are when you die?" Marijana asked, wondering if her parents would grow older in heaven. When she grew up, would they recognize her?

Her grandmother dabbed her eyes with a handkerchief.

Marijana realized that loss connected them as much as blood.

Baka chopped onions in the kitchen. Her eyes watered while she worried about her granddaughter and the situation in Yugoslavia. After Tito's Partisans marched into Zagreb, she'd heard that Partisans burst into hospitals and thrown wounded soldiers out of windows, she'd heard of mass executions on the border of Austria and Slovenia. A friend had written to Baka about her neighbor, a poor mother of six, who was accused of being a spy; the police came, and the youngest children tried to hold on to her skirt as she was led away. Later they learned that she was killed. Six children, motherless. Baka shook her head as she tried hard to concentrate on the drum of her knife hitting the board.

Tito's framed pictures appeared in all the schools and offices. On the tram, she read signs saying: *Dok traje obnova—nema odmora.* During the rebuilding of our country—no rest whatsoever. On the bus: *Comrade Tito, we swear never to leave your path.* There was an underlying fear that she could see in everyone's eyes. Yet people still managed to keep a sense of humor. Her friend told her this joke: *Comrade Tito, it's not clear to me why it's my cow, but you're getting the butter. After three years in prison, now—it's clear to me.*

Still you had to be careful. People had their phones tapped or their mail opened. It took little to be accused of being a collaborator. There were informants everywhere. If you hadn't been on the Partisans' side during the war, or if you were anti-communist, the UDBA (the communist-run secret police) could end up pounding on your door. They kept lists of people's names. If you were suspected of anything, you could be denied a state job, or lose the position you had. Since Tito had split from Stalin in 1948, he was determined to crush all opposition (especially those who'd been active in the Croatian Peasant Party, or the Catholic Church) in order to force his one-party state into existence. Macedonia, Montenegro, Bosnia and Herzegovina, Slovenia, Serbia, and Croatia were the six republics of Communist Yugoslavia. In Tito's Yugoslavia, he suppressed any differences or tensions between the ethnic groups to encourage a Yugoslav identity.

Baka thought that if her youngest sister Victoria and her husband Ivo were here, surely they'd have been arrested.

Ivo had been active in the Peasant Party and during the war had been part of a secret pro-Allied movement. *Thank God, they made it out*, Baka sighed. If they hadn't escaped to Italy and then made their way to South America, there was no doubt that they would be in prison now. She knew of a young woman who had made a joke about Tito, and a day later had been arrested. She was sent to Saint Gregory Island, a women's prison camp for a year. Bakica was certain if Ivo was here, he would have been executed or sent to Goli Otok, the barren island camp where political prisoners were enslaved, re-educated, and forced into labor.

Bakica's thoughts turned to a friend who, each month, sent parcels to her husband in one of these prison camps. The conditions were unbearable and people often died from hunger, typhus, tuberculosis or torture. Enemies of the state, those who sided with Stalin instead of Tito, those who were anti-communist, those who had accidently said the wrong thing at the wrong time, could disappear for years. One month her friend's parcel was returned unopened; her husband had died.

Sometimes it seemed to Baka that it was even more difficult to buy food in the post-war years. Everything was rationed. One pair of shoes was supposed to last for more than two years. For hours, she waited in endless lines for a few potatoes and a kilo of flour. When someone tried to break into the queue, there were loud arguments. Sugar, meat, and coffee were impossible to buy.

Baka remembered how right after the war everyone was delighted when Truman eggs and dehydrated milk came in the American food parcels. Marijana could hardly wait for Bakica to prepare them. She added piping hot water to the powdery flakes, Marijana stirred them, and they became eggs! So many Croatians were hungry and nothing made Baka happier than watching her granddaughter eat. Marijana never complained, but Baka could see she was growing thinner, and in recent months Marijana had several colds that lasted a long time. Baka worried. Oftentimes, her granddaughter seemed tired.

Baka dropped the slices of onion into the bottom of a pot and then peeled the garlic. She thought how they were lucky to have their little house. She had watched the Communists nationalize private businesses and private farms. The Party also confiscated flats or suddenly sent a family to move in with you, and then you had to share your home with strangers. So far private houses had been left alone. Her son Anton had made certain they owned the house before he died. "We'll look for boarders. We'll manage," she told Marijana. And they did, although they often struggled to get actual rent. Yesterday a squawking chicken was produced instead of *dinars*. This morning she had killed that chicken and plucked all its feathers. Now she cut it up into pieces and added them to the pot of water along with chopped carrots, celery, and potatoes. As the soup boiled, she added the salt and felt relief that today, finally, she could provide food for her granddaughter.

While the soup simmered, Baka walked outside to get water. Her granddaughter should have a hot bath when she came home. Better to start heating up the water now. She wiped her forehead and lugged the wooden bucket with slopping water to the house. Later she needed to wash their clothes, which meant getting more buckets of water and heating it on the stove. Her wrist joints ached.

Most days she got on her hands and knees and tended their garden. With her hands covered in earth, she'd pray to God to help them find enough to eat. She recalled the afternoon, when two nuns dressed in black and white habits had startled her. They asked for a donation. "God needs your help in these desperate times." She blinked in astonishment; she couldn't feed her own granddaughter. She was an old woman without work, without an education. "If you want money, why don't you go to work?" she snapped at them.

Communism couldn't stop her from being a deeply religious Roman Catholic. It was hard for professionals, teachers, lawyers, and doctors to attend mass, because the Party members harassed them. They'd get passed over for a promotion or they'd lose their job. Many became Party members. But she was an old woman and no one really bothered her. She wondered if Communist Yugoslavia was going to outlive her.

Her third-grade village education proved to be enough to read to Marijana each night from the worn Bible that she hid beneath her mattress. She'd heard of children getting in trouble at school, accidentally mentioning their parents' Bible, when a teacher asked about their family's beliefs. But Marijana was too smart for that. Baka was astounded how quickly her granddaughter could read people's characters.

One of Baka's friends had recently traveled from her village to visit them. Her daughter had played outdoors with Marijana, while they spoke in the kitchen. Her friend described hearing political prisoners being tortured in the cellar of a neighboring house. Sometimes she walked by the window and could hear the screams, the moaning. One afternoon, she put bread into her daughter's hands and told her to play nearby the house. "I told her to throw some bread through the window, when no one was looking. She didn't understand, she was hungry and would have liked to eat the bread herself." Anxiously, the mother watched her daughter walk toward the house with the prisoner. Her daughter pretended to play, squatting beside the window. She made certain no one was looking when she tossed pieces of bread through the small holes in the window.

Such suffering, Baka sighed.

Marijana had been required to join Tito's *Mali Pioniri*. All children had to join Tito's Pioneers and there were no exceptions. From the doorway, Baka had watched her granddaughter leave the house in a white blouse, blue skirt, red scarf tied around her neck and red bows on her braids. The costume of a young communist. When Marijana returned home, she marched around the kitchen chanting:

Pioniri Maleni,
mi smo vojska prava,
svakog dana ničemo
ko' zelena trava.
Smrt fašizmu
a sloboda narodu
i meneće moja mati
za brigadira dati.

Little Pioneers,
We are the righteous army
Every day we are growing
like green grass.
Death to Fascism
and freedom to the people,
my mother would be proud
to have a brigadier child.

When Marijana had seen the dismayed look on Baka's face, she'd laughed. The thought of her Marijana becoming a communist deeply upset Baka. Breathlessly, Marijana had sat on a kitchen chair and told her grandmother that she'd been bored listening to lectures about the liberation of the people from fascism.

"They give us liberty to live in prison," Baka snapped.

10

THE HOSPITAL

The doctor pointed to a chair outside his office. He nodded for Marijana to sit there and wait. Obediently she sat down, while her grandmother followed him through the door. Marijana noticed that the door didn't quite latch when it was closed. She nudged it open ever so slightly.

"…white spots on her X-ray," the doctor said, and then added, "it was only a matter of time. Seems like the whole country. Her parents? Yes?"

Her grandmother nodded wordlessly.

Marijana held her breath outside the door.

"Well," the doctor continued, "it's possible that she was exposed then, and it's been dormant till now. Though, she could have contracted it anywhere, anytime. Someone coughs, sneezes, laughs, talks, cries out…and then bacteria is there, invisible, floating in the air, and then, someone breathes it in. Look, no one is to blame. It's not your fault. It's not her parents' fault."

Marijana saw her grandmother's shoulders shake. She looked away from the door and slouched down in the chair.

Sušica disease that dries you up. Thin like a mummy. She stared out the hospital window at a chestnut tree. She was only fourteen. Why her? Why would God do this?

"She'll have to stay in hospital for months at the least, possibly a year. It's hard to know, really. We must take this very seriously," he warned Baka. "I've watched whole families disappear… brothers, sisters. It can worsen without anyone becoming aware, and then it's too late."

Marijana imagined herself running away from this place, sneaking back into the bedroom that she shared with Baka and stealing a few *dinars* so she could go to the cinema and see Ingrid Bergman.

She overheard the doctor say that she needed rest and lots of good food. When they came out, Marijana quietly followed the doctor and her grandmother down the corridors and climbed the hospital stairs, stopping every once in a while to catch her breath. The overpowering scent of cleaning fluid hit her nose; the floors had just been mopped. She passed a nun in a stiff white wimple that framed her face. There was a Party sign on the wall: *Tko ne radi, taj ne jede. Those who don't work, don't eat.* At the top of the stairway, she saw another girl about her age, sitting in a wheelchair. She was extremely pale; her eyes were light blue, and she caught Marijana staring at her.

"One more victim has arrived," Marijana joked.

The girl giggled, then drew in her breath through her teeth, and gripped her right side ribs with her hand.

They both waited for her pain to subside.

"I'm Ružica," the girl finally said.

"How do you do? I'm Marijana. That's my grandmother over there," she said, tilting her head toward her granny. They both watched Baka, listening intently to the doctor.

Ružica smiled shyly and asked, "And how are you?"

Marijana blinked. She was alone in the world except for

her Baka. Marijana's throat ached. "Fine," she answered. "I wish I could go home, I don't want to be here, but I promised my grandmother I'd come. She says they'll make me better."

"Where are your parents?" Ružica asked curiously.

"They're gone. My grandmother looks after me," she said, noticing that her own voice had become harder.

"Oh," Ružica said, pressing her lips together. She began to cough, she dug her hand into her right ribs as she curled forward.

Marijana kneeled beside her. "Are you all right?"

"Yes…this, it's so, unpleasant," Ružica whispered breathlessly.

Marijana nodded sympathetically. "I agree."

"A few nights ago, I couldn't stop. My mouth was full of blood. Hemorrhaging, the doctor said. I kept coughing and coughing. I thought it would never stop. They've taken me for more X-rays, and now back to bed. I must be on complete bedrest, only resting. Sometimes it's hard," Ružica said bravely.

In the hospital, Marijana fought the impulse to venture outside. Endless days in bed meant boredom. Days turned into weeks into months of being propped up by pillows. She longed to go for a walk. Sometimes after school, she'd walked around Zagreb with her friend Dragica, and they pretended that they were American tourists so they could practice their English.

Here she was assigned to bed rest, with the occasional sputum test or X-ray. "Let your lungs rest," the nurse ordered. There were so many rules; it was worse than school. Everything was limited to a certain amount of time or not allowed. The nurses said that if you broke the rules, you would be sent home to die.

"They're so uplifting," Marijana said sarcastically.

Ružica arched one eyebrow at Marijana and chuckled.

One afternoon during visiting hours her grandmother and Ružica's mother came, as they often did, bringing them soup, crusty bread, and carrots. "I feel like a rabbit, we're eating so many carrots," Ružica said under her breath to Marijana.

"Eat, eat, eat," Baka urged. She believed that the more you ate, the better your chances were. "Lots of butter, milk, fat, and rest makes all the difference. *Slušaj me*, try bacon in milk. Fatten her up as much as possible," a neighbor advised Baka, and then added, "When she comes home, hang her sheets and blanket in the sun. The sunlight will kill the tuberculosis bacteria."

When they were finished eating, Baka bundled up the leftover food in a cloth, and the girls hid it behind the radio that they kept between their beds. Baka reminded them how lucky they were to be in the hospital. "You're eating much better than the rest of us out there." It was true. Outside, they had often felt hungry. Here, every once in a while, they even had cucumber salad or wild goose. The girls sipped from mugs of warm chamomile tea that Bakica had brought them, while they chatted about the young patients in their ward.

From her purse, Baka pulled out *Filmski Svet*, a film magazine. "Bakica!" Marijana cried in surprise, and then threw her arms around her grandmother. Ružica and Marijana slowly went through each page, examining the black-and-white photographs of their favorite Hollywood actors: Greta Garbo, Fred Astaire, Leslie Caron, Ingrid Bergman, Clark Gable, Elizabeth Taylor, Gina Lollobrigida, and Jane Russell. Marijana felt a burst of energy.

While Marijana chatted with Ružica's mother, Baka went over to Ružica's bedside. She whispered to her, "Please, please, promise to keep an eye on Marijana. Sometimes she can get into trouble. She does too much and doesn't rest. I want her to get well, despite herself. Do you understand, my dear Ružica?"

Ružica's blue eyes widened and nodded seriously. "I will. You have my word."

Marijana glanced over at them. "What are you two talking about?" she asked suspiciously.

Her grandmother patted Ružica's arm tenderly. "Nothing, nothing, my little one, I was telling Ružica how lucky you are to have each other."

At night, Marijana listened to the rattling breaths of the other patients. It seemed as if when someone coughed, it spread throughout the ward. The urge was overpowering. She tried to resist, but often she would break out into hacking coughs herself, until it felt as if her ribs were about to shatter. A nurse appeared in the doorway and whispered, "Cover your mouths, control your coughs, rest your lungs!" Marijana groaned and then rolled over, trying to fall asleep in the quiet spaces.

One morning Marijana's excitement consisted of listening to the occasional sound of a automobile rumbling past on the street. A steady stream of nurses checked in on them, but as soon as the room was empty, she slipped out of bed so that she could move her legs about. When she heard the familiar squeak of the doctor's shoes coming down the hallway, she ran back, leapt into bed, and slipped beneath the sheets.

Ružica appeared in the doorway, smiling, showing Marijana a new pair of black suede shoes that her mother had brought her, one foot placed in front of the other. It had been years since Ružica had new shoes. Marijana put her hand on her chest and said, "My God—you made my heart stop! You scared me! I thought it was the doctor. I thought I'd get into trouble."

Ružica laughed.

Marijana started coughing and laughing. "Model them for me," she said, directing Ružica from her bed. Ružica smiled as she twirled around, with one hand on her hip, like a Hollywood actress.

That day they visited the ward with the younger patients. They sat around a table with a few little girls. They sketched and cut out paper dolls with them. Marijana designed elaborate dresses for each one. Ružica colored the fine details on the dresses. As they drew and scissors snipped away, Marijana recounted stories from the Shirley Temple films she had seen. The children were delighted. Magdalena, a rosy cheeked girl with long dark braids, requested that Marijana also make a night gown for her paper doll.

"Why a night gown?" Marijana asked.

"I want to play hospital. I need to take X-rays of her chest," Magdalena told them.

"Splendid! So are you her doctor?" Ružica asked.

Magdalena nodded proudly and then smiled.

Marijana laughed and patted her head. "I will design the fanciest hospital gown you have ever seen!" Ružica hugged Magdalena, who grinned at all the attention.

When Ružica and Marijana returned to their own room, they flopped onto their beds and stared out the window. Only a few moments passed when their friend Miro burst in. He announced, "Today I'm going home. I'm leaving, and I'm never coming back here."

"What? Did the doctor say you could go?" Marijana asked.

"No," Miro said, "But I'm cured."

"How do you know? Do you feel different?" she challenged.

"Because I'm not coughing anymore; my fevers have vanished. I feel better and I don't want to stay another day."

"Are you sure? I mean, sometimes you can feel better, but you aren't. That's how TB is."

"No, I'm certain. I'm cured. I don't need to lie in bed all day long. I can go home now. I miss my Mama's cooking."

Miro's face was glowing. Marijana wondered was it from happiness or fever.

"The nurse tried to talk me out of it, but no one can stop me."

"What did she tell you?" Ružica asked gently.

He paused, looking away from them.

"Go on, tell us," Ruzica urged.

"She said, 'If you go, that's it. You can never come back. There are plenty who need your bed. If you leave, you'll end up in the grave.' My dear friends, don't worry. I'll never set foot in this hospital again."

Marijana and Ruzica looked at each other. There was nothing that they could do to talk him out of it.

One week later, two nurses helped Miro back into a hospital bed. When Marijana went to his doorway, he was lying on his side, defeated. He didn't seem to see her. She took a deep breath and walked straight up to his bed. She held a tattered copy of a Karl Maj novel. Maj was a German writer who wrote adventure stories about the American West. She'd been surprised to hear that he'd never once visited America, still she loved his books and it was the only thing she had that she could give Miro. She placed it on his bedside table. She took his hand and held it for a moment. For the time being, he was unreachable and he didn't speak. Marijana wondered, were they all on the edge of death.

A fifteen-year old blind boy named Mate arrived on the ward. His dark hair jutted in different directions on the top of his head. He brushed his hands along the hospital walls and walked slowly, drawn forward by the voices. He noticed that Marijana's voice could be heard above the others. She could make people laugh, people who hadn't laughed in a long time. Sometimes he tried to predict whether someone would live or die by the sound of their voice. He was certain that Marijana would survive.

"Mate, how are you today?" Marijana said when she saw him standing in their doorway.

"Much better now that I've heard your voice," he sighed.

She laughed and then rolled her eyes. "Well, are you going to come in or not?" She waved him into the room as if he could see her every gesture.

He followed her laugh to the end of her bed.

Ružica shook her finger at Marijana for teasing him. The night before, she had said, "Marijana, he's a nice boy, don't you like him?"

"You can have him," Marijana had said then added, "I'll be leaving soon. I want a healthy boy."

"Marijana!" Ružica protested, but couldn't stop herself from smiling.

"Mate, you know Ružica, don't you?" Marijana asked him now.

"Yes, of course," Mate replied.

"She's the most lovely girl in the entire hospital, did you know that?" Marijana told him.

"Marijana!" Ružica protested. She blushed. She put her hands to her warm cheeks and sputtered, "It's not true, Mate, not true at all."

"Of course it is," Marijana said with such conviction that she slapped the sheets with her hands for emphasis.

Mate and Ružica timidly exchanged a few words. And after a while they began to exchange stories. They talked about Jack London and his book *Call of the Wild*, and soon they were so comfortable that they interrupted each other. Ružica glowed, and Marijana felt happy as she turned on the radio so that they could listen to Ivo Robić, singing a romantic ballad.

It was still dark when Marijana woke up. She watched Ružica lying on her back, her head turned to the side, her curly blond hair draped over the white pillow. Marijana rolled to her other side, she rubbed her hands together, trying to warm them. She wished that she hadn't woken up yet. She felt miserable. There was nothing to look forward to, nowhere to go. Another long day in bed stretched endlessly in front of her. She closed her eyes and then blinked them opened, staring at the young woman across from her, a new patient who'd come to the hospital only the night before.

Marijana noticed that the girl's eyes were slightly open; she was perfectly still. Was she awake? Marijana threw back her sheets and tiptoed over to her bed. The floor felt like ice against her bare feet. She touched the girl's arm; her skin was cold. Marijana shook her a few times and the girl didn't wake up. Marijana ran to the door and cried out for the nurse.

"Go back to bed," the nurse ordered Marijana once she entered the room. "Go, go." The nurse took Marijana by the arm and helped her climb back into bed. Ružica sat up, startled. They both watched soundlessly as the girl's body was taken away. Sheets were stripped off the bed. It was as if she never existed.

"She was our age," Ružica whispered once they were alone.

"I know," Marijana said huskily.

"We never even got to know her name…"

They burrowed under their covers, their faces peeking out from their blankets. Marijana shivered. She rubbed the sides of her arms quickly, trying to get her blood to circulate. The nurses insisted on keeping the windows open. Fresh air was part of the cure. Lately, she thought she was getting worse. She felt tired all the time; she often woke up in the middle of the night covered in sweat.

Streptomycin was nearly impossible to find in Yugoslavia, but their doctor had managed and while they were staying in the hospital, they were given some. After they left the hospital, it would be more difficult. "What if I'm next?" Marijana said aloud. "I'm so young, how can I just lie here in bed all the time?" she asked, her voice got caught inside her chest.

Ružica shook her head. "No, Marijana, we're going to get better. I know we are."

"Some people never leave."

"Yes, yes, they do," Ružica told her. "One way or another they do."

This was true. Each week at least two or three beds opened up, mostly because children died of the disease.

"Ružica, are you ever afraid?"

"I am. All the time. But I pray to God and that helps me." She swallowed, and then whispered, "I remember when I was about five years old, during the war, suddenly the floor was rattling beneath my feet. A bomb fell. Debris flew, broken glass everywhere. It was so loud, the sound of everything breaking. I couldn't see anything. My dad pushed me down to the ground and when I touched my head, and looked at my hands, they were full of blood. I ran crying to a neighbor's house."

Marijana caught her breath, as her own wartime memories rose up.

"Marijana, I felt more afraid afterward; if I saw a bomber plane, my hands would start to shake. Afterward I started sleepwalking."

Marijana nodded. She thought of the war, of her parents. She remembered the wail of a siren and the way she ran to an air raid shelter. She sat with strangers along the walls; she could hear nearby explosions. She could feel the rumble as clumps of dirt and pieces of the ceiling fell onto her hair and shoulders. It was strange to know that death could come at any moment. When an old man in the corner pulled out his accordion and began to play, she calmed down.

They heard footsteps out in the hallway of the hospital. Marijana held a finger up to her lips and Ružica nodded. The footsteps grew fainter and fainter until they could no longer hear them. Ružica tilted her head thoughtfully. "Some go home and some go to heaven, that's all," she said softly.

Marijana stopped holding her breath.

They whispered to each other until the sun stretched through the windows, until it was safe to go back to sleep.

11
MARIJANA'S BRESTOVAC

After three months in hospital, Marijana returned home to her grandmother. And in the year that followed, Ružica would often visit Marijana and her grandmother. At the kitchen table, they ate Baka's black cherry strudel while they sipped tea with *šljivovica*. Baka insisted that it would improve their health. Marijana and Ružica flipped through the latest *Filmski Svet* and chatted about when they would go to the cinema next, while Bakica fussed about the kitchen, bringing them more food, encouraging them to eat.

Marijana told Ružica about her art classes at the secondary school in Gornji Grad, the old city. There was a life drawing class, where students sketched a nude model. While Bakica was out of the room, Marijana explained to Ružica that the model was shaved, and when the art teacher left the room, the boys took their charcoal pencils to their sketches and began shading in the hair between her legs as fast as they could. They both laughed and rolled their eyes.

They were relieved to be out of the hospital; they avoided talking about their health. As they spoke about everyday things,

Marijana felt close to Ružica. She imagined this was what it must be like to have a sister. She imagined that they would always visit each other, when they were grown up, when they got their first jobs, when they became mothers, when they became grandmothers.

The doctor used the stethoscope to listen to her lungs. He pressed lightly against her back and told her to inhale and exhale. When he finished, she buttoned her blouse and tucked it back into her skirt.

The doctor was busy writing something down. He motioned for her to sit.

"Marijana, how are you feeling?"

"So-so I guess," she told him, nervously. The truth was she had felt some signs of breathlessness. Sometimes she was coughing, but still, it was not serious, she was sure of it. She was seventeen now.

"The lungs. Your X-ray. They don't look as they should."

"What do you mean?" she asked tentatively.

"Young lady, what I think you need is a good rest outside the city," the doctor told her.

"I don't want to go back to the hospital," she said, trying to convince him.

"The X-rays show evidence of TB, Marijana. There is no denying the spots on your lungs," he told her gently. He explained that Brestovac, the sanatorium on Sljeme, the mountain behind Zagreb, would be the best place for her now.

She shook her head. What would her grandmother say? She didn't want to tell her this. She would be devastated.

"Marijana, look, you're sick. People relapse with this disease and it's important to catch it before…" He leaned back in his chair.

"Before it's too late," she finished his sentence.

"We will get you better. Your grandmother can't manage to get you enough to eat at home. At the sanatorium, you can rebuild your strength. You will be healthy again."

She crossed her arms.

"Your friend Ružica is there."

"I know." She began to tremble slightly. They had been writing letters to each other.

"So," he said, and then looked at her thoughtfully, rubbing his closely shaven chin.

She glanced at the ceiling for an instant. She wondered if there was any way out. "Okay, what else can I do?" she relented.

"Good. This is exactly what you need."

"Thank you," she said. She knew that she should be grateful, but instead she felt angry.

He gave her a tired smile. There were so many like her; there were so many that would spend years dying.

From their semi-reclined cure beds, Ružica and Marijana could see the stone buildings and huts scattered through the forest. Alongside the mountain, there was a veranda, where patients were lying on cots in the open air. They spent many afternoons outside; the fresh air was supposed to do them good. The nurses said that there were more days of sunlight up on the mountain of Medvednica than down below in the city of Zagreb. The state-funded TB sanatorium Brestovac was nestled on the slope of the mountain. In the crisp winter air, Marijana smoothed her short light-brown curly hair and then slipped back on her winter cap. Ružica pulled her woolen blanket up to her chin. "Wait, so then what did you tell your teacher?" she asked Marijana.

"I simply told her that she was incorrect."

"You didn't. Marijana!" Ružica scolded.

"Well, she was. Listen, she should study her English more before she tries to teach us."

"Maybe if she went to the cinema as often as you did, she would speak better English," Ružica teased.

Marijana rolled her eyes.

"Really, I miss school, but instead we're stuck here," Marijana said regretfully.

"Imagine we're somewhere else," Ružica suggested.

Marijana smiled. "Today we're visiting the Swiss Alps on holiday."

"Oh, yes, I can already see the view, the snow-capped mountains," Ružica said, extending her arm, gazing beyond the pine trees.

"Can you give me a light?" Marijana asked, holding up an imaginary cigarette to her dry lips.

"Of course." Ružica dug her hand deep under the blanket and pulled out an imaginary matchbook; she leaned over and struck the match. Marijana could almost smell the sulfur. She inhaled deeply, and then tilted her head back as she blew the smoke out.

"Put it out!" Ružica whispered in a panic as a nurse approached, carrying a stack of starched sheets. Marijana threw it to the ground, sat up and stomped it out with her foot. They laughed, and each time they looked at each other, they laughed harder until they were both breathlessly coughing and choking and laughing. Snowflakes drifted down from the sky, catching on their eyelashes.

In the springtime, they took walks, venturing past the sanatorium grounds, on the trails of Sljeme. Marijana liked the moment she could no longer see the stone sanatorium buildings, when she was surrounded by trees. Sometimes they came across wild cyclamen, snowdrops, crocuses, and primroses bursting from the earth. They picked a few, and Ružica arranged them in a vase back in their room. Marijana would take out her charcoal pencils, and pastels, and sketch the flowers. Ružica noticed that when she was drawing, Marijana seemed to find a particular kind of quietness. She peered over her shoulder and admired her work.

"Marijana, as my uncle would say, 'When God gave out the talent, you were sitting in the front row.'"

"No, it's horrible. I'm out of practice. I've got so much to learn," Marijana said hopelessly.

"No, really Marijana, not everyone can draw that well."

Marijana shrugged and stared at the flowers, then let her pencil take over.

With a basket of food, Marijana's grandmother came to visit. She bustled about their room, rearranging things. "It's been so long since you've been home, my little one," she told Marijana as she folded her granddaughter's cold hand into her own.

"I miss you, Bakica," Marijana blurted, feeling like a child once again. She had been in the sanatorium for half a year.

Baka smoothed the bed sheets and asked, "My little Marijana, are you taking care of yourself?"

"I'm fine. Ask Ružica, she'll tell you." They both glanced toward the doorway. Ružica was taking a walk with her mother.

Baka looked anxiously at Marijana. "Bakica, don't worry," Marijana said.

"I am worried. I'm writing to your aunt and uncle in Argentina. I'm trying to figure out a way to get you out of this country so you can get better treatment."

"I'll never leave you."

"Marijana, please be reasonable. You need a better life

than the one I can give you. If you stay in this Godforsaken country, you'll never get better."

"You can't make me go."

"What is going to happen if you stay here, Marijana?"

"I don't care. I'd rather die," Marijana answered firmly.

"Come on, stop talking that way. I don't want that. Do you understand? I don't want that for you. I'd do anything so that you get well again."

"We only have each other," Marijana pleaded, and then she turned away from her grandmother. She felt a sharp ache in her chest. She was well aware there wasn't enough money for both of them to leave. How would they get permission to leave Yugoslavia anyway? She knew that her grandmother saw her escape as a chance to survive. Her father once told her, "Your Bakica has the most common sense of anyone I know. Make sure to listen to her." But now Marijana didn't want to listen.

Sometimes Marijana slipped out of the sanatorium at night with Čija, Ružica, and her fellow patients. They wandered through the forest, admiring the city lights of Zagreb in the valley below, eventually settling down for a midnight picnic, spreading out a blanket they'd stolen from an empty bed. Someone would break off pieces of bread and pass them around, and sometimes they even managed to get their hands on a bottle of wine. When they couldn't get wine, one of the boys would sneak into the dispensary and make their own concoction. They lounged on the blanket, forgetting why they were there on that mountain, yelling out in delight when a bat swooped down.

One young man with dark brown hair and a pointy nose named Željko liked to tease Marijana. Some afternoons he stopped to visit her. She blushed as they sat outside together, while a nurse mopped the wooden floor of her hut with strong disinfectant. Crickets trilled as they spoke about Vivien Leigh and Clark Gable in *Gone with the Wind*. After the nurse left, he told her about Milivoj Dežman, the physician who had helped build this sanatorium. Dežman's childhood love, a famous Zagreb actress named Ljerka Šram, had been stricken by TB. She had been married and had a child, but her husband abandoned her. Milivoj had brought her to Brestovac and taken care of her. "Finally Ljerka died in his arms," Željko told Marijana.

She sighed, shaking her head. She felt badly for Željko. Recently his good friend had been taken for surgery and never returned. There were rumors about new treatments, including removing ribs, or blowing up a small balloon into the lung. Marijana shivered. "Let's promise each other that we will never let them take us for an operation," Marijana told him.

"Agreed," Željko said. And then he confessed to her that when his mother visited, she would whisper to his younger sister to not sit too close to him. "We must be kept away from the world, I guess, Marijana. We are too dangerous." As he spoke, Marijana noticed how pale and handsome he was. The afternoon sun fell upon their faces. He pulled out his guitar and gently strummed a song; they both sang along.

After he left, she confided in Ružica that she wouldn't mind having him as her boyfriend. "Marijana, you know you are supposed to stay as calm as possible and lie in bed and rest like the doctors tell us. No excitement whatsoever, remember? Because it just wears you out. Girls with TB aren't supposed to have boyfriends," Ružica told her.

Marijana rolled her eyes.

"Listen, Marijana, I'm serious. Do you want to get better or not? It is a small sacrifice."

"I might as well be in the grave already. You can light a candle," Marijana snapped.

Ružica bit her lip.

"Ružica, look, I don't care. I'm so bored here. I'm tired of waiting. Wait for what? I want to live now, not later." Marijana slipped on her shoes, and walked away down the stone road, down a trail into the forest where she could no longer see any of the patients. Her heart pounded in rage; her cheeks burned. The crickets' maddening chatter made her want to scream, but after a while it faded into the background and she could only hear tiny branches and dry pine needles crackling beneath her shoes. She felt the thread of a spider web brush against her cheek, and another brush against her arm. She stopped and stood still until she was able to take a deep breath.

"No one will even know. Come, please," Marijana tried to entice Ružica in their room.

"Absolutely not. How can you even consider walking all the way down there to see a film? In your condition?"

"You could use a bit of fun, come on. We'll go to *Kino Sloboda*, or *Kino Zagreb*," she said, naming their favorite theaters. Marijana remembered how it felt the time that she and her friends had slipped down the mountain to see a snake charmer performing in the city. She desperately wanted to escape again. She wanted something to look forward to. She wanted to be free from all of this.

Ružica sighed. She could see there was no talking Marijana out of this. "Listen, I won't go, but if someone comes asking for you, I'll make up some story." Ružica grabbed Marijana's arm. "Don't stay too long. Don't come back too late, okay?"

Marijana nodded.

The next morning Ružica got up and ruffled Marijana's sheets to make the bed look as if it had been slept in. She'd been awake half the night worrying. Why hadn't Marijana come back? What if she collapsed somewhere from exhaustion?

A nurse popped in and asked about Marijana. Ružica took a deep breath and said she'd gone to the toilet. An hour later, Marijana crept into the room and sank into bed. She looked feverish; her cheeks were flushed.

"Ružica, are you sleeping?" Marijana whispered.

Silence.

"Ružica?" Marijana could sense her anger. "Are you upset?" she asked.

"What do you think?" Ružica answered.

"Please, please don't be angry with me. Don't you want to know where we went and what we saw?"

"No, I don't care. You are going to ruin your health. Don't you care about that?"

Marijana swallowed.

"Did you at least go visit your grandmother?"

Marijana didn't answer.

"You went all the way to the city and didn't even stop and visit your grandmother?"

"I'm sorry."

"You know how hard it is for her to come here. All the trams and buses she has to take, and it's hard for her to walk."

"I know."

"I'm never going to make excuses for you again. Look, Marijana, even though I'm younger than you, your Baka wanted me to look out for you, because sometimes you push yourself too hard, because you will push yourself into the grave if you aren't careful. Your grandmother told me she just wants to protect you from yourself."

"Ružica, I'm really sorry," Marijana's voice cracked. "I'll never sneak out again. I know it's not good for me. Look how tired I am. I was coughing all the way home."

"You were?" Ružica saw that Marijana's green eyes looked bright, her lips looked dry and pale.

Marijana nodded, she wiped tears from her cheeks.

"You promise?"

"I promise," Marijana said quietly.

After eight months at the sanatorium, Marijana was released and sent home. There was a long waiting list. They needed the bed even though the X-rays said otherwise. Still, her grandmother was grateful to have her granddaughter at home. She sat beside Marijana, who lay quietly in bed.

Marijana glanced up at her grandmother. "Come on, *Bakica*, streptomycin is hard to find," she said, shrugging her shoulders.

"Everything I could think of…even if we had the money… it is so impossible here, everyone is scrambling for it, scraps of meat on the black market."

Marijana nodded. Streptomycin meant life. Even on the black market, once it appeared, it disappeared. People were desperate. Her entire body ached. She'd overheard the doctor whisper to her grandmother, "Can't you get her out of here? Don't you know someone abroad? Send her away. It's her only chance."

"Yugoslavia is so backward. Why is it so difficult to get medicine here? It is all Tito's fault—things were so much better before," her grandmother said angrily.

"Before the war?" Marijana asked her.

"Yes, in our little peaceful village."

Marijana suddenly laughed—hysterical, tired laughter.

After a moment, her grandmother joined her, chuckling loudly, slapping her knee, her chest heaving up and down. There was nothing left to do but laugh.

"Oh, *Baka*, shhhhh, shhhh, someone might hear you," Marijana teased. They both stared at the closed door. Suddenly Marijana imagined one of the boarders, pressing his ear against their door. Would he report them to the Party? "Anti-communist" was broadly defined. In Tito's Yugoslavia there was no room for dissent. You had to be careful about what you said outside the house, and sometimes inside the house. Some families were broken; a son would denounce a father, and then the father would be taken away.

"You never know," her grandmother warned. Marijana thought about something her friend told her, "If you aren't a member of the party, you are considered suspicious. If you aren't a member of the party and are a Catholic, you are considered even more suspicious. If you aren't a member of the party and are a Catholic and celebrate religious holidays, you are an enemy of the state."

One of her classmates at school had tried to push Marijana into joining the Communist Party. He would constantly show up at places she liked to go, at cafes, or while she was in line at the cinema. Her grandmother told her to keep her distance from him. "Never join," her grandmother said. "I told your father that and he listened." She thought her grandmother was probably right. Anyway, it was her dream to go to America one day, and everyone knew Americans hated communists.

From another room they heard one of the boarders shuffling in his chair. A student. Months ago his parents had stopped paying his rent. Her grandmother couldn't get any money from him, and he wouldn't leave. It was useless, but still each month she tried, knocking on his door, reminding him that it was time to pay. They needed the money, for bread, for medicine, to get out of this country.

Marijana knew that her grandmother was determined to get her a tourist visa for Italy; then it would be up to her aunt and uncle to find a way to get her a visa so that she could go to South America. It seemed far away. Marijana couldn't imagine it yet, but maybe she could, maybe it would be like *Casablanca*. She imagined Ingrid Bergman going toward the plane.

"I'm going to see a film tomorrow," she announced. Her tired eyes looked up at her Baka.

"Marijana, you need to take it easy," Baka tried to talk her out of it. Too much too soon, and her granddaughter would end up back in the hospital where she should be anyway. Who knew when they would have an opportunity to get her out of the country? Better to have her at home, so she could put her on the train when the window of chance opened. When she looked at her granddaughter's pale face, she couldn't find it in herself to say no. Let her have this, she thought to herself. Let her have a little fun, she's still so young. She's spent so much time in hospitals.

Her grandmother nodded and sighed. "I'll find you some money so that you can go, but promise me you won't walk too much. You take the tram, my little one, okay?"

"Mmmmm," Marijana murmured, her eyes already closed. Lying in bed with Baka beside her was peaceful. And then, as an afterthought, she told Baka, "I'm never going to another hospital."

"Of course, my little one. So you missed my snoring, eh?" By the time her grandmother pulled the covers over Marijana's frail shoulders, she was fast asleep.

The next day her grandmother carried the heavy bucket to the house, and heated the water in a large pot on the stove, so her granddaughter could have a hot bath. Marijana washed her hair slowly, and her grandmother poured water over her head. Marijana liked to listen to the sound of the water falling. "I want to stay for a while," she told her grandmother, who nodded and said, "Not too long, when it gets cooler, come out."

Marijana leaned back and stayed in the tub until her fingers and toes puckered and her nails grew white. When the water grew cold, she climbed out. She wrapped a towel around her body and combed her short wavy brown hair. It was a luxury to be at home with Baka. Nurses couldn't barge in.

"Hurry and get dressed. Stay out of the draft. And come eat. Eat!" Baka called to her. After Marijana dressed, she sat at the kitchen table and spooned chicken soup into her mouth. It tasted good, but she didn't feel hungry. Bakica brought her some black bread, and then sat across from her. She reached up and felt Marijana's forehead and sighed. Marijana pushed the bowl away. "I'm sorry, Bakica, I'm not hungry."

"You hardly ate. You'll turn into a sparrow."

"A sparrow with bad lungs," she giggled, and then coughed into her hand.

Her grandmother chuckled.

"Baka, I thought you were going to read my cards," Marijana said, smiling as she changed the subject.

"I don't believe in any of that."

"I know, for fun. Please. I love it when you read my coffee grounds at the bottom of my cup. Come on, read my cards."

"The future is in God's hands."

"I know, I know, Baka." She'd heard her grandmother say that a thousand times.

Baka scooted her chair back and disappeared into the small kitchen. She returned with the deck of cards and set them on the table. She divided them, set out a few, then took some back, then set out some more cards face up. She turned two toward her granddaughter: the ace of diamonds and the ten of clubs.

"A letter is coming," she said slowly.

"From whom?" Marijana asked, leaning forward on her elbows.

"From someone important to your future," her grandmother said.

Marijana pushed her short brown hair off of her forehead then scratched her cheek thoughtfully and asked, "And the other one?"

"A journey by water," her grandmother said, leaning her head to one side as if looking at the card from a different angle would give her a different interpretation.

"Really?" Marijana said, captivated.

"Maybe you will travel across the Atlantic," her grandmother shrugged.

Instantly Marijana could see a ship moving across the ocean, waves breaking against the bow. Then she stared at her grandmother suspiciously.

"I'm not going. I'm not leaving you here alone."

"Marijana, it is only in the cards." Baka sighed and lightly patted the table with her hand.

"I know you're trying to tell me something." Marijana looked up at her. She felt a slight burning on the inside of her nose. She took a short breath and said, "I'm going to get some fresh air."

"Just like your mother," her grandmother said under her breath.

"What?"

Her grandmother was silent.

"What did you say?"

"It's that drop of gypsy blood that made your mother stubborn."

Marijana narrowed her eyebrows and clenched her jaw. She knew her grandmother would never have said that about her own son.

"Well, I don't mind having gypsy blood flowing through my veins." Then she added, "Especially my mother's."

Her grandmother got up and went to her room. Moments later she came back with a few *dinars*. She pressed them into Marijana's hand. "Here, for the cinema tonight."

Marijana had a half a mind to say she didn't want to go anymore, but she took the money.

Several young men stood up to let Ružica and Marijana pass. They sat down in their seats and drew their coats across their chest; there was a draft. The dark and musty cinema filled quickly. Each time Marijana shifted in her seat, she bumped elbows with the young man beside her. He offered her a cigarette and she shook her head. Marijana and Ružica giggled. Someone on the other side of the audience stood up, shouted and waved as he recognized a friend. The heavy smell of human sweat hung in the air. Someone began coughing in the second row.

Most people could hardly afford to go to the cinema, but somehow they managed. In a darkened theater, they could escape the grimness of communism and dive into glamorous Hollywood pools with Esther Williams, listen to hooves drumming against the dry earth as John Wayne held the horse's reins. Marijana told her friends that the actress Linda Darnel was her aunt, and soon she'd be on a plane to California to visit her.

"Did you see *Viva Zapata*?" Marijana asked. Mexican films like *Mamá Juanita* inspired Croatians to learn Mexican songs.

"Of course," Ružica said, letting her chin dip lazily into the palm of her hand.

Marijana leaned back into the wooden seat. The click, click, clicking started slowly, and then picked up speed as the film wove its way through the projector. A ray of light appeared from the projector to the screen. The newsreel began with Tito, dressed in a white suit, visiting schoolchildren. He clasped his hands behind his back and smiled broadly as he greeted his little communists. Another young man in front of her rolled a cigarette and lit up. He inhaled before passing it to his friend. Marijana let her eyes close.

When she opened them again, she saw Orson Welles' name on the screen. Everything was silent except for the steady hum of the projector and the occasional cough. Light flickered over the lifted faces. Little Jane Eyre entered the cruel Lowood School for orphans and was sentenced to walking endless circles in the rain with her beloved, ethereal Helen, who was destined to die in her sleep from TB. Tears fell down Marijana's face as Jane collapsed atop Helen's grave, sobbing for her dear friend.

A young woman now, Jane (Joan Fontaine) heard the distant drumming of hooves growing louder and louder as her eyes searched the fog. Suddenly a horse was rearing above her, a man was thrown to the ground. Marijana smiled when she saw Orson Welles, his large figure hurled himself back onto his horse and galloped away. Rochester.

When Marijana was in the theater, she could make time stop. Her own story faded as she became engrossed with the one on the screen. Jane returned to the burnt remains of Thornfield only to see Rochester once again, limping and blind, making his way through the rubble, leaning upon his cane. Once he realized who she was, he called to her, "Jane, Jane…"

In a daze, with images of the film still flashing though their minds, Marijana and Ružica wandered out of the theater onto the streets of Zagreb, blinking beneath the flickering lamp-light. They stumbled over the cobblestones, arms linked. The woody smell of roasted chestnuts floated past them. A boy sat on the side of the street with a small stove. He lifted the pan and stirred the glowing embers. They gave him the last of their coins, and he filled a paper cone with warm chestnuts.

They walked by a shop window with a Party sign: *We are Tito—Tito is us: Workers of the World, Unite!* They relived their favorite scenes as they turned down an empty side street. A hundred yards ahead, they saw the silhouette of a man. He walked slowly with a limp and Marijana heard the faint tap of his cane. She called out to him, "Rochester, Rochester…" She wanted someone to rescue her from this life of hunger and sickness. Ružica grabbed her arm and pulled her away; they ran off, stumbling over the stones.

On a cold October afternoon in 1954, Marijana and her grandmother took the bus to Mirogoj. They walked toward the high ivy-covered wall that encircled the old cemetery and passed beneath the domes by the entrance. Marijana slipped her arm into her grandmother's. The wind picked up and brown leaves swirled over the graves. They took their time as they made their way past avenues of cypress, chestnut, and oak trees. Marijana breathed in the smell of pine. Branches creaked in the wind. They saw an old woman sweeping a grave with a whiskbroom. Most Croatian families visited their dead often, but her grandmother worried that it wasn't good for Marijana when she was fighting against death herself.

Silently they walked beside the gravestones. Marijana shivered. Sometimes she struggled to remember things about her parents. Her mother seemed blurry, but Marijana remembered how it felt when her mama held her; she remembered being in the kitchen as her mother made pastries at Christmas time. And, of course, she could remember more things about her Tata, the way he played with her, the way he walked quickly. She felt a longing for them now, knowing that she might leave her grandmother.

They descended a slight hill and Marjiana thought about November 1st, All Saints Day, when people from near and far traveled to Mirogoj to visit their family graves. By evening, the graves were covered with burning candles and bright yellow and white chrysanthemums. She loved the smell of melting wax and seeing flickering flames. Everything floated in breathing light.

Baka and Marijana stood in front of her parents' grave. A wooden marker said *The Kanjer Family, Katica Kanjer 1906-1943, Anton Kanjer 1907-1945*. Her grandmother padded her forehead with a handkerchief and put down the basket she was carrying. She knelt down to sweep away the dead leaves and flowers. Marijana knelt down beside her. In her hand, the dried leaves disintegrated into tiny pieces. Baka took two candles from her basket and lit them. One day Marijana planned to give her parents a proper gravestone. If she hadn't been sick for so long, she would already be working to help.

"Will this be the last time I come?" Marijana asked. She began to cough. Her grandmother handed her a handkerchief.

"Someone is helping us get you an Italian holiday visa." Baka heaved herself off the ground. She rubbed her knees, which had gotten stiff. Marijana stared at her parents' names. "You always wanted to go to Rome," Bakica reminded her softly. Marijana looked at her. She wondered how could she leave her grandmother. Yet it was true, she always wanted to see Rome. And her grandmother also knew that it was her dream to live in New York City and study art. "Where would I stay?" she asked cautiously. Everything was spinning beyond her control. A couple strolled past them on the way to another grave. Baka lifted her finger to her lips. When they were far enough away she whispered, "Your aunt and uncle will figure that out. They will find a place for you to stay while they find a way to get you a visa."

"How long will that take?"

"I don't know."

"What about you?" Marijana stood up. Blood rushed to

her head; she felt dizzy and weak. They hadn't had enough to eat today. She thought about Rome and felt excited and nervous all at once. She pushed up her coat collar. "Baka, did you hear me? What about you?"

"I'm fine here, my little one."

"No, you aren't, we're barely making it, Baka. We're always hungry. Why can't you come? Isn't there some way?"

"For an old woman like me? I have spent seventy-six years on this earth. Marijana, you're only nineteen, you need to get out of this country. If you stay…who knows what will happen? What I want more than anything is your health. I would do anything for that. Every night I pray to God to make your lungs healthy."

Marijana put her arm around her grandmother and rested her head on her shoulder. Her teeth were beginning to chatter. "I'm tired, Bakica. I want to go home."

"We've been here long enough," her grandmother agreed.

"Baka?"

"Yes, my little one."

"I'm going to send for you as soon as I can. I'm going to take care of you. I promise."

Her grandmother nodded, putting her hand on Marijana's flushed cheek. "Of course, we can't be apart for very long. I'll come wherever you are."

"Not too many things," Baka told her, adding, "We don't want anyone to be suspicious." Marijana had packed some of her clothes, a pair of shoes, and several photographs of her parents and her grandmother. Baka carefully folded a tablecloth that she had crocheted and placed among Marijana's things. The visa had finally come through, and then her grandmother discovered that the woman who lived on their street, the informant who reported everything to the

Party, was away on holiday. Baka decided now it was time. The following morning, they went to the train station.

"What will you say when she gets back?" Marijana asked.

Baka shook her head. "I'll say that you are taking a holiday. You'll be back in a week."

"What will you say when I don't come back?"

"Don't worry my little one, I'll think of something."

Marijana had heard that the police came and interrogated the family left behind. Or they took you to the police station for questioning. Where did she go? Why isn't she back yet? Has she written you any letters? Let us see them. What contact have you had with her? How did she leave? When will she return to Yugoslavia? The police seized personal property or did worse. Sometimes phones were even tapped. Luckily they didn't have a phone. Marijana shuddered and tried to stop herself from thinking about what would become of her grandmother. Instead she thought about Ružica; she'd met her one last time at a nearby café.

When she whispered into Ružica's ear that she was leaving for Rome, Ružica was stunned. Finally she'd managed to say, "Marijana, how will I survive without you?"

"You will! We both will. I promise you, we will both be healthy one day. We will sing and dance in the rain like Gene Kelly and Debbie Reynolds."

Ružica couldn't stop herself from laughing even though she already felt the loss of her dear friend's departure.

At the train station, Baka insisted on helping Marijana carry her small suitcase. "Give it to me, Baka," Marijana pleaded. Reluctantly her grandmother handed it over. They stood facing each other, people rushing past them; train windows were opening and closing. It was cold and gray and the smell of coal smoke hung in the air. Baka held Marijana's arm; her eyes welled with tears. "My little, little one, you take care of yourself, and promise me you'll eat, and rest."

Marijana nodded, unable to move. She was abandoning her grandmother. She wanted to say so many things. Her chest ached. She wanted to tell Bakica that she would see her again soon. But would she? Once you escaped, she wondered, could you ever return. She threw her arms around her grandmother. "I love you, my dear Bakica," she whispered. She took a few steps backward, holding onto her suitcase with both hands, then turned and bravely walked toward the train.

Her grandmother dabbed her eyes with a handkerchief. She stared at the back of her granddaughter's knees, which bowed slightly. Marijana had suffered from rickets as a child. They couldn't manage to get enough milk during the war and afterwards. Marijana's bones had grown soft. As she watched Marijana board the train, Baka shook her head and thought to herself, now her granddaughter really was in God's hands.

The train whistled and slowly moved out of the station. Marijana pushed open the window and waved until she could no longer see her grandmother. She had a painful lump in her throat as she pushed the window closed. She sank back onto the wooden bench in the third-class compartment. Marijana held tightly onto the image of Bakica standing at the train depot, a shawl over her shoulders, her white hair pinned in a bun at the back of her head. Marijana closed her eyes and she could still see Bakica's round face, her high cheekbones and sloping eyes, her double chin and broad forehead. Marijana repeated to herself, *don't forget.*

The October cold penetrated the smudged glass. Marijana buttoned up her woolen coat. In the rows of wooden benches in the crowded compartment, people leaned upon their suitcases and each other. A man dozed off and began to snore behind Marijana. Someone coughed in front of her, holding a handkerchief to his mouth. One woman held a basket with one arm while she readjusted her hat.

At the Italian border, a guard came over to check on everyone's papers. Marijana avoided looking at him. He grabbed documents from people's hands, and then flung them back on their laps. She glanced down at her worn shoes, trying to maintain her composure. For a second she couldn't breathe. After the police guard left, a train attendant entered. She pulled out her train pass. Since her father died while working for the railroad, she'd gotten a lifetime train pass, third class, of course. Her eyes flew over the letters, the dates, her signature *Marija Kanjer* and her childhood picture. The photo had been taken after her Tata died. She wore black and her hair was in two tight braids; her thin lips pressed in a frown, her light eyes looked gravely into the camera's lens. An unhappy child, she thought to herself. Maybe this train pass was her father's way of telling her to go, to leave everything behind, and start a new life. She leaned her forehead against the cool glass. Someone in the compartment pulled out some sausages and cheese; the smell of salt and grease filled the air. The movement of the train lulled her into a moment of calmness; she felt a pulse of hope. It was her first time leaving Yugoslavia, her first time traveling to another country. She was on her way to Rome.

12

CATHERINE'S BRESTOVAC

Inside the Croatian tourist office in Jelačić Square, I asked the young woman behind the counter how to find Brestovac, near Sljeme. "We only give information about Zagreb, not villages outside," she explained dryly.

"It's not a village outside of Zagreb," I said earnestly in English. "It is an old TB sanatorium on Medvednice." I pointed in the direction of the mountain behind Zagreb. She shrugged disinterestedly, then asked some women chatting behind her. Someone kindly handed me a map of Medvednice Nature Park and suggested that I visit the hiking society office. I hurried out the door, through the square, zigzagging through the tiny cobblestoned streets. When I finally arrived at the hiking office, it was closed.

The next morning I returned. I pressed my cupped hands against the window so that I could peer inside. It was dark; I knocked. "Hello," I called out. Once again, I glanced at the military-time schedule taped onto the window. I double-checked the hours. It was supposed to be open. "Oh God," I sighed, turning around, leaning against the door with a thump.

How was I ever going to find it? I only had this afternoon left. Tomorrow I planned to visit the village where my mother was born, and then I would leave Zagreb and make my way by bus to the Dalmatian Coast. I didn't have the money to rent a car, plus I couldn't drive stick shift. Vaguely I recalled that Courtney (my friend who often visited her aunts in Zagreb) had told me that the number 14 tram would get me to the base of the mountain.

I walked back to the street. At that exact moment, a number 14 clamored past, swinging into the curve. I hurried toward the tram stop and thought about the fact that Brestovac was in ruins. Courtney had read somewhere that it was probably going to be torn down soon. I didn't know when, if ever, I'd have the money to come back. It was now or never, I told myself as I climbed onto the tram. "Sljeme?" I asked the conductor. He grunted in the affirmative.

As soon as I sat down, I pulled out the map from my backpack. The maze of tiny lines seemed designed as a keepsake for tourists who were not planning on doing actual hiking. I scanned it and found Brestovac in small black letters. It was hard to tell from the map, but I made my best guess and approximated that Brestovac was halfway up. When the tram pulled into the last stop, at the city's edge, I followed several people down a walkway to the entrance of a tunnel. They disappeared inside the darkness.

I followed them, and on the other side, I discovered a fairytale forest with beech, oak, and chestnut trees. The trail curved until I arrived at the cable-car entrance. I got in line to buy my ticket. Everything had a 1950s feel to it, the muted, mint-green color of the walls, the glass booth, the worn floors, the elderly people waiting in line, the framed topographic map on the wall. I walked over and examined it. It was much more detailed, and when I found Brestovac, I was surprised to see that it was much closer to the top. It made sense to take the cable car. I asked the ticket clerk about Brestovac. He looked confused, as if he'd never heard of such a place. He pointed to the topographic map. I nodded and paid for my ticket.

At least I'm here, I thought to myself as I sat inside the bubble-shaped cable car. I didn't know how I'd pay my rent next month, but finally I was here in Croatia. I glanced down at the lush forest hundreds of feet below. I couldn't see through the tops of the trees. Once Courtney had told me, "When I was taking the cable car up, I could see Brestovac below." It must have been autumn, when the branches were bare. I felt the cable car lurch forward. Every once in a while, it stopped, silently dangling in the air. The system had been built in 1963.

When the cable car reached the top, I headed upward in hopes of finding a forest ranger or hiker who might know which trailhead I should take. My heart raced. I stopped a few people. No one knew. For a moment, I gazed at one well-worn trail where many groups of people were headed. That's definitely not it, I told myself. Nothing in my life had ever been that simple. I was tempted to drop my backpack down in frustration, then I caught a glimpse of a young man, a possible hiker (jeans, hiking boots), gathered with his friends beside the cable car port. I walked over. "Do you speak English?" I asked.

"A little," he said, smiling, raising his eyebrows curiously.

I explained where I was headed and showed him on the tourist map. "I need to find the trailhead," I said.

"I think it's right here," he replied, looking up, pointing directly in front of me.

I was actually standing at the trailhead. "This is it?" I said in disbelief.

"Yes, here." He once again pointed ahead of me at an empty trail heading down directly below the cable car port.

Pine needles crackled beneath my sneakers. Something settled inside me. I was on my way somewhere. I passed two hikers using ski poles, the older man was fit and barefoot. We nodded at each other solemnly. Nothing seemed strange anymore, especially to someone who had traveled all this way to find a forgotten TB sanatorium. For the next five hours, they were the last people I would see.

No one in the world knew where I was today, and it was a strange and liberating feeling. As I began making my way down the trail, I thought of my father. Before I was born, before he got polio, he climbed mountains in Washington State and Oregon: Mt. Rainier, Mt. St. Helens, Mt. Adams, and Mt. Hood. He had drilled the hiking rules into me: never go hiking alone, always bring water, a first aid kit, snacks, wear good shoes, make sure someone knows what trail you took (in case you disappear), and so on. At least I knew that if I headed down on this side, eventually I'd hit the city of Zagreb. The only thing that troubled me was that I could easily pass Brestovac without realizing it. I concentrated on the sound of the branches and leaves beneath my shoes. A cable car silently ascended overhead.

On the trail I kept a steady pace, walking beside beech and pine trees, breathing in the dry summer air. I thought about my mom and Ružica on this mountain. The morning after I arrived in Zagreb, Ružica's husband Iv and her son Igor, picked me up and drove me to their house in Štubice Toplice, where I stayed for a couple nights. I had not seen Ružica in ten years.

I stood in the entrance with her, bursting with words, asking Igor to translate. I blushed as Ružica answered. I had spent so much time with her and my mom in the stories that I had written about them, I felt that I knew her differently now. It was an imagined relationship, yet it felt real. As I spoke, a look of astonishment appeared in her blue eyes. She said something in Croatian and her son translated, "Your voice, it sounds exactly like your mother's."

"It does?" I asked amazed.

Ružica nodded.

Ružica held me for a long time when I said goodbye. As the car drove away, I turned and looked though the rear window. She stood in the middle of the empty street, waving and crying.

I stared at the divide in the trail. Right or left? "Which way?" I asked myself. I walked around, searching for trail markers, signs, stacked stones, paint on a tree trunk, something signifying the name of the trail. Nothing. Both trails were heading downward. I bit the side of my lip and put my backpack on the ground. I sipped some water, then looked back in the direction of the cable car. I had crossed beneath it and now it was no longer visible. I unfolded my map. I traced the red-lined trails with my eyes. Go with your instinct, I told myself, and turned left.

I let my mind rest on the large spring pool Ružica and Iv had taken me to. They could not speak English, and I could not speak Croatian, but somehow we communicated. "Kateerine," Ružica said, pointing to where I should leave my towel. In the water, Iv and Ružica gestured arm movements, and spoke to me in Croatian. They kept patting their hearts with their hands. Suddenly I found myself, standing alongside fifteen elderly Croatians in the water. A girl, about sixteen, with light brown hair, golden skin, and a peppy attitude, stood by the edge of the pool. Obediently, with the others, I began doing leg movements underwater, raising my arms up and down, splashing, twisting, kicking, and side bending. "*Dva jedan, dva dva, dva tre, dva četri, dva pet, dva šest, dva sedam, dva osam,*" the girl called out, leading us through the exercises. I laughed, hopping in the water, moving my arms. Beside me in the pool, Ružica and Iv nodded in cheerful encouragement.

Now I listened to the birds rustling through the bushes. I imagined people wandering these trails, mushroom hunting in the spring when there were primroses, cyclamen, and dog-tooth violets. I imagined the autumn when yellow and brown leaves covered the ground. There would be people picking up chestnuts. Suddenly I could imagine the smell of roasting chestnuts. My mind returned to Ružica. She had pulled out bound collections of old movie magazines, the same ones she and my mom used to look through when they were convalescing as teenagers. We flipped through the pages, admiring the actors: Grace Kelly, Rita Hayworth, Jane Wyman, and Ingrid Bergman. And finally I mustered up the courage to ask her about Brestovac. Her blue eyes became grave. Her son translated as she said, "That time was a disaster for so many of us. Every week, two or three beds would open." She sighed, smoothing the white tablecloth with the palm of her hand.

My mom had never talked about the dying.

Ružica continued, "Your Baka, your mom's grandmother, only wanted Marijana to get better, despite herself."

Despite herself, echoed in my mind. I nodded and felt a slight ache behind my heart. My mom wanted to live even if it made her die. Ružica shook her head and said, "Kateerine, we tried so hard to forget. We spent our whole lives trying to forget that time." Crickets trilled around me. I listened to my footsteps and checked my watch. I passed by a tree with a red *S* painted on it. It must stand for *Šestina*. At least I'm on the right trail, I told myself. I paused and stared into the forest on my left. How will I know if I'm passing it if I can't see it? Should I go off the trail? Not yet, something told me. As I walked, the thread of a spider web brushed against my cheek.

I looked up at the sky and said, "Mom, I could really use

some help down here." I kept my steady pace and after five minutes, I felt a strong presence to my left. Out of the corner of my eye I caught a glimpse of something, but when I stopped and looked into the trees, there was nothing there. This happened again. The faint outline of a building appeared at the edge of my vision, but it disappeared as soon as I turned my head. I gazed into the empty space between the leaves.

"Is this it?" I asked.

Moments later, I saw a stone road on my left that branched off the trail. Once again there was no sign. I paused, holding my breath for a few seconds. I glanced down the trail, then back at the stone road. This could be it. I could always come back and retrace my steps. I turned.

After only walking a little way, I saw a small crumbling stone hut. My mom and Ružica had shared a hut when they stayed in Brestovac, but she was certain that theirs had been torn down. Maybe a few still existed. Stone crackled beneath my shoes. The road sloped upward. I glanced up and stopped abruptly.

Ahead, a large four-story stone building rose up from the ground on the hillside. Branches twisted through the glassless windows. Trees stretched out through a broken roof. Gray stones were piled in a heap. The building was part of the forest, fading into the trees. It was Brestovac.

"Oh my God," I whispered. A feeling of awe passed through me. Finally I said aloud, "I found it!" to my dad across the continent and Atlantic Ocean. I scrambled up the mountainside and made my way through the brush alongside the building so that I could glimpse through one of the windows. I leaned into the warm stones and peered inside. The floor had disintegrated into the earth. Large trees grew upward inside the stone building. Vines were winding up the walls. I sighed with great relief.

I scanned the nearby forest and saw another building, and another after that. It was like a Colorado ghost town, only made of stone. Plants brushed against my calves as I made my way to the next building. I laughed giddily.

I circled behind, looking through the glassless windows. There were broken bottles on the ground, an old battered mattress, and a rusty white stove. Brestovac opened in 1909, a hundred years ago. The sanatorium, in the middle of the forest and on the southern slope of the mountain, seemed like a perfect spot for patients stricken with tuberculosis. The first building turned out to be too small for the increasing number of TB patients, so it was expanded twice. It had been used as a military hospital during the World Wars. At the end of World War II, Partisans killed 200 wounded soldiers here and their bodies were probably buried nearby somewhere. My mom was about seventeen when she stayed here in 1953; she escaped Yugoslavia the following year, but continued to fight the disease. In 1968 Brestovac closed; medicine was used to treat tuberculosis instead of nature. The sanatorium was completely abandoned.

I watched shadows of branches dancing against the stone walls, geometric shapes of sunlight shifting over the earth. I wandered through one of the buildings and climbed down some stairs through the blackness until a doorway of sunlight blazed in front of me; I leaned through it and saw a small overgrown courtyard; vines climbed the walls, a tangle of bright green plants and weeds covered the ground. For a moment I felt as if my story and my mother's story were intersecting.

I went back up the stairs and wandered through the empty hallways until I came across a wide, curving outdoor walkway that connected one stone building to another; an open veranda shaded it. It faced down the mountain. For an instant, I saw the faint outlines of patients lying in lounge chairs, the sicker ones in cots, covered with gray woolen blankets. A nurse, with a stiff white cap on her head, held a tray; she bent over to give someone their medication. I could see patients playing chess, reading novels, trying to pass the time, occasionally staring into the forest. In those trees, I could see my mom walking with Ružica, arm in arm. I could hear their laughter. I could feel their fear. Here they had battled against the white death.

I turned back and retraced my steps until I made my way through another dark corridor. I glanced left and right into tiny rooms. I imagined freshly painted white walls and hospital cots. A bat burst out from a hole in the floor and flew across the ceiling. I cried out, startled. It swooped down into another room. "It's just a bat," I told myself, laughing, though my heart pounded. I was completely alone.

As I explored the grounds of Brestovac, I was reminded of something that my dad once told me about climbing Mt. Rainier. When he finally stood on the snow-covered top, everything below seemed so small, the rest of the world so far away. He realized that he was a tiny part of everything, and he was struck with a feeling that he didn't want to remain up there too long. There was a pull to go back down, to return to what he had left below.

Outside in the sun, I stood in front of the buildings. Far in the distance was the hazy outline of Zagreb. I imagined that it must have taken my mother hours to walk from Brestovac to Zagreb when she snuck out at night. I shook my head in amazement at my mom's determination to live her life.

I took a deep breath and sat cross-legged on the road for a while. I felt a rising sensation in my chest, then calmness descended upon me; my breath became steady. I felt the stones and packed earth beneath my bare calves. I thought about why it had been so important for me to come here.

As I finished graduate school, I had lost faith in myself,

and my writing life seemed impossible. I wondered why I was making my mom relive everything all over again through my writing. Hadn't she suffered enough? I carried that burden. I was much closer to the dead, to the people in my stories, than the living.

When I had first considered traveling to Croatia, the idea had seemed so impossible, financially, emotionally, logistically. I wondered how I would find things on my own, when I didn't speak my mother's language. I had struggled through depression and severe anxiety, so I was frightened that I wouldn't be mentally strong enough to travel alone in another country. Perhaps it was the impossibility of everything a few years ago that allowed me to feel such bliss and freedom now.

Ružica's voice echoed in my mind: "We spent our whole lives trying to forget that time." The contradiction of everything settled upon me. My mom almost died here. She tried to keep all this separate from me. She tried hard to forget, and I needed her to remember. Even after her death, I didn't want her to suffer alone. In this way, our relationship continued. As I sat there looking at the abandoned stone buildings of Brestovac, I could finally glimpse the truth of my history.

A bee buzzed, landing softly on a wildflower. A bluebell fluttered in the breeze. I traced the earth with my fingertips and felt in every molecule of air around me that she understood. More than ever I felt her living through me, a steady oneness. Suddenly I realized that I didn't need to know what was coming next. I knew that I'd stayed here long enough and it was time for me to walk toward the living.

13

BETWEEN COUNTRIES

After the train entered *Stazione Termini*, Marijana quickly pulled down her suitcase and slipped her hand into her coat pocket. Her Yugoslav passport was still there. She pulled it out; her eyes skimmed the dark red cover: *People's Federal Republic of Yugoslavia*. Then she shoved it back. As she climbed down the stairs of the train compartment, she wondered who would meet her at the station. From Argentina, her aunt and uncle had made arrangements for her to stay at a center for refugees. She needed to obtain a visa. Her lungs were the problem. To be admitted into Argentina, one had to prove good health with a clean chest X-ray.

Marijana stepped onto the endless platform and searched for something familiar. An elegant lady walked by wearing a straight skirt with a small felt hat pinned to the side of her head. Her hips were swinging. A mother ran after her son, grabbing hold of his hand. Two men spoke loudly in Italian, arguing, waving their hands at each other. A woman embraced a man wearing an overcoat and a grey fedora hat, as if they been separated for a long time. An elderly gentleman glanced at Marijana and tipped his hat at her. She smiled and retied the thin scarf around her neck. She felt shabby and suddenly alone; she wished that she had family here. There was no one to celebrate her escape from Yugoslavia or her arrival in Rome.

A little boy tugged on her sleeve, interrupting her thoughts. His cheek had a streak of dirt. He was dressed in tattered clothing, his trousers were too short and his dirty bare ankles were exposed. His right shoe had a hole on the side of it. He said something in animated Italian; she smiled at him confused and shook her head. He pointed at her case on the ground.

"He wants to carry your suitcase," someone said in Croatian. She glanced up and saw a middle-aged priest, wearing a cassock, a close-fitting ankle-length robe. He tilted his head slightly as though he were trying to recognize her. He asked, "Marijana? Marijana Kanjer?"

She nodded. "You know my Aunt Victoria and Uncle Ivo?"

"Through letters," he said, nodding, and they both smiled, relieved.

The priest turned to the little boy and patted him on the head; he pointed toward the exit and said something in Italian. The boy happily lugged the suitcase, hurrying forward. Marijana learned that the Croatian Monsignor was from the Vatican. He was going to help her get all the documents in order for her journey to South America. In Rome, he explained, she was considered a political refugee, fleeing communism. Her aunt and uncle had sent some money to hold her over until her visa for Argentina came through. "How long do you think it will take?" she asked anxiously. He didn't answer her question, instead he suggested this would be a wonderful opportunity to learn Italian and visit the museums. "In Italy, everything takes three times longer than predicted. We must be patient," he said.

Marijana asked him about the Vatican, and he described

the walled, 108 acres of the Vatican City, where he spent much of his time. "In the library, we have manuscripts dating back to the 4th century. The basilica of St. Peters… the mosaic there is breathtaking. I will take you there when I have time. I am sure you will want to see Michelangelo's *Pietà*."

Marijana nodded. She sensed that the Monsignor would be busy much of the time, and that she would be able to explore on her own. Here, there was no one to really worry about her or watch over her.

Signorina, Kanjer Marijana, Via Bobbio 30, Roma, Italija. Her eyes flew over her friend Mira's enthusiastic greeting: *Draga Marijana! I got your congratulations. Every day I expect to hear from you, but nothing comes. I hope when something new happens you will write to me, and I will too.* Marijana missed her friends in Zagreb. She put the postcard back into her purse and began to walk down the Spanish Steps. She paused in the middle of the wide butterfly stairway; a young Polish woman, Klara, from the refugee pension, had told her that there were 137 steps; she had counted them. Marijana loved the way it opened and spilled onto *Piazza di Spagna*. From above, she admired *Fontana della Barraccia*; fresh water poured from the eyes of a fish-like, half-sunken boat. Klara, who was passionate about Italian history, explained that in 1598, the River Tiber had overflowed and there was a great flood; everyone traveled through the city by boat. When the flood waters receded, one boat was marooned in the square, the artist's inspiration for the fountain.

It was early springtime and a boisterous crowd of students descended the stairs; they laughed and sang together. Marijana daydreamed about being a student once again, studying art in Rome. Maybe her documents wouldn't go through, maybe she could stay here. There was no need to travel so far away from Baka. Perhaps one day her grandmother could visit and stay here. Marijana walked down the rest of the Spanish Steps filled with hope. She tried to walk like a Hollywood film star and laughed at herself. She paused again, staring alongside the stairs at the houses. A suntanned young man dressed in a dark suit stopped beside her and lit a cigarette.

"*Americana*? *Inglese*?" he asked, curiously, turning toward her.

She laughed and shook her head. "I understand, little, English."

"School?"

She nodded.

"But, no Italian?"

"Now learning."

"I'm Angelo. I teach English to Italians, and Italian to the English, or American travelers."

"Marijana," she answered, careful not to say too much, so she wouldn't make mistakes. She didn't like her accent.

"You like British writers?" he asked.

"Dickens, Austen, Brontës, I read in my country," she said and smiled shyly.

He pointed over the side of the stairway. "You were looking at the house where Romantic poet, John Keats lived…" In a dramatic voice, he began to recite, "Darkling I listen: and, for many a time, I have been half in love with easeful Death, Call'd him soft names in many a mused rhyme, To take into the air my quiet breath; Now more than ever seems it rich to die, To Cease upon the midnight with no pain, While thou are pouring forth thy soul abroad, In such ecstasy!"

She clapped her hands together and asked, "Please, name?"

"Ode to a Nightingale," he answered and smiled thoughtfully.

An impromptu performance. Poets took a breath each time their words were spoken aloud, she believed. She stood in silence. Angelo pointed to the apartment once again. "Keats died there, tuberculosis, only twenty-five."

"Young," Marijana said sadly.

He nodded.

She stared into the apartment window. She was nineteen, on her way to somewhere unknown. She wondered if she would make it to twenty-five. She wondered if it was easier to appreciate life when you lived beside death. She sighed. The steady sound of the fountain pulled her attention back to the square.

"He could hear the water from his window," Angelo added.

"Beautiful," Marijana murmured. They both paused there, gazing at the fountain and the people crossing the square.

He looked at his wristwatch and began to hurry down the remaining stairs, turning back toward her. "Will I see you on the Spanish Steps again? Next time, you recite poetry for me."

She waved and laughed at him. "*Ciao*, Angelo!"

Things like this could only happen in Rome. Here, painters worked on their canvases outdoors, painting the spires, towers and domes against a pink Roman sky, musicians played on the streets, dancers practiced their steps in the square, and without a second thought, a man could stop and recite poetry to a young woman.

She strolled through the square, gazing at the European tourists sitting at tables in outdoor cafés, a young couple held hands, waiters served espressos, fruit juices, and gelato. Small children played beneath a table. A man rode his bicycle through the square. Two *carabinieri* with their feathered tricorn hats and flowing capes turned into a cobblestoned alley. The sound of a violin drifted from an open window. She left the square in search of a nearby bakery. She followed the criss-crossing narrow streets with no true destination in her mind. Wet sheets flapped above her, hanging between two buildings.

Marijana smelled baking bread and saw a bakery. A woman with an apron leaned against a doorway, stroking a white cat, with an orange tail, in her arms. She set the cat down and stepped aside, so that Marijana could enter. The sweet aroma of almond cakes filled the air, and it reminded Marijana of her mother. She asked the woman for a crusty loaf and paid. She said, "*Grazie mille*," as she took the warm loaf from the woman. She wandered around outside, breaking off the heel of the crusty loaf and chewing, remembering all the times Baka had sent her to the bakery in Zagreb.

The twists and turns of the narrow Roman streets led Marijana past a crumbling stone wall. From the apartment buildings, she smelled cooking garlic. From an open window, someone leaned out and waved to a friend below. A man in dark sunglasses flew past on his Vespa, his girlfriend sitting sideways behind him, holding onto his waist tightly.

At a local outdoor café, Marijana ordered an espresso. Her legs were tired. When the waiter left, she pulled out Mira's postcard again and squinted at the letters, blinking away the bright sun. *These days in Zagreb, Gerard Philippe visited, unfortunately I haven't seen him in person*. Marijana giggled. Gerard Philippe was their favorite French actor; she wondered which of his films had come to Zagreb. *Marijana, do you remember all those times that we strolled together on Strossmayer Promenade*? Marijana flipped over the postcard and stared at the picture: the view of the cathedral, with its spires, from the promenade in Gornji Grad, where she had walked so often with her school friends, arms linked. Only months ago, she had been there. It seem like a lifetime ago.

Now Rome was reshaping her memories: the fountains, waterfalls of sound, splashing and foaming, the open squares, the broken aqueducts, the screeching automobile brakes, blaring horns, horse-carriage-wheels rattling… The colosseum with its deep vertical corridors, the street sweepers, the children selling roasted chestnuts, and Piazza Campo De' Fiori with its stalls of fresh fish and clams, artichokes and tomatoes, umbrellas and dolls. The place where sellers and buyers raised their voices, bargaining shrewdly with each other.

She thought of her new home, a crowded room full of cots. Poles, Hungarians, Croatians, Serbs, Czechs, young, middle aged, and old, women, beginning again after war, after concentration camps, escaping communism, escaping poverty, escaping hunger. They found work as cooks in local restaurants, as housemaids and seamstresses. They gossiped and argued; they laughed and cried together.

On the second floor, her friend Klara exchanged stamps for *lire* with her. She laughed at Marijana's lively stories, like the time that an Italian man had followed her for blocks until she finally slipped into a church. She crossed herself, lit two candles for her parents, and walked toward the front of the church where she sat on a bench, kneeled and prayed for her grandmother. She waited a while, before she stood up to leave, and then she saw he was sitting in the last pew. He grinned and said, "*Ciao, Bella*!" She hurried out of the church; he followed.

"Marijana, when it comes to women, Italian men don't get distracted," Klara had told her.

At the café Marijana sipped her espresso, she watched an elderly woman lean out her second story window to wave at her granddaughter below. The little girl with thick pigtails looked up, shielding her face from the sun. Her grandmother motioned for her to come back upstairs. She'd forgotten something. The little girl scampered back into the building. It was strange how Marijana appreciated these small scenes of life. She felt longing for all those evenings sitting at the kitchen table with Baka. Marijana wanted to get those familiar light blue envelopes that the other Croatians received. But her grandmother could barely write, and only communicated with the help of a neighbor writing for her. "Just a third grade education—still I read the Bible each night," she would often tell Marijana.

Several weeks ago, much to her surprise, Marijana had received a simple letter from Bakica. Now she carried it with her everywhere. Marijana pulled it out of her purse and unfolded it carefully, placing it gently it on the small round table. Baka's child-like, rounded, uneven letters filled one page.

Draga moja Marijanica,

Here is a hello from myself, your grandma—you are afraid but now I'm fine and don't feel pain anymore, feel much better than before, I had flu and now I'm fine I have appetite and feel good and don't work and take care of myself, I wish I could see you, take care of your health—čuvaj se i bog će te čuvati—take care of yourself and God will take care of you, I'm afraid for you especially when spring comes, those who are sick on the lungs must take care and don't walk a lot, it's better you lie down, It's not very cold here, but it's muddy because they are always moving something across the road and the roads get bad, I wish everything good for you, and good health, if you have good health everything will be fine, my dear angel, I always pray to God for you, my sweetheart, many greetings from your grandmother, Zbogom, Baka.

Marijana's short brown hair hung down over her tearful eyes. She dabbed her nose with the cloth napkin and stared out into the street. She could imagine her Baka and the neighbor together, one young and one old, huddled over paper, drinking strong Turkish coffee while they composed sentences. They were careful about what they wrote. "You never know who's reading your mail," Bakica had warned.

Marijana's skin felt warm; she closed her eyes and lifted her face toward the April sun. She sat in a blanket of light.

She was between sickness and health, between hope and despair, between two countries, between two lives.

Sometimes she imagined writing letters to her friends. In them, she could pretend to have confidence, she could be carefree, she could feel a connection to her past. *Dear Mira, I love Rome! Though I miss Zagreb, and my friends, especially strolling with you along Strossmayer Promenade. I'm learning Italian. It is such a wonderful language. My aunt and uncle in Argentina are trying to arrange for me to travel there. Truthfully, I might not come back to Zagreb for a long time. If you can believe it, my aunt even found some man in Argentina to marry me, so that I could get papers. But at the last minute, she wrote saying that she had called the whole thing off because she didn't trust the man and was afraid, when the time came, he wouldn't divorce me. I don't want to get married to a stranger, even if it isn't real. The Croatian Monsignor, the one who is helping me, is going to send me to a doctor who might be able to give me what I need to leave Italy. Before I really leave, I'll visit Trevi Fountain and throw in a coin so I'll come back to Rome one day. Think of me and visit my grandmother as often as you can. Send her my love. I miss her beyond any words that I could write here.*

Greetings from your dear friend,
Marijana Kanjer

A young and exuberant Croatian priest dropped her off in front of the building and told her, "*Lire* can fix anything. Don't worry. I'll be back in a couple of hours." She climbed up the stairs and found the doctor's waiting room full of people. Marijana looked at a little girl crying, her face flushed. She sat on her mama's lap. There was a young man beside her who couldn't stop coughing; he held a white handkerchief against his mouth. He seemed embarrassed of his illness, turning away, avoiding eye contact with anyone. A couple of men stood as they talked; one leaned his shoulder against the drab wall. There weren't enough chairs so Marijana stood as she waited to see the doctor.

The plaster peeled off the walls in places. A simple wooden cross hung over some chipped paint. A little boy ran across the room to his mother, and she said to him softly, "*Bambino, bambino*," as she ran her hand through his black hair and then took out a grubby handkerchief and rubbed his runny nose. Marijana wondered what her own mother's voice sounded like. The memory seemed to have evaporated. Sometimes Marijana felt trapped in this constant reaching for something beyond her grasp.

She pushed up her sweater sleeve to scratch the side of her arm, and then she pulled both of her sleeves down over her wrists, covering her palms. Restlessly, she shifted her weight back and forth. Finally, she stepped outside and sat on the stairs in the dark musty stairwell. There was music, the rich sound of a cello, floating upward. She could hear car horns blaring and Italians yelling at each other. She laughed. Italians were quick to lose their tempers like Croatians, and she quite liked their spirit.

She wondered what would happen if the doctor wouldn't give her a good X-ray. She wondered if anyone had contacted him like the Croatian Monsignor promised. What if the doctor called the police, and she was arrested and deported back to Yugoslavia? Then she'd be sent to prison and then grandmother would have to take several trains to visit her. Everyone knew that if you had TB and ended up in a Yugoslav prison, you were as good as dead.

This plan had to work. Her aunt and uncle were waiting. She had somewhere to go where she could get better. She wasn't supposed to die like her parents. The smoke from a stove filtered through the hallway. In a nearby flat someone was cooking. She started coughing. She stood up, pressing her hand against the cool wall.

Back in the waiting room, she stood by the window. The wooden shutters were open. As the sky darkened, she leaned forward, breathing in the April air. Two nuns dressed in white habits walked across the square. The rain began to pour down; umbrellas popped open, one by one. The nurse called her name.

In the examination room, she sat down, waiting for the doctor to appear.

"*Buon giorno*!" said the large man in a white coat as he entered. The tips of his moustache were twirled at the ends. He looked like an actor from an American comedy film.

"*Buon giorno, Dottore*," she said and attempted to stand.

"No, sit, sit." He gestured for her to remain in the chair.

"What can I help you with today?" he asked, arching his eyebrows.

"I…need," she stuttered, confused, was she supposed to explain, or did he already know?

He waited.

"An X-ray, to travel," she stepped carefully onto her words.

"Ahhhh," he nodded slowly, "you're the one who needs the improved X-ray."

She nodded nervously. The doctor pulled out a recent film of her chest that had been taken in Rome, one she'd given to the nurse when she arrived at his office. With one hand, he held it up at an angle against the light. The X-ray made a cold, hollow sound each time he moved it. He peered at the white, gray, and black shadows that were her lungs.

Then he declared, "I'm going to make your lungs look so healthy that no one will ever know."

She felt her eyes water with relief.

"Come back tomorrow, young lady, and I'll give you a new X-ray. I'll fill out the health form for you. But, my dear, I want you to promise me something…"

She waited.

"Wherever you're going, you're going to get more treatment, yes?"

"Yes," she agreed.

"We're finished, I'll take care of it. That's it."

"That's it?" she repeated, confused, opening her purse, reaching for her money. She knew this was going to cost her and she hoped that she had enough to pay him and pay for her journey.

"No, no, no," he said, shaking his hand. "The priest, your Croatian friend, he's already taken care of everything. Unless of course you want to increase my salary?" he joked.

She raised her eyebrows and laughed with him. She felt lighter as she firmly shut the door behind her and left the examination room. She ran down the stairway and opened the door. The rain was falling more gently now. She had forgotten her umbrella, but she stepped out into the open, feeling the raindrops hit her cheeks, her nose, her hair, her palms. She hurried down the street, past the cypresses, allowing a girlish skip here and there.

14

GIULIO CESARE

Seagulls squawked and hovered in the air as Marijana climbed the gangplank of the *Giulio Cesare*. It was the 7th of May, 1955, and she was about to begin her first transatlantic journey from Genoa, Italy, to Buenos Aires, Argentina. Inside her purse, she kept her official health documents. As she went through customs, she held her breath. She felt as if the officials could see through her chest, but they only flipped through her documents and motioned for her to pass.

As the tugboats towed the ocean liner away from the quay, people waved to their relatives, grandparents, aunts and uncles, mothers and fathers, sons and daughters. There was no one was out there saying goodbye to Marijana, but still she waved and cheered with the other passengers. She waved to her grandmother back in Yugoslavia.

The *Cesare* stopped in Cannes, Barcelona, Dakar to pick up more passengers, before it began its long journey across the Atlantic Ocean toward South America. Her aunt and uncle had sent her money for the passage, and Marijana shared a small cabin with several other young women in third class.

Quickly, the women learned about each other's origins as they joked and gestured, searching for common languages, or words they could recognize in each other's languages: Italian, Portuguese, Spanish, French, Hebrew, and Croatian. They were off to Argentina to visit family, to begin a new life, to escape an old one or to forge a new identity.

Six of them slept on bunkbeds in the cramped cabin, and they washed their hands in the same washbasin, and shared a bathroom with the cabin next door. This twenty-one-day journey felt festive to Marijana. They chatted about the handsome stewards who worked on the ship, taking away empty glasses from their dinner table and emptying their ashtrays. Marijana hadn't expected so many people. Over 1,400 passengers, Alma, a young Spanish woman, informed them. Marijana listened to a flurry of languages, but the women often made their way back to English. It seemed they had all studied it in school or spent too much time at the cinema. She discovered that she could easily communicate in Italian or English now.

Through the porthole, Marijana could see the water surging alongside the ship. Alma had been on this journey before in order to stay with her relatives, who had a vineyard in Mendoza on the eastern slope of the Andes. She explained that they could all look forward to the festival when they crossed the equator, the invisible line that divided the earth into the northern and southern hemispheres. Twirling, she told them about the costumes that the passengers came up with, Greek and Roman gods and goddesses, white sheets draped like a toga. She held one arm up and placed one on her hip, looking at them from the corner of her eye, and described how many dressed like Neptune, god of the water and sea, or sirens, whose singing lured sailors to their deaths.

Whenever Marijana could go outside, she did. She loved

to see the glittering water beneath the bright ocean sun. Each morning the empty decks were damp with dew and held the lingering smell of cigarettes from the previous night. A black felt hat was lying forgotten on a deck chair. An elderly woman walked her dainty little dog; its nails scratched the wooden deck. A man sat at a table, writing a postcard. Marijana gazed at the water and thought about the previous evening, when she sat beneath the night sky, beneath countless stars, watching a film. The sound of the reel clicked away, as people laughed, smoked, and leaned toward each other; the audience pulled blankets around their shoulders as they were magically transported to a world that was so different from their own.

When the wind picked up, white crests fanned endlessly outward. The deck began to sway beneath her feet. She had learned not to fight it, but to lean into the movement as she held onto the railing. There was always the sensation that she wasn't on solid land. For some of the passengers, it was difficult and they never quite adjusted. They disappeared into their cabins and never emerged.

One day a storm came, water rose over the railings, spilling onto the deck and the air filled with salt water. Marijana slid like an ice skater across the deck, wrestling the door open and forcefully closing it behind her. In the dining room, plates shifted across the table. Wine and vermouth spilled onto the white tablecloth. The ship creaked in the wind. The bow rose and then dipped downward. She hurried through the dark narrow corridors, getting tossed from one wall to the other, until she reached her cabin, and stumbled onto her bunk. She tried not to slide off and held onto the side, while her roommates groaned, holding their stomachs, vomiting into little metal pots. Marijana breathed slowly, keeping her chin perfectly level with her belly button; she'd heard that this prevented seasickness.

After the storm, the sun seemed brighter. She ventured out onto the wooden deck. An elderly man smoked and played chess with his son. Two young men played ping-pong. When the ball flew off the table and landed at her shoes, Marijana tossed it back to them, and they thanked her. She strolled by women in hats, lounging on deck chairs, reading novels with their legs crossed. A priest sat beside a table, studying his *diccionario de español.* A little boy and girl scampered after a bouncing red ball. When Marijana wet her lips, she could taste the salt. She found a chair by a table and sat down, writing postcards to her Croatian friends and Baka. The ship spent nine days in open sea, with no dry land in sight.

There were nights where she would sneak up to second class with a young Italian man named Octavio, and they'd sit outside and listen to the live orchestra playing Italian and Argentinean music. Once a porter secretly handed them two tickets to enter, and they spent the evening dancing the Tarantella, Tango, and Bolero until they could hardly stand. When they didn't know a dance, they watched the more experienced dancers and did their best imitation of the intricate footwork.

Afterward they went outside and sat on deck chairs, watching waves shimmering beneath the moonlight. Octavio explained to Marijana that he was the eighth boy, and so his mother had named him Octavio. He was traveling all this way because he wanted to be a mechanic for the famous Argentine race car driver Juan Manuel Fangio.

"Are you sure he'll hire you?" she asked.

"Of course! How could anyone not want to hire me?" He raised his eyebrows, charmingly, and then added, "I'm an excellent mechanic, the best."

They both laughed. Octavio enthusiastically told Marijana that Juan Fangio had been racing with Alfa Romeo and Maserati, but now he was driving for Mercedes Benz.

She smoothed her white skirt with her hands and listened to his melodic voice. Marijana told him that she was supposed to convince someone at the Argentine Consulate in Italy that she was going to Buenos Aires to study dressmaking. Her aunt had even sent her money to buy a small sewing machine, so that she would be more convincing. She hated sewing, but her grandmother had taught her things like hemming a skirt and sewing buttons. If she ever had a daughter, she swore to herself that she'd never teach her how to sew!

Hanging lifeboats swung midair alongside the borders of the ship, and Octavio admitted that one night he had looked inside. "They each have a rubber lifeboat and some wrapped chocolate. It's very hard, and dark and bitter; I only took a tiny nibble, Marijana. There's also a sail, so as not to be stuck out at sea forever, and a compass to help guide you to dry land." He joked, "I thought about taking the chocolate, but then if I ended up on the open ocean, there would be nothing to sustain me, so I put it back. Of course, if that happened, I would share my chocolate with you, Marijana."

"Hopefully this ship won't sink," Marijana chuckled and then glanced at the lights of the tall radar mast at the top of the bridge.

"Marijana, do you know anything about this ship?"

"Nothing," she proclaimed.

He pointed one way and said, "This is the bow," and then pointed the other direction and said, "this is the stern of the ship."

She rolled her eyes. "I know that, Octavio!"

He grinned. "Of course you do, Marijana, but did you know this ocean liner towers 49 feet over the sea? And it's powered by two diesel engines constructed by Fiat. It has

13,000 horse power! Can you imagine? This ship can go up to 23 knots. Incredible!"

"23 knots," she repeated, smiling at his passion. He went on about the power of the 682-foot-long ocean liner. When he stopped talking, she looked directly into his dark eyes. His curly black hair hung loosely about his forehead. She reached over and pushed a curl off his forehead. He took her hand and then leaned toward her, his lips brushed against hers; she closed her eyes. For a moment, she stayed in the stillness of his kiss, surrendering to the feeling of floating, until she remembered. She pulled away from him and laughed.

"What's wrong, Marijana?" Octavio asked her, placing his warm hand on her arm.

"I promised the girls I would come back, they're probably worried." She stood up. "I have to go. I'll see you tomorrow."

He nodded. "Shall we continue our evening walks?"

"Who else would teach me everything about cars and ships?" she teased, before whirling away. She pushed her way through a doorway, walking through the maze of narrow corridors, until she was back outside on the decks. She held onto the railing and looked into the dark vastness of the sea and began to cry. Octavio was young and healthy. You couldn't say, I can't kiss you, I'm afraid I'll make you sick. She couldn't let anyone get too close because she wasn't sure how long she had. She began coughing, her chest heaving with emotion.

When she finally caught her breath, she decided she didn't want to go back to her room; she couldn't imagine making conversation with the girls. Instead, she wiped her eyes and listened to the waves. Soon she would see her aunt and uncle after so many years. Baka had sent them photographs, so they knew what she looked like now, and of course, they had been corresponding through letters since the war. Still, she felt nervous. They were strangers even though they were her relations. She wondered if she would recognize them. Baka told her, "They are saving your life, my little one, by getting you out of this God forsaken country."

On the last day she had seen her aunt and uncle, she played in their garden, galloping, circling their blooming lilacs. She remembered that when she had gone inside, her Uncle Ivo had smiled at her as he sipped his strong Turkish coffee and smoked a cigarette. Her Aunt Victoria bustled about the kitchen happily because Ivo had come home alive after two years of fighting on the Russian Front. During one battle in the trenches, men on both sides of her uncle had been killed. Somehow he'd survived.

At the kitchen table, Uncle Ivo began telling Marijana about the winter holidays during a cease-fire. Soldiers from both sides met on the battlefield; he had spoken Russian and drunk vodka with the Russian soldiers. A sudden knock at the door interrupted his story and German soldiers entered their house; she could hear sharp words and the sound of heavy boots in the other room. They were speaking to Ivo. She leaned toward the doorway and for the first time, she heard her uncle speaking German.

Marijana stared out the kitchen window and suddenly wondered about the people she had seen yesterday, riding in the open-air trucks. She'd overheard her parents saying something about Dotrščina forest and executions. She wasn't sure what that meant. As the trucks rumbled past, Marijana had dared to look at the people. Some were standing, their arms crossed, some were sobbing, their heads bowed; some gazed expressionless into the distance. She couldn't take her eyes off of them, until one man smiled at her, raising his bound wrists. He waved, trying to take her attention away from the others. She lifted her hand and waved back to him.

As she sat in her aunt's kitchen, chewing on her bread,

she thought about her aunt and uncle's whispers. If she was very still, she could overhear a lot of things. Last week, Ivo told Victoria that soon the war would be over. He was certain that the Germans couldn't hold out much longer. Marijana thought that her uncle was a wise man because he had studied in Paris and his shelves were filled with books.

Now she strained to listen to her uncle as German soldiers spoke to him. The kitchen had a wooden half-door with a ledge at the bottom, wide enough for a child to stand on. She stepped onto the ledge, pushing off with one foot, sending the door swinging into the other room, then swinging back into the kitchen. As she pushed the door forward, she listened to the halting words of the soldiers. She didn't understand what they were saying, but she was certain that her uncle understood because he spoke many languages, six to be precise.

She swung on the door. Back and forth, creaking, back and forth, creaking. She made up a song about the Germans losing the war. She sang, her voice ringing out.

Aunt Victoria, who was standing nearby, caught a few of Marijana's words. She spun around, grabbed her niece by the arm and dragged her back into the kitchen. The voices in the other room stopped for a moment as Marijana cried out. Her uncle firmly shut the door. Aunt Victoria's fingernails dug into Marijana's skin. Victoria leaned forward and said in a frantic whisper, "What are you doing, Marijana?"

She pushed Marijana down into a chair. "They could have heard you." Her eyes were wide with fear. "Your uncle could be sent away forever, he could be killed. Never, never repeat what we say. Do you understand? Marijana?"

Marijana nodded. She stared down at the floorboards; her eyes welled with tears.

At nineteen, she stood on the decks of the ocean liner gazing at the endless waves. Marijana understood why Victoria had been so terrified then. Ivo was part of a pro-Allied, anti-communist underground movement within the Domobran. He believed in the Croatian Peasant Party. Years after the war, her grandmother told her that Ivo had been helping Czech refugees who were in hiding. Victoria's former husband was a Jewish banker, and Ivo had helped him obtain false papers so that he could escape the country while others were being rounded up and taken to the island of Pag or Jadovno camp in the Velebit Mountains. If suspicions were aroused, he and Victoria would have been arrested.

On the 9th of January, 1944, Ivo and Victoria boarded a small plane and escaped to Allied-controlled Bari, Italy. Ivo was on a special mission. He had documentation that the Chetniks were collaborating with the Nazis. He was to convince the Allies to invade through the Dalmatian coast with Domobran support.

But Ivo was too late. A month before, the big three Allied leaders had met at the Tehran conference in Iran. British Prime Minister Winston Churchill, President Franklin Delano Roosevelt, and the Soviet Premier Joseph Stalin discussed military strategy; they would invade through northern France.

Before the end of the war, Churchill had switched his support from Mihailović's Serbian Chetniks to Tito's communist Partisans. Baka told Marijana that when Ivo reached Italy, Tito demanded that the British arrest him and hand him over. Fortunately, the British refused, instead interning him in Rome. Afterward, Ivo and Victoria boarded an ocean liner and traveled from Genoa to Argentina to begin their life of exile.

Now Marijana listened to the ship cutting through ocean waves and wondered if her aunt and uncle would ever be able to return to Yugoslavia. She tried to breathe more deeply as she stared at the moving water. She still thought about the man who had waved to her from the back of that open-air truck. She understood that he had most likely not survived the day.

So few had been able to flee. Many more had been rounded up and taken deep into the forest, their wrists tired with wire. They were forced to sing. They were silent. They stood completely alone. They stood tied together. They stood huddled in the snow. They stood beneath the canopy of leaves. They stood under the open sky and bright sun. They stood in the morning mist. They stood shivering beneath the shadow of clouds. They stood in the middle of a meadow. They stood on the edge of ravines. They stood on the banks of a river. They stood beside a karst pit. They sunk the dull metal edges of shovels into the earth. They disappeared into the waves of the sea, beneath stones, beneath leaves, beneath branches, beneath the earth.

The *Giulio Cesare's* horn blared on the 27th of May. On land, people waved their white handkerchiefs into the air, cheering as the ship entered the busy port filled with passenger steamers. As the ship docked, Marijana looked at the enormous cranes swinging, tall concrete buildings, railway tracks, and trucks moving down roadways to warehouses. She scanned the crowds, worried that maybe her aunt and uncle weren't there. They had not seen each other for ten years.

Immigration and customs officials boarded the ship. The passengers readied their documents. Nervously, she pulled out her passport and her health documents, proof that she was free of tuberculosis. She held her breath while a stern immigration clerk glanced through all her documents. He shrugged and handed everything back to her. Hurriedly she put it all away.

She went down the gangway and made her way through

the people. A family rushed over to a grown man, his weeping mother reached to embrace him. Brothers slapped each other on the back, laughing heartily, and then broke down in tears. Suddenly, she felt lightheaded; the ground beneath her moved and swayed as if she were still on the ship.

Finally, she saw her aunt and uncle standing together. Victoria had a small white hat pinned to the back of her head, and was dressed in a dark checkered skirt and jacket and high-heeled shoes. She was a small round woman with a large bosom. There were some similarities between her grandmother and her aunt, but it was hard to believe that they were sisters. Ivo wore a brown suit with a white shirt. He was tall and thin. His long face was sun-tanned and his ears stuck out.

They looked almost the same as they did when she was seven. Baka had told her that her aunt was now in her mid-forties and her uncle was almost fifty. Marijana watched her aunt clutching her purse beneath her arm, her eyes searching the crowds as she said something to her uncle, who nodded. He looked into the faces of the people. Marijana picked up her heavy suitcase and became aware that they had seen her. She heard them call her name, "Marijana!"

She bit her bottom lip and smiled timidly. She was filled with emotion; they recognized her! Her aunt waved, her purse still in hand. Uncle Ivo navigated his way through the crowds, *perdóname, perdóname*, and suddenly he was there, in front of her. "Marijana, you're here," he said, smiling, taking the suitcase from her hand. "*Tetak*," she said as he kissed her lightly on each cheek. He guided her through the crowd until Aunt Victoria rushed to her, throwing her arms around Marijana, kissing her on one cheek then the other, holding her by the arms. "Marijana, I could hardly sleep last night. Thank God, you're here. Your grandmother will be so relieved when we write to her. How are you feeling? How's your health? Here, we will take care of you. Don't worry! You're here!"

"*Tetka*, I made it!" Marijana exclaimed as she felt the urge to tell them about everything all at once, about her grandmother, about what they had endured together, the hunger of everyday life in Zagreb, about the sanatorium, but she felt so overwhelmed that she couldn't summon one word, she could only smile at them. She was filled with the longing for her grandmother; she should be here, Marijana thought.

15
BUENOS AIRES

Ivo and Victoria showed Marijana the house that they rented in the small town of Pilar, 58 kilometers north of Buenos Aires. There were high ceilings, the kitchen had running water, and there was even an indoor toilet; Bakica would be thrilled! Marijana loved the warmth of the parquet floors. Light poured in through the wide windows; growing vines hung from the balcony. Ivo placed Marijana's luggage in *el dormitorio* and left her alone. Marijana pushed back the heavy drapes and the sun spread onto the bed with its freshly ironed white sheets and pillowcases. This was her first time sleeping in a room by herself. She sighed delightedly and sat with a bounce on the bed, falling backward, her arms spread.

Later she wandered into the courtyard and found her aunt and uncle. After vegetable soup and crusty bread, her aunt placed a steaming cup of coffee in front of her. Marijana felt exhausted from the journey, but too excited to sleep. She thought about how many people helped her get to Buenos Aires and what her grandmother had sacrificed.

Her uncle put a plate of Argentinian pastries in front

of her. "We must celebrate your arrival, my dear Marijana. Finally, you are here," he said. The three of them sat around the table, while her aunt and uncle asked about the ship, her stay in Rome, the situation in Zagreb. They wanted to know about her grandmother, the shortages, what people were saying about Tito. As she spoke, Uncle Ivo watched her with serious eyes. When she paused, he'd stare into the distance as if he were remembering his home. His dark hair was slicked back. His unruly eyebrows and protruding ears made her smile. She listened to Ivo describe the life they had built for themselves in Argentina.

Here, her uncle explained, the landscape was incredibly vast. He described the geography, the rainforest, Iguazú Falls along the border of Brazil, and the snow-covered Andes along the western border of Chile. He told her about the grasslands, the Pampas, the windswept Patagonia like the west of America, and the enormous glaciers in the south. Many of these places he had yet to see. Maybe they could all travel together and explore more of the country once her health improved.

The longer they talked, the more she sensed that although he appreciated his home of ten years, he still longed for his country of origin. Part of him lived in the past, holding onto his Croatian identity. She understood his longing for home. She longed to go to the market for Baka and carry home the warm bread. She longed to taste her grandmother's peasant soup.

Ivo told her that he still received letters from his nephew who lived in Žabno. He sighed. "He would like me to come back home and see my family…" He cleared his throat. "The situation there prevents us." He knew that his life would be in danger if he returned to Tito's Communist Yugoslavia.

Victoria changed the subject. "We're happy you're here, Marijana. Everything will be better for you now." Marijana could sense her aunt's relief. Was it lonely for them without any children? Her aunt struck a match and lit a cigarette, and then handed it to her husband. She lit another one for herself. Ivo poured some dark vermouth in crystal glasses for each of them. Oftentimes, her aunt's small dark eyes glimmered mischievously like a child's when she spoke. Victoria was her grandmother's youngest sister by thirty years. She was really Marijana's great aunt, and Ivo, her great uncle.

Victoria explained to her niece that here around 11:30, Argentinians enjoyed their two-hour lunches of salads, steaks, and bottles of red wine, after which they took a *siesta*. "All the stores close between eleven-thirty and two in the afternoon," Victoria explained. Ivo described *asados*, ranch-style barbeques where they grilled ribs and sausages. "The chef is very passionate about making the grill a precise temperature, so that the embers cook the meat to perfection. You will eat well here, my dear niece. I have no doubts." They all chuckled.

Marijana felt relieved and confused at the same time. Only seven months ago in Zagreb, she and Baka had struggled to have enough food each day. Many times, she had walked to school lightheaded with her stomach growling.

After they sat silently for a while, Marijana took a deep breath and said, "I'm…" and paused, swallowing back her emotions, "I'm grateful for everything you did. Helping Baka to get me out, arranging for me to stay in Rome and come here. Thank you." She stared at the floor tearfully.

"What? What for?" Victoria said quickly, patting Marijana's hand, reassuring her. "We wanted to help you." Ivo added, "Even though you haven't seen us in many years, each day we would think about you, and wonder how you and your grandmother were. We looked forward to the day you would arrive. You're like a daughter to us. We would do anything to help you." He took one last drag from his cigarette and then tapped it carefully on the edge of the ashtray. Ivo reached out to her, resting his hand on her shoulder in comfort.

Ivo often traveled to the Andes in order to survey locations for power line towers for a Russian engineering company. He spent his days squinting through a small telescope atop a tripod called a surveyor's level. He measured distances and elevations, deciding the precise place for each tower, writing down the figures in a small field notebook, which he kept in his pocket.

Later, in his home office, he'd do the calculations necessary to plot the locations on a map. At his desk, Marijana showed him her sketches of passengers from the ship, of the scenes she captured in Rome, a little boy playing in a square, tossing a ball to his mother, a woman ironing sheets, a man riding his bicycle. Ivo admired her charcoal sketches and encouraged her to continue to develop her art. "Marijana, I'm certain that with dedication you will go far." Then he came up with the idea that she could help him with his own work and earn some money for herself. "Many young people here do correspondence courses. Instead I can teach you the art of drafting, if you are interested."

First, he showed her how to trace the exact location of the towers on the map in pencil. Then he opened a black leather case, where his ruling pens rested in soft green felt. He filled one carefully with India black ink. She held the pen with her right hand and learned to keep the bird's beak point almost vertical, so that the single stroke came out evenly on the map. Her uncle demonstrated how to adjust the width of a line. She learned that if she filled the pen with too much ink, it created a bubble when she stopped at the end of a line. And if she filled the pen with too little ink, the line would fade before she reached the end, and when she began again, it would look uneven. She had to be steady and work quickly, so that the ink didn't dry before she finished a single stroke. And somehow this work satisfied her. She got lost in the quietness and in the perfection it demanded. Before long she surpassed even her uncle's abilities.

A little over a week after Marijana arrived, there was an attempted coup. On a cloudy day, the 16th of June in 1955, Ivo adjusted the antenna on the radio, and they learned of an aerial bombardment. The Argentinian Naval Air Force had targeted *Casa Rosada*, the presidential building where President Juan Domingo Perón had been in the early afternoon. Ivo explained to Marijana that *Casa Rosada* overlooked *Plaza de Mayo*, where there had been a large crowd of Perón supporters assembled, along with other men, women, and children enjoying the city's central square. Hundreds had died or were injured. A trolley bus, filled with passengers and schoolchildren on a special trip to visit the city, was also hit. Civilian rebels had taken the communication centers and declared a democratic revolution. But within hours, the revolution was quashed.

Ivo, Victoria, and Marijana stayed by the radio all evening until Perón's address, where he reassured the people that the rebellion had been suppressed and his government was in complete control. He expressed his wish to ease the tension that had been growing between his government and the Church. Ivo and Victoria both looked worried. At the table they smoked one cigarette after another, filling the metal ashtray. Ivo urged Marijana to go to bed. "You need to get your rest. Tomorrow we will know more."

That night, Marijana listened to the rain drumming on the rooftop as she fell into a restless sleep. The next morning, the chirping of birds woke her up. Outside the window, everything looked calm. A stray cat scampered across the street. She could smell coffee. Downstairs Ivo and Victoria were sitting around the table, their coffee cups half-full; there were stacks of newspapers. Ivo had gotten up early to go out for bread and the latest news. Marijana sat with them, wondering if this meant civil war. It was strange that this explosion of violence had occurred right after her arrival.

Ivo told his niece that he'd heard rumors about the navy being dissatisfied with Perón. "Look, he's made the Church upset, and most Argentinians are Roman Catholic. He's putting through his *Peronista* measures, taking religious education from schools, making divorce and prostitution legal…" Ivo glanced over at Victoria. She shook her head, distraught. Marijana thought that in Communist Yugoslavia such a public display of religion or protest would have been suppressed immediately.

"I'm so sorry, my dearest Marijana, you come here and this happens. We want a peaceful life for you after everything you've been through," Victoria said hoarsely.

"You can't control life. There's no way of knowing what will happen in the future. Don't worry about me," Marijana said firmly, but then she shuddered as she thought of the children in the trolley bus. They were looking out the windows, teasing each other, excited about their school trip. Today, their parents must be inconsolable.

Victoria sat down beside Ivo, blowing her nose loudly into a handkerchief. "How could this happen? Is it war? Will we have to escape? I can't start over, not again…" Ivo did his best to calm Victoria; he brought her a drink to steady her nerves, and poured one for Marijana and himself too. "At least we are outside the city. We have to wait and see what happens," he told them as he lit a cigarette for himself, and then shook out the flame of the match.

The following week, Marijana could see that her aunt was still shaken. She jumped at the slightest sound. When Victoria and Marijana traveled to Buenos Aires for her first treatment, they took a *colectivo*, a red and blue jitney bus that avoided the part of the city that had been bombed. The driver took corners recklessly, tossing the passengers from side to side. Marijana hung on and couldn't help but laugh; the crazy driving reminded her of Rome. Her aunt rolled her eyes and told her niece, "They all drive this way." The *colectivo* wove its way through lots of traffic; the exhaust fumes made Marijana cough. On the streets, Marijana saw shopkeepers throwing buckets of soapy water onto the sidewalks. Waiters carried large baskets of bread into restaurants. The bus passed tree-lined plazas, construction workers chatting and reading newspapers on a park bench, and a group of children in white smocks running toward a school.

They got off the bus and changed to the *subterráneo*, underground trains that traveled across the city for two miles. Below, there were slot machines and a newsstand where Victoria stopped to buy several papers. Marijana looked at her curiously while Victoria rolled them up together and stuffed them into her bag. "Your uncle," Victoria laughed, and then explained, "he wants to read all the perspectives." While they waited on the tiled platform, Victoria rearranged the scarf tied about her neck. Marijana tried to imagine that they were on their way to the cinema instead of the hospital. A blue train glided in and they moved with the crowd toward the entrance.

At the hospital, Victoria spoke with the doctor in Spanish while he glanced at Marijana's most recent X-rays; he pointed to the white patch in her right lung. The doctor sat behind the wooden desk and leaned forward. His instruments, bandages and medications were in a glass cabinet in the corner of the room. Marijana watched Dr. Molina's fluid gestures and listened carefully. She understood some Spanish. She'd been studying on the ship. The words and rhythm reminded her of Italian, which she'd picked up quickly. Her aunt translated his explanations into Croatian: Marijana would receive artificial pneumothorax treatment. Gas or filtered air was introduced into the pleural cavity, collapsing the lung and giving it time to rest, so that the tuberculosis lesion could heal. No matter what, he emphasized, Marijana was to stay still during the procedure.

Panic flooded her body. Her thoughts flew wildly as she imagined what collapsing a lung entailed. Dr. Molina tried to reassure her by explaining some more of the process in Spanish. "*No te preocupes.*" It was quite simple, he told her calmly, and she wouldn't feel much because they would use Novocain. When the oxygen supply was cut off, the TB bacteria would suffocate and die; she would get better. He smiled with confidence at Marijana. "You will be fine! I'll send a nurse to come and get you in a few minutes."

"*Tetkica*, I'm afraid," Marijana confessed. Victoria took Marijana's hand and squeezed it protectively. A nurse bustled in with a squeaky wheelchair. Marijana sighed; she stood up resigned and went over and sat down in it, surrendering to the familiar feeling that she was losing control of her life. Her aunt patted her on the cheek and went to wait outside. A nurse pushed Marijana to the surgical room.

Marijana unbuttoned her blouse and handed it to the nurse, who hung it up on a hook by the door. Then Marijana covered herself with a thin medical gown. She hated feeling as if she were sick, and the wheelchair was a strong reminder.

Two nurses and Dr. Molina entered. They instructed her to get on the operating table and lie down on her left side. One nurse moved her right arm up, so it was out of the way.

Marijana felt as if her body were no longer her own. Her skin tingled. She heard movement behind her, something was lifted off a tray. She closed her eyes and listened to the water running from the faucet. A sheet-covering was placed over the side of her chest; through the opening, the nurse scrubbed her with a sponge and then used a gauze to brush the reddish-orange mercurochrome all over her skin. Dr. Molina came over. His gloved hands felt her ribs, and he stepped away. Then she felt the sharp pinch of a needle between her ribs.

She heard movement behind her. And then it was almost as if someone had shoved her. She gasped a little, struggling to remain still and clenched her fists. The needle pushed its way through the membranes and muscles, until there was a burst of pain. Everything closed in on her as if she couldn't bear another moment—and she tried to think of something, anything but being there in that room. She thought of the ship and the endless ocean, an eternity of white crests. She tried not to hold her breath, but she did. She stole a glance. Dr. Molina was attaching the large needle to a small rubber hose. She felt nothing for a time, until a painful sensation rose up around the side of her neck. Dr. Molina carefully removed the needle; the nurses huddled around Marijana, placing bandages on her side ribs.

Dr. Molina slipped out of the room to talk to her aunt. The nurses helped Marijana into her wheelchair. She was now breathing with one functioning lung, while the other was collapsed. Marijana strained to listen to the doctor in the corridor.

"The process will reverse itself on its own. She will stay here in the hospital for the rest of the week, then she can go home to you, only if she is on complete bed rest. Understood?" Victoria agreed to follow his exact instructions. "Bring her back in two weeks, so I can check on her progress. At her more advanced stage of the disease, this is our best option. She will respond to this treatment," he added.

Marijana suddenly felt exhausted. Her aunt bustled through the doorway, rushing to her, carefully taking hold of her cold hand. Dr. Molina came into the room, gazed down and told Marijana, "Rest, eat well, and not too much excitement, Doctor Molina's orders." Marijana nodded obediently and ran her fingers along her collar bone. The right side of her neck and right arm ached. She thought to herself, at least I don't have to stay in the hospital long.

For the first few days in hospital, Marijana felt wrapped in stillness. When she coughed and took the white handkerchief away from her mouth, she noticed blood and felt terror. Sometimes, she'd feel stabbing pain in her chest and an intense ache on the side of her neck. The nurses made her lie quietly. "Try not to move," they told her, using sign language even though she could understand them. Other patients attempted to talk with her, but she couldn't, not again. She pretended not to understand them, but in truth she couldn't bring herself to be friendly because too many hospital memories flashed through her mind.

When she finally came home at the end of the week, she crawled into her own bed. She sipped tea and stared out the window. Marijana lay there, imagining her lung re-inflating, little by little. Sometimes Marijana stared out the window; there were hours she would not speak to anyone. *Tetak* would be at work, *Tetkica* busy in the kitchen making their meals.

Ivo ventured into the city to the library to find books for Marijana. She wanted to improve her English; she was certain one day she would make it to America. Ivo came home with the play *Our Town*; he told her that a few years before, it had been performed in a Buenos Aires theater to great success.

Marijana lay in bed wandering through Grover's Corner. In Thornton Wilder's play, she could imagine Emily and George on the stage; their voices rang out in her head. She wondered if this is what an American village was like. Everyone seemed to trust each other, take care of each other; they stayed in the same place for their whole lives. No war, no violence. She came from a world of suspiciousness and unrest.

Strangely, through the characters she could feel the slowness and quickness of one's life. When Emily, still a young woman, looks out at her world from her grave and chooses to relive a day from her 12th birthday, Marijana began to feel breathless. What would it be like to touch one's mother and father again? To hear their voices? It's too painful for Emily and she turns to the Stage Manager, her guide, and says, "I can't. I can't go on. It goes so fast. We don't have time to look at one another. I didn't realize. So all that was going on and we never noticed. Take me back up the hill… to my grave."

Marijana placed the book on the sheets beside her, and brought her hands to her face and wept. She coughed; her body shuddered. What would she think and feel when she stood at the end of her own life? Would she have regrets? Would she know real love? Would she have a son? A daughter? Marijana picked up the book and began to read. Emily asks, "Do any human beings ever realize life while they live it? Every, every minute?"

After too much time in bed and books, separated from the world, Marijana grew restless. She moved through the house carefully. In the early evenings, she sat with her aunt and uncle around the table, discussing different things until inevitably they found their way to the topic of her health.

"Marijana, you must take care to keep out of the cold drafts. *Propuh* can cause you to relapse; we must be very careful with your health. When you recover from this treatment, you must remember to dress warmly when it's damp and whenever you go outside," her aunt advised.

Ivo teased them, "My dear Marijana, you know the root of every illness according to a Croatian woman is that you sat too long in a draft. I only believe you must try to eat a bit more. You are much too thin."

She nodded silently because she couldn't admit that she wanted to be slender with a small waist like a Hollywood actress.

"We know you are a grown woman now, but still, you're still only twenty, which is young, and we worry," her aunt said, leaning over to push Marijana's short hair away from her forehead.

"Of course," said her uncle, holding up his hands for a moment, "we don't want to interfere with your decisions, you are a young lady now. Know that we have good intentions. We suggest things because, well, we have more life experience." He rubbed out his cigarette into the metal ashtray.

"I know. I know," Marijana said quietly.

"Marijana," her uncle cleared his throat, "we are only afraid for you. You must be cautious. We are asking you to be reasonable. *Polako, polako, poco a poco*, you will recover. Your *Baka* worked so hard to get you to us, she would want you to listen to our advice."

When she was able to return to the office where her uncle worked, in order to draft maps again, she began to feel more like herself. On afternoons when she wasn't helping her uncle, she'd write to Bakica, wondering when she would see her again. If only she could help her in the garden. Sometimes Bakica's back ached, and Marijana would do the bending and digging for her. The tip of the ink pen glided over the fragile onionskin paper and the words poured out. Occasionally she paused, gazing out the window at the red geraniums. By the fence, her aunt had planted *madreselva*, honeysuckle, and she told Marijana that in spring and early summer, she could see the slender pink petals. Marijana wrote to Bakica that now in August, strangely, it was winter, but it was mild and nothing like a Zagreb winter.

Marijana wrote to Bakica about the times that she felt healthy. She told her about the Sunday mornings when her aunt and uncle had taken her to the market where books, stamps, and coins were sold. She'd discovered an Edgar Allan Poe book in English, and she'd bought it with the money that she earned helping her uncle. That afternoon she sat in their courtyard, among the red geraniums, sipping at her *café cortado* and reading, listening to the leaves rustle in the breeze.

She gazed out the window again and felt her grandmother's presence. If she wrote long enough, she could hear Bakica's voice; she could hear her hearty laugh. Marijana looked down at the translucent paper again and continued describing how they celebrated her twentieth birthday, on the 28th of July. Her aunt and uncle had taken her to Buenos Aires for dinner with their friends, *porteños*, those who were proudly from the city. So many arrived from elsewhere who now called Buenos Aires their home. They came from Spain, Italy, Belgium, France, Ireland, England, Syria, Portugal and Eastern Europe. They now embraced their Buenos Aires identity. Marijana sat with intellectuals, writers, poets, artists, and musicians. A waiter brought them a bottle of red wine and *platitos* to snack on. Ivo encouraged her to try *matambre*, flank steak rolled with hardboiled eggs, red peppers, and green olives. This is what killed the hunger before a late dinner, which took place between the hours of nine and midnight. Marijana enjoyed listening to the live orchestra playing tango, and when they took a break, another orchestra *tropical* took their place and played mambo and cha-cha-cha.

Carmen, a young woman, leaned over and told Marijana that on *Avenida Callao* they offered tango lessons, and that she could lend Marijana her Carlos di Sarli record. Marijana smiled and thanked her. She loved dancing and wished she could learn more forms of dance. For tonight, she would imagine that she was perfectly healthy and could do whatever she wanted. When she was a girl, she dreamed of being a ballet dancer, but there were no opportunities. Maybe one day she could still take ballet classes and wear pink ballet slippers and leap through the air. She listened to the lively voices at their table and laughed with the others. Ivo gestured for the white-jacketed waiter to bring over more drinks. He returned with another bottle of wine and flirted a little with Marijana before he left. She listened to Ivo and Victoria's friends passionately discuss their politics, philosophy and their love lives. They smoked cigarettes and teased each other about drinking too much the last time they had gotten together. One man, a Spanish guitarist, blamed them for his splitting headache. Ivo told him, "*Calavera no chilla.*" Carmen explained to Marijana, "Those who love to go to parties shouldn't complain about the consequences." They all laughed, and Marijana felt a wave of freedom, different than she had ever experienced at home.

She wrote to Baka that there was no need to worry about her anymore. She took long walks each day and got her fresh air. Uncle Ivo said that it's the Argentinian steaks that were making her stronger. She couldn't bring herself to tell Baka about the pneumothorax treatments or the uncertain political situation.

Instead, Marijana described the exotic fruits to her grandmother like the sweet bright-orange mangoes, and what it felt like to stroll down the wide boulevards, lovely parks, and past people sitting in sidewalk cafes, men smoking cigars, the smell of cooking meat coming from open windows. She described the languages, Spanish, English, Italian; she described the exquisite French architecture. She told Bakica about the central market with neatly stacked fruits in the shape of a pyramid. She told her that the cobblestone streets reminded her of Zagreb. She told Bakica how her aunt had taken her to a dressmaker; she wanted to sound young and frivolous and full of hope.

Here, she told her grandmother, when she walked to the market and passed by a group of men, they would say, "*Por Dios*, how pretty you are." And it made her laugh. She ignored them. She wasn't afraid of their flirtations because that was part of the culture here, how they gave compliments to women. *No, Bakica, I promise that I'm not overdoing it*, she reassured her, then sealed the letter and posted it that afternoon.

One evening, Ivo gave her a glass of red wine and placed a record on the phonograph. The needle lowered, and the phonograph crackled for a moment before a rich voice filled the room, a tango song called "*Madreselva*." They sat at the table, listening together. Ivo, who clearly enjoyed sharing Argentinian culture with her, explained that the music and lyrics had been written in 1931.

de mi niñez sin esplendor/ throughout my humble childhood
la amiga fue tu madreselva/ your honeysuckle was my friend
Cuando temblando mi amor primero/ When I trembled with my first love
con esperanzas besaba mi alma/ with your hope kissing my soul
yo junto a vos, pura y feliz,/ I was together with you, innocent and happy
cantaba así mi primera confesión./ singing my first confession of love.

Marijana listened to the melancholy song, wondering how

you could trust love. It seemed so fleeting. She could hear the longing and loss in the male singer's voice. She picked up her little notebook from the table. It was here that she jotted down new words and expressions in Spanish. She copied down the final verse of the song.

Madreselvas en flor que me vieron nacer/ Blossoms of honeysuckle that witnessed my birth…

…Madreselvas en flor que trepándose van,/ Honeysuckle blossoms that keep climbing upward

Es tu abrazo tenaz y dulzón como aquel…/ your sweet embrace is as strong as his

Si todos los años tus flores renacen,/ If every year your flowers bloom,

¿Por qué ya no vuelve mi primer amor?/ Why doesn't my first love come back to me?

Marijana stopped copying the lyrics… She wondered if she would ever fall in love. Her aunt reminded her not to speak to anyone about her condition. It made Marijana ashamed at her body's inability to heal itself. Still, she noticed that there was resilience in the song; through suffering and longing, the flowers continued to bloom again and again, despite the pain.

The following week, Marijana, her aunt, and uncle strolled along *Calle Florida* where she looked into the fancy shop windows. They walked past women in button-down dresses, men in gabardine trousers, jackets, ties, and polished black shoes. Young people held hands, pensioners strolled beside their grown children and grandchildren. The street, blocked from traffic, was filled with shoppers, many only browsing because the fashionable shops were too costly. She smiled as she smelled the floral perfumes of the women walking by. Near Plaza San Martín, they stopped briefly to look at the posters displayed in the large glass windows of the library. Marijana visited as often as she could to borrow books; sometimes she sat reading beside university students and pretended to be one of them.

Ivo and Victoria took her to a *confitería* to meet friends. They sat at marble tables drinking *café doble* or *café cortado* in tiny white cups. A little boy walked from table to table selling red carnations; Ivo bought two, one for Marijana and one for Victoria. Marijana broke off the stem and put the flower behind her ear like a flamenco dancer. Carmen encouraged Marijana to try *facturas*, pastries. She described the *pastafrola*, the latticed pie filled with quince jam or sweet potato, or the *bolas de fraile*, a doughnut filled with *dulce de leche*, milky caramel, dipped in powdered sugar.

Carmen encouraged Marijana to go to the cinema with her. Marijana was thrilled. Finally she had a real friend in Argentina; maybe she was making a home here after all. Carmen discussed Tyrone Power and Linda Darnel in *Blood and Sand*. Marijana confessed to her that she hated dubbed films. "I want to hear Greer Garson's voice in *Pride and Prejudice*, not someone else's. How can I practice my English if they're dubbed?"

"Who would want to hear Clark Gable impersonated? You need to hear his actual voice to fall in love with him. Have you seen some of Van Johnson's films?" Carmen asked.

Marijana nodded, laughing. Carmen's enthusiasm for films reminded her of Ružica. She missed her friend and wondered about her health. Was she getting more treatment? Did her TB linger and rise up unpredictably? Even with all the excitement of trying to fit into this new life, she carried the suffering of her dear friend.

On the other side of the table, Marijana overheard Ivo discussing the rumors circulating about Perón. Would there be another coup attempt? She'd learned from her aunt that since his wife Eva Perón's death in 1952, things had taken a turn for the worse. The poor and the working classes had supported Perón, and he had improved the social programs for the people, but now inflation was soaring. Devout Argentinians were upset that he was trying to separate the church and state. Ivo and his friends discussed how Perón was controlling the press, and the economy was collapsing.

As Marijana lay on her bed that night, she wondered about the political unrest.

Change did arrive. In September of 1955, Perón was overthrown by a military *junta*. General Lucero read Perón's open letter over the Argentine state radio, where Perón gave his resignation. He expressed that he wanted to spare Buenos Aires from being bombed and save innocent lives. Four generals overtook the government. Perón boarded a Paraguayan gunboat and sought political asylum.

Ivo wondered how long the military government would last. "When will there be elections?" he asked.

Within a brief period of time, Ivo's work came to a standstill: the military halted many foreign companies' work in the country. Ivo had not anticipated that they would struggle to get out their *pesos* from the bank; their savings was lost to them now that they needed it the most. Croatian friends living in Caracas wrote to Ivo, encouraging him to move to Venezuela. Victoria was resistant. She wanted to stay in their home, but Ivo could foresee how impossible it would be to sustain his family during this latest political upheaval. He made the decision that he would travel first, and then his wife and niece would follow.

"Look my dear, these things happen and we knew there was a chance we might not stay here. I think if I go first, you can settle everything here, then you and Marijana can follow me," he said steadily.

"What will we do? How will we manage? Always, always, something happens. When will we ever have some peace?" Victoria's voice rose.

"Victoria, we have no other choice. We must leave. Who knows how long this will last? Please my dear, calm yourself. We will start again somewhere else. We've done it before, we can do it again. If we stay, we will lose everything. *Más vale pájaro en mano que ciento volando*. Better to have one bird in the palm of your hand than one hundred flying away," Ivo said. Marijana met his eyes, motioning to him, asking if she should leave the room. Instead he nodded toward the empty seat, so she sat down beside her aunt.

"How long? How long will we be apart?" Victoria cried.

Marijana could see that everything seemed impossible to her aunt. The life that they had spent years rebuilding in a foreign country had already begun to vanish.

"I don't know…" Ivo lit a cigarette for Victoria and handed it to her.

Before she placed the cigarette to her lips, she asked, "What if something happens to you? What if we get stuck here? What about Marijana? We have to find somewhere to continue her treatments. In a new city, everything will be so complicated. Ivo, you'll be far away."

"Victoria, think rationally." His patience was running out.

"I can't believe it. What if things improved in Yugoslavia? We were going to use our money to go back home one day," she said helplessly.

Ivo shook his head and said, "My dear, what can we do?" He lit his own cigarette now.

"*Tetkica*, we'll figure out something. Maybe we won't have to wait here that long. I'll help you. You're not alone. I'm here, remember?" Marijana jumped in.

Victoria examined her niece. "Marijana, you need to eat more, you're much too thin." She sighed.

"*Tetkica*, but I've gained weight here. You're making me eat too much." Marijana smiled because if her aunt was nagging her about something that meant she was feeling less anxious.

"Yes, yes, maybe we should all eat something, while we still have something to eat," her aunt said.

Ivo and Marijana laughed.

16
TRANSANDINE RAILWAY

Within the month, her uncle headed to Venezuela in search of work. Marijana felt sadness sweep over her each night. Here, her health would return; here, she wanted to take tango lessons; here, she would learn Spanish. She tossed and turned in sleepless uncertainty.

Over the next couple of months, her aunt sold everything in their home and came up with a scheme to make some money for their new life in Caracas. She bought several blue leather suitcases, which she planned to sell in Caracas for a profit. Victoria used them to pack their things and told Marijana that Argentine leather had a worldwide reputation. No one could say her aunt wasn't resourceful, Marijana told herself.

"God willing, we will be on a train to Chile in a few days," her aunt said happily.

On the day of their departure, her aunt pushed her way through the throng of people and bribed someone at the ticket window for passage on the *Ferrocarril Trasandino*. They would travel by train from the Atlantic to the Pacific, 900 miles to Valparaíso, Chile, where they would board a ship bound for

Venezuela. Marijana watched as grannies and aunties cried as they kissed their relatives goodbye, uncles and fathers helped carry luggage, a little girl in pigtails reached her arms up to her grandfather, who wept as he picked her up. Marijana noticed how expressive South Americans were; she watched people hold on to each other for dear life; they showed their love with openness. Victoria broke her reverie as she pulled Marijana through the maze of people on the platform.

The train whistle pierced the air, and their journey began through the Pampas, endless plains to the foot of the Andes. For hundreds of miles, the train seemed to travel straight. Through her window, Marijana watched herds of cattle meandering across pastures, one raising his head to gaze at their locomotive. White wisps of clouds moved against a vividly blue sky. The flat landscape was endless until it met the horizon. Someone in their compartment joked that he was *más aburrido que perro en bote*, more bored than a dog in a boat. Every once in a while, there was a cluster of trees around a farmhouse surrounded by wheat fields. On the *estancias*, there were herds of cattle directed by the *gauchos* galloping on horseback. The dust of the landscape penetrated the closed windows and doorway of their train compartment. Victoria covered her mouth with a scarf, and she urged Marijana to turn away from the view, protecting her eyes. Marijana coughed, the dust particles aggravating her lungs, but still, she couldn't tear her eyes away from the window at the unchanging landscape and giant sky. For hours, she stared and wondered how people lived here, so far from the sea.

A herd of rheas, ostrich-like animals, swept across the plains like long-distance runners with a feathery bellies. Marijana laughed out loud at the silly and graceful nature of their movements. Victoria pulled the scarf from her face, and asked Marijana, "What? What was it?" Marijana pointed to the window, but they were small dots in the distance now. Victoria pulled out a thermos filled with steaming coffee and poured some into a cup for her niece. Marijana leaned her head against the vibrating windows and dozed off.

The shriek of the train awoke her as they veered toward the eastern slope of the Andes. They stopped in Mendoza. There they would change to the narrow-gauge railway. They were able to get off and stretch their legs. She saw an ox pulling a wooden wagon, and it suddenly made her think of her village Oriovac. A mule carrying barrels of wine, went past. In Mendoza small white-washed houses lined the wide streets. In contrast to the Pampas, Mendoza was an oasis of green vineyards, peach orchards, terraced farms, and a system of canals. Before he left for Caracas, her uncle had explained to Marijana that the Huarpes Indians had designed these irrigation systems where the snow was channeled into canals. The Mendoza streets were particularly wide and the houses built low because of earthquakes. She couldn't imagine being in an earthquake. It felt otherworldly, until she remembered how the ground felt when the bombs were falling during the war. The choking dust, the debris, pieces of the ceiling crashing, flying glass, the earth crumbling beneath you, the smell of burning houses, and burning flesh. She began to cough into her hands. Strange how it could come back so quickly; she shook the memories away. She believed that she could bury the pain deep inside, where one day even she could no longer find it.

As Victoria and Marijana boarded, they overheard two women whispering "*Espero que no tengamos mala suerte.*" Marijana raised her eyebrows quizzically at her aunt, and she explained that trains on this line occasionally derailed; they had friends who had been stranded for days because their train had struck a snowbank. Victoria gave Marijana a sharp, worried look, and did the sign of the cross when they sat down in the passenger compartment. Marijana noticed that the train was crowded with other foreigners fleeing Argentina to visit relatives in Chile, Bolivia, or Peru.

On the foothill of the Andes, a grandfatherly Chilean man sat down across from them. He introduced himself as Ernesto Peña, and they learned he was a professor in Santiago. He pointed out their window and told them about *Cacheuta*, a hot springs he had visited as a young man. "The train used to stop right there. There was a lovely hotel, but then a glacial flood destroyed everything in 34. Such a pity! Miles of this railway were swept away by gushing water. It was horrible. Many, many people were lost. But, I do remember before all that, the thermal baths were marvelous. You should have seen them! Once you spent time in that water, all your ailments healed," he said, sighing nostalgically.

Victoria raised her eyebrows at Marijana, who shrugged. She knew her aunt believed that the hot springs could help Marijana's lungs.

Señor Peña turned politely to Victoria. "May I ask, dear lady, where you are going in Chile?" Victoria explained that her husband had secured work in Caracas, Venezuela. They would take a ship from Valparaíso and go through the Panama Canal.

"How interesting! What an experience your daughter will have."

Victoria nodded and smiled; she didn't correct him.

Marijana thought maybe it was easier this way, less explaining to do. Sometimes she felt as if she were abandoning her parents' memory in order to become someone else.

Victoria asked Señor Peña about his journey, and he explained he had been visiting his daughter, who lived in Buenos Aires with her Argentine husband. He pushed himself up to standing; he was heading to the dining car. Quickly, Victoria stood to help him through the moving passageway. Marijana said she would join them momentarily. She was grateful for time alone to study this barren landscape with its scrub brush, stunted trees, and massive peaks in the distance to the north and the west. As they moved to higher altitude, the temperature dropped drastically. The air became cool and dry. Marijana shivered.

When she stepped into the narrow passage of their train, she felt slightly breathless. The floor vibrated beneath her feet as the train continued its ascent. She passed the saloon car, where men were sitting in leather armchairs. One gentleman was reading *La Prensa*; another group of men were playing cards as they smoked cigars. A young couple, who spoke with British accents, sat beside the long rectangular windows. The train puffed its way up steep canyons with rocky precipices; the wind howled outside. Luckily, she had put on her coat. She buttoned up as she walked and accidentally bumped into a young man, who was chatting in Italian with his friends. The train jostled again, knocking her down, her knee banged into the floor. She laughed through the sharp pain, and the men leaned over with concern. The stocky one with black-rimmed glasses reached to help her up. She stood, wobbly, brushing off her coat, hoping there wasn't a tear in her stockings.

The Italians were brothers, she learned. They were traveling to work in their uncle's sombrero factory. They headed to the dining car with Marijana. She took a seat beside her aunt and Señor Peña. The Italians sat at an empty table behind them. Victoria leaned over. "Marijana, what took you so long?" Marijana shrugged and motioned to the window. "I was looking at everything. I've never seen anything like this." Her aunt smiled approvingly.

One of the Italians turned and asked in Spanish what language they were speaking.

"Why do you want to know?" Victoria asked suspiciously.

"*Tetka*, they're just being friendly; they aren't spies," Marijana said quietly, cutting her off in Croatian. Then she turned sweetly to the brothers and asked, "*¿De cuál provincia de Italia son ustedes?*"

The eldest brother, Antonio explained that they were from Verbania beside Lago Maggiore, below the border of Switzerland. Antonio and his brothers, Lorenzo and Luka, had traveled by ship across the Atlantic and would take this train and another one to Santiago. Señor Peña asked them about their uncle, who they were visiting in Chile. Antonio, the one with a thin moustache and wavy black hair, answered, using his hands to describe the different styles of *sombreros* and the different materials his uncle used. Luka explained to Marijana he didn't want to work in his uncle's factory, he wanted to make films and move to Hollywood; for now he would learn from the world, so he could tell stories on the screen. Lorenzo, the teenager, who was lanky with a thin face and an angular long nose, told Marijana that he wanted to swim in the Pacific Ocean and become a fisherman like his grandfather.

Marijana was intrigued by the brothers. After they had chatted for a while, Victoria invited the Italians to join them. It was a long train ride and easier to pass the time talking to these entertaining young men. The smell of coffee filled the compartment as the train wove through the rugged landscape, finally reaching an arid valley and the town of Uspallata.

Beside craggy slopes, beneath overhanging cliffs, they moved. Long shadows cast over the train until it burst forth from the narrow canyons to a magnificent view of snow-capped mountains that were tinged by violet sunlight. Señor

Peña pointed out the massive Aconcagua, the highest peak in South America; he explained that it reached 22,841 feet above sea level and the severe weather on the mountain made it nearly impossible to explore. The Italians spoke about their own treks through the Italian Alps as the train zig-zagged slowly, hugging a rocky ledge of a gorge. They peered down to see a terrifying drop, the roaring river, fueled by snow melt, snaking through the rocks.

The wind rattled the windows. After so many hours together, Marijana could hear the train travelers around her revealing the true nature of their journeys: a job in another city, searching for work, visiting a sick aunt, leaving behind a lost love. She listened as their talk turned toward who was being left behind—a son, a wife, a grandmother. She heard regret; she heard hope and excitement. She realized that everyone on the train was grappling with some sort of loss—loss of home, loss of language, loss of family. Marijana watched her fellow passengers' expressions and gestures. Through scraps of language—Italian, Spanish, French, English, and Croatian—she realized that people were not only retelling their histories, but they were reinventing themselves in this new landscape.

The last stop on the Argentine side was *Puente del Inca*, where there was a naturally formed arch, a stone bridge, high above the *Cuevas* river. The Italians admired the stripes of rusty colors on the rocks beside the bridge. Señor Peña explained that a glacier had most likely formed the seventy-foot-long bridge and how the sulfuric waters created the yellow and orange lines. Victoria admired the fashionable spa hotel below the bridge. Marijana listened thoughtfully as Señor Peña told them of the Inca legend. A chief, whose son was paralyzed, had searched long and hard for a way to help his son. Nowhere could he find a cure to help his son walk again, until he heard of the hot waters that rose from deep inside the earth. With his warriors, he traveled to the faraway Andes. A torrential river stood between him and the healing hot springs. His warriors offered to make a human bridge, and the chief walked over their trembling bodies, carrying his son in his arms. On the other side, finally, he was able to place his boy down in the magical hot springs. His son was healed; his legs moved and splashed in the water. The chief turned with joy to tell his men; he wanted to thank them. But to his horror, they had turned to stone creating *Puente del Inca*, a bridge that would last for centuries.

Marijana's eyes watered as she stared at the desolate landscape and the snowy summits surrounding them. The air felt thin and cold. She thought about sacrifice, and one image appeared from her childhood. She was standing at the bedroom doorway, looking at her mother lying in bed, dying. She saw longing in her mother's eyes because she wanted to hold Marijana one last time, but she couldn't allow herself that final wish. Marijana stood powerless in the doorway, watching her mother's anguish. Now Marijana understood that her mother was trying to protect her from tuberculosis. But it had all been in vain. In her mind, she rushed into her mama's arms one last time. They held each other.

Marijana began to cough as she sometimes did when she would get emotional. Her lungs felt tight; she couldn't quite catch her breath. She pulled her coat tightly around her. Wordlessly, she nodded to her aunt, and they both returned to the train.

Inside everyone spoke of the altitude. It made some people feel light-headed, or they complained of headaches and nausea, but it only made Marijana sleepy. Victoria took out some cards and began to play solitaire. Marijana looked out the window at the high ridges, vertical planes, and domes of icy rock. Like the ocean, the snowy precipices and sharp angles of the rocks transformed as the clouds cast moving shadows on the earth. Marijana marveled that the Andes didn't seem locked and motionless as she had imagined; instead the view was ever-changing shifts of sky and clouds, darkness and light.

When they reached the *Cumbre* pass, the train entered the two-mile tunnel. They passed into Chile in blackness, a bell clanging to prevent another train, from the opposite direction, from crashing into them. Marijana squinted when dazzling sunlight flooded their compartment once again. A government official checked their passports. She felt her heart race, but there were no issues.

As they moved through the Andes, the conductor stopped the train occasionally to allow the engine to cool down. Everyone shifted restlessly in their seats, their bodies tired from sitting in the same position so long. Marijana tried to distract herself by looking for life in the treeless, snowy landscape. After an hour or so, she finally saw a condor soaring above an alpine valley. He circled, his enormous black wings gliding on the wind. She watched until he disappeared in the distance. She dozed off into a half-sleep, the train bumping her awake from time to time.

Hours later, she awoke disoriented. The train was inching forward like a caterpillar; the snowy mountains with sharp pinnacles still loomed around them. Outside her window, the Italians jogged breathlessly beside the train. Antonio stopped and bent down to rest. She laughed. Her aunt pushed down the window, stuck her head out, and shouted in Spanish, "What are you doing? *¿Están locos?*"

"Look, we can run faster than the train," Luka said, jogging and waving his arms. Antonio called out, "We live near the Alps, so we're used to the altitude." Luka hopped on one foot, comically; Lorenzo placed both his hands behind his head, feigning sleep. Her aunt sat back down, and Marijana stuck her head out and shouted, "Hey, get back on! The train will leave you here in the middle of nowhere, and you'll freeze to death." They all ran to catch up to the train. When Antonio reached Marijana's window, he clasped his hands together in front of his heart and said, "*Signorina*, I promise to get back on the train only if you, and your aunt, of course, have dinner with my brothers and me in Valparaíso!"

"*Tetkica*, should we let them have dinner with us?" Marijana joked with her aunt.

"Why not?" Her aunt grinned.

Marijana leaned back out the window and said, "Okay. But come on, you better get back on or you'll be lost forever."

The three Italians jogged breathlessly; one by one they leapt onto the ambling train; a trail of white smoke drifted into the mountain air.

17

THE LETTER

He admired her lines, the contours on the map unrolled on the drafting table. He was mesmerized by the fact that he couldn't detect the exact place where she lifted her pen in order to refill it with ink. She maintained the width so precisely. For a moment, his eyes lingered on the cloth, spotted with black ink, sitting on her desk, and then he took a deep breath and smiled; he gazed into her striking light green eyes. It was a December afternoon in 1956; he had just arrived in Caracas, Venezuela, and didn't speak a word of Spanish. Marijana glanced down shyly, smoothing her white smock, which protected her clothes from the ink.

That first morning in Caracas, someone had picked him up at the Waldorf Hotel and walked him to the United Geophysical Company office. Now Dave watched his new co-worker Osvaldo lift his chin in an upward nod and say, "*¿Qué tal?*" to the young lady. She stopped drawing, and looked at them inquisitively.

"Dave, this is Marijana. Go ahead, try your German." Osvaldo nodded encouragingly at Dave, laughing. Dave glanced at the floor bashfully; immediately he regretted that he had admitted to Osvaldo, his new friend, that he could speak a little German. He glanced for a moment at Marijana, and then he stumbled over the only language he'd studied in high school.

Marijana smiled, confused.

Osvaldo laughed again and asked Marijana, "*¿No hablas alemán?*"

She shook her head and arched her eyebrow.

"*¿Inglés?*" Osvaldo prodded.

"*Sólo un poco*," she responded cautiously and said, "Daaave?" testing out his name, letting the aaa hover over her tongue.

Dave nodded, smiling, entranced.

She noticed his dimples.

Within a week of his arrival, Dave disappeared from the Caracas office; he traveled sixty miles east of the city into the field in order to map the layers of the earth, so that the company could determine where to drill for oil. He watched the crew bury dynamite and listened to the dull *whooomph* when the explosion went off underground, sending seismic waves diving downward (as deep as twenty thousand feet), bouncing like a rubber ball off the rock layers only to be caught by geophones attached to cables lying on the ground as still as a sunbathing snake. He mused over the fact that the geophones could sense even a breeze brushing over the grass. Dave spent his days calculating the depths of the various layers.

When he ate dinner outside the small motel, the parrots mesmerized him, noisily chattering away as they perched on tree branches. Their unexpectedly bright green feathers made him feel wonder. He never imagined that he'd celebrate his twenty-eighth birthday in Venezuela; he was so far away from his home in Washington State. When his airplane had taken off, snow was drifting downward, and now he was sitting outside in the tropics, in a short-sleeved button-down shirt. He thought about his former girlfriend, Billie; they'd been together three years. She'd broken off their engagement. Not ready for a family yet, she told him firmly.

She wanted to work, to see the world, and he had wanted to stay in Washington State. During the war, he'd worked as a park ranger at Mt. Rainier National Park. When all the soldiers returned, they claimed the park ranger positions, and Dave had been put on a wait list. It was then, he learned of an oil company searching for a geophysicist. Although he'd only just graduated from the University of Washington with a degree in geology and didn't know much about geophysics, he thought why not give it a try. It seemed like an adventure: a new job, a new country, and a new language. Still, memories of Billie flashed through his head; he could see her standing beside her Arabian horse or skiing at Snoqualmie Pass. Before he left for Caracas, she'd written to tell him that she was going to get married.

Dave traveled to *Los Llanos,* the rugged grasslands, and stayed at a camp beside the Santo Domingo River with the other company workers. He surprised himself when he casually asked, in his two-week-old Spanish, about Marijana, the Croatian girl with green eyes who worked in the Caracas office. Did anyone know anything about her? He was told by one of the men that a relation of hers worked in the camp.

In the evenings, Dave found himself playing chess with Ivo, who gracefully moved his wooden pieces: pawns, knights, bishops, and rooks, while the cicadas' chatter filled the air. After a long day's work, they each sipped *Cerveza Polar* and spoke in English, one of Ivo's many languages. At first, Ivo didn't speak much about himself, Dave could tell he was a private man. Somehow though, as the evenings progressed, Dave's earnest questions disarmed Ivo, and he began to open up a little about himself. Dave learned that Ivo had been born in Žabno in Yugoslavia, educated in Paris at the famous École de Guerre Militaire, and escaped from Yugoslavia during the Second World War; he had been interned in Italy, and after the war, eventually traveled by ship to Buenos Aires. "The situation there is too unstable, so I brought my family here," he explained. It was Ivo's job to survey the seismic lines, and sometimes, due to the shortage of surveyors, he had to take someone off the street and teach him to be a surveyor in two weeks. "An unfortunate aspect of the job," he told Dave, wryly, his unruly eyebrows arching. Ivo was a tall thin man with high, angular cheekbones. Dave could sense he was an intellectual, a man who spent his evenings reading.

They peered at the chessboard together, each devising his next move. Ivo had his legs crossed and his left foot trembled ever so slightly. Nervous energy, Dave thought to himself. By the time Ivo finished one cigarette, he'd said "checkmate" with a thoughtful smile.

Dave threw his hands up in surrender and shifted his long legs, one foot in front of the other, glancing downward, building up his courage. He asked about Marijana. "Who is she?"

And Ivo, about to light another cigarette, replied simply, "My niece, but like a daughter to me."

Nothing more and nothing less was said about her for the rest of the evening. Dave didn't ask for more information. Still, before they finished their work in that location, they had built a mutual respect for each other.

Dave's tent was a canvas draped over a wooden pole frame, and he quickly learned to sleep with his legs bent, otherwise his feet hung out over the edge of his cot. For the first time, he tried to get accustomed to the strange taste of olive oil (his mother only used Crisco) and the bland food that the two Chinese cooks served each night. He easily befriended the locals who made up the crew; they were pleased he was trying to learn Spanish. One night they confessed to Dave that they had nicknames for everyone in the camp. The Canadian party chief, who refused to learn Spanish and was forever calling out "Ivan! Ivan! Ivan!" so that Ivo could translate something, had been named *El Niño Perdido*, the lost child. "Y usted, Señor David, se llama, Enano," they informed him, gesturing and showing him what it meant. "Dwarf?" he asked, a very unusual nickname for a six-foot-five man. He laughed at the irony, and they joined him.

Some mornings while he stood outside in the thick humid air, peering into a mirror at his chin lathered in shaving cream, he'd hear howler monkeys, as they hung from their tails off the branches, or swung from tree to tree. Their low and incredibly loud, guttural voices would often awaken him in the mornings. He learned that the howlers had a bone in their throat that amplified the sound. More than once he'd seen a howler monkey take a handful of their own shit and throw it at a crew member, often hitting him, unexpectedly, on the head. The crew member would shake an angry fist in the air and shout obscenities at the howler. An effective defense mechanism, Dave thought, smiling to himself. He'd never been hit, at least not yet.

Slowly and methodically, he ran the shiny razor over the sides of his cheeks and below his chin, the blade scraping his tanned skin. He thought about the day someone on the crew had killed an ocelot, *tigre*. He watched her exquisite black-spotted golden fur being slit open with a knife. A lump rose in his throat as her lifeless babies slid from her belly. They were covered in blood and fluid. In one shot, her life, family, and future had been ended.

In Los Llanos, he could look up at the sky and see five red macaws flying overhead, or a capybara, the world's largest rodent, which looked like a small hairy hippo, waddling across the dusty road. He marveled how the details of his life had changed. On the weekends, the men would say to each other, "Let's go to town," which meant crowding into the company truck and driving to the closest village to drink whisky and stagger to the local brothel. Once he'd accompanied them, but he never returned. He was disillusioned by the crudeness of the place and the sadness of the women. For the first time in his life, he got really drunk; the crew handed him one beer after another, and this, on top of the whiskey, left him in bed the next day, tossing in his cot, wrestling the incredible nausea of a hangover in the heat and humidity.

After a couple of months, he returned to Caracas. Back in the office, he quickly became aware how he looked forward to seeing Marijana each day. He'd found out that she was twenty-two, and didn't have a boyfriend. He glanced up from his desk to watch her working at her drafting table. Carefully, she examined the lines before placing her pen against the paper. Sometimes he'd overhear her speak Croatian on the phone with her friend Marica. He became entranced by the sounds of her language. He smiled to himself when sometimes she exclaimed, "*Ma, ne*!" He understood that this meant she didn't believe something being said to her.

Every once in a while, he accompanied his fellow workers to lunch, and once he found himself walking right behind her. She wore a black and white striped blouse that reached her elbows. Her full white skirt swished from side to side. He watched her shapely calves as she took confident steps on the sidewalk. From time to time, she'd turn to say something to her friend. She had high cheekbones, and the sun made her smooth skin glow. In the office she was so serious, but outside he caught glimpses of her when she was unguarded, when she laughed and tossed her head back carelessly.

The office phone rang. She reached for another pen and accidentally spilled some ink. She grabbed her blotter to wipe off the table. As the phone kept ringing, she thought, my God, why does it always have to be me? Why won't they pick it up? She stayed at her drafting table and pretended not to hear, pretended she was too busy, even though the endless ringing grated on her nerves. She didn't care what they said about her, she wasn't going to pick it up this time. The office was full of men, Americans and one Englishman, who, although they'd been living in Venezuela for quite some time, couldn't seem to learn Spanish. Suddenly she overheard someone pick up the phone and answer it. The tall American, Dave. She sighed, and peeked over her shoulder for an instant and glanced at him.

She looked back down at her work, and then stared out the window at big American cars with tailfins: red Chevrolets, mint-green Oldsmobiles, and pink Plymouths. In the plaza, she could see little boys in dirty clothes, carrying boxes and rags to shine someone's shoes. She wondered if they lived in the *superbloques*, the multi-colored high-rise buildings, which the government had recently built for the poor people. She'd heard that for some reason water didn't reach the top floors and people carried buckets of water up to their apartments. She imagined her own grandmother using both her hands to set the heavy bucket on the ground. "Wait, wait!" Marijana would rush out of the house. "I'll carry it, Bakica." Now she wished that she had helped her more often. Her grandmother must feel so alone. Thank God for neighbors, she thought to herself. At least her friend was looking in on her Baka daily.

She glanced back at her work. She overheard one of the Americans say to someone else in a low voice that he thought she was moody. He thought she didn't understand English, but she understood everything. She'd kept her eyes fixed on her drafting table. A line of ink on her map bled slowly into another line. What did he know about her anyway? No one knew anything about her life, her past.

When she came home that day, sullen, her Aunt Victoria asked what had happened. "I don't want to talk about it," she said, pushing her short hair behind her ear, angrily.

"I know it is about a man," Victoria said knowingly.

Marijana pursed her thin lips and looked away. Her aunt would never understand her.

"Look, Marijana, you'd better learn how to cook, or you'll never find a husband."

"But you don't really know how to cook," Marijana protested and laughed.

"Yes, I do. Well, I've got a husband so I don't have to worry. But you, I worry about."

"Well, I don't want one. Who would want to marry someone with TB anyway?" She sighed and crossed her arms.

"Marijana," her aunt said sharply, "we're not going to tell anyone that you have TB. No one has to know."

"What? What do you mean?"

"No one has to know," Victoria whispered, her forehead crinkled.

"Of course they have to know," Marijana said sharply. "You can't marry someone and not tell him. That's wrong."

"We will tell him afterward."

"That's crazy!"

"Marijana, listen to me, I'm not crazy; I know this world. I have many life experiences. I know how the world works. Afterward is better. No need to know everything. Of course, it's up to you. You have to make your own decisions. I'm only asking you to listen to my advice."

"Maybe by the time I get married, I won't be sick anymore."

Her aunt shrugged. Marijana walked to her room. She had been fighting this disease since she was a child, and it was long enough.

The office phone rang and startled her. She nearly jumped out of her seat. "*Por favor*, Marijana," the Englishman called out nonchalantly, as the phone rang again, interrupting his conversation about which camera lens was the best to buy. She noticed that Dave was busy, working at his desk. She turned her head sharply and glared at the rest of the men, who stared at her expectantly. "It is not my job to answer the phone. I'm not a secretary! I do the same work you do. If you want the phone to stop ringing, you answer it." Her green eyes blazed. She grabbed her things and left for lunch.

The next morning, she found a wrapped box and a note on her drafting table. She glanced up bewildered to see all the men working quietly. The note said: *Marijana, forgive us*. She opened the box and saw seven shimmering gold bracelets. One had all their names engraved inside. She noticed Dave's name and smiled, then slipped them over her hand and held up her wrist to admire them.

During their lunch break, Dave and Marijana sat together at a small Italian café with polished terrazzo floors. They were alone for the first time. She glanced up at Plaza Candelaria; couples strolled hand in hand, or with arms linked. After they ordered, she asked how he was getting to work now that he'd moved into his own apartment. "*Por puesto*," he answered, and she couldn't help but smile. His American accent. She liked listening to the way the Spanish words tumbled off his tongue.

He explained to her in great detail that a *por puesto* was a taxi that followed a particular route, and picked up more than one passenger, and that you were only obliged to pay for your seat. She nodded, pretending she hadn't known all of this, even though she'd been living in Caracas for a couple of years.

She told him that she lived with her aunt and uncle down the street from the office. She could walk to work every day. In Zagreb, she had walked everywhere; she spent entire days exploring. She sipped her cappuccino and he sipped his espresso, admitting that it was the first one he'd ever tasted and that it was quite bitter. She noticed that he grimaced slightly when he took the next sip from the tiny white cup. He asked her if she ever spoke English. "I only have a little English," she lied. She didn't want to make any mistakes. And so they continued their conversation in Spanish.

Before they returned to work, he asked if she would mind if he took her to dinner. His shoulders were slightly raised in apprehension. "I don't mind," she said as they walked back to the office together, her seven gold bracelets bouncing on her wrist.

After one dinner, she invited Dave to her aunt and uncle's apartment. She walked him through the courtyard, and told him how a dressmaker lived above them, and how sometimes they talked to each other from the windows. She motioned for him to sit on the sofa, and walked across the terrazzo floor to the kitchen, where she took a bowl from the table and came back to offer him some green grapes.

"Thank you," he said, shyly, plucking one off the stem. He wasn't accustomed to eating grapes. He teased good-naturedly that no woman had ever offered him grapes before. She asked if they had grapes where he was from. Of course, he told her, then admitted that at his house, his parents didn't usually have grapes. In fact, grapes seemed rather exotic to him. He tried to explain that after the Depression things had been difficult for his family; they lost their house, his father lost his job as an engineer, and they moved from Duluth, Minnesota to Takoma, Washington where they'd eaten many potato chip and tuna casseroles, he joked.

"What is a casserole?" she asked. And they spent the rest of the afternoon trying to think of a Venezuelan equivalent.

On another afternoon, she asked, "Dave, tell me more about Washington State, about what you did there."

He stared at the wall, smiling, and she knew that he was seeing something in his mind that she could not. Animatedly, he told her about his home, and his dream to someday return to the mountain where he had found indescribable beauty. Mt. Rainier, Marijana understood, was a part of him—a mountain he had climbed more than once, a mountain he longed for. His voice fell into a steady rhythm. And she could see the trail that he had climbed, weaving through an alpine meadow with wildflowers and slender firs. They ventured across his stories together, and she felt as though she could almost breathe the crisp air of his mountain. She sensed that there was something unreal about it, as though it had been painted onto the sky.

She was captivated by the fire lookout; a wooden hut on stilts, perched up high upon a rocky precipice, where he'd lived months at a time. Sometimes he would go down into the forest and gather huckleberries so he could bake homemade pies, carefully following the recipe in his mother's cookbook. Once, he told her, he climbed up a tree and rescued a lost black bear cub; once he recovered the body of a fisherman, who had drowned. When the man crossed the river, the forceful current and slippery rocks had caused him to tumble downward; his heavy backpack pinned him beneath the icy water. "I'll never forget his red hair," Dave said, shaking his head at the memory.

He told her about his shy and gentle blond-haired sister Nancy, and his older brother Jack, who had been an incredible golf player, semi-pro. Halfway through college, Jack went into the infantry during the Second World War. At twenty-one, he had been sent to the island of Okinawa in Japan as an army scout. On the 16th of May in 1945, he'd been leading a group of men up a mountain near Naha. "He heard a mortar shell coming, and shoved the men beside him out of the way. The mortar shell hit. Jack found himself on the ground. He looked around and saw his army boots in the distance. The explosion took off both of his legs above the knee," Dave told her gravely, motioning to his own knees.

Marijana gasped, tears springing to her eyes.

Dave rested his eyes on the floor for a moment, and then continued softly. Marines stationed in the foothills had scrambled to carry Jack off the mountain; he went from island to island in the Pacific until he made it all the way to Letterman General Hospital in California. There he stayed for two years while the doctors tried skin grafting and other treatments, but nothing seemed to work. "Until his legs were finally drained of infection and fully healed," Dave explained. "Finally he was fitted with artificial legs. They were so heavy to maneuver, he told me, but he actually walked out of that hospital on his own. Jack never gave up, and it's amazing how much he can do, even drive a car with his artificial legs! He was honored with a purple heart medal."

Marijana continued to ask questions and Dave told her more about his childhood. Early in the mornings when he delivered newspapers in his neighborhood, he could hear a foghorn from Puget Sound. He would toss each paper so that it landed perfectly in front of each doorway with a thump. He told her about the Japanese family who owned a nearby local store. He went to grammar school with their boys. One day, when Dave was thirteen years old, his Japanese friend came to school and brought gifts of colored pencils and chocolate bars for each student in class. "And after that day, he never came back. We never saw him again. The store closed and they disappeared. I never knew what happened. I didn't know about the internment camps for the Japanese until much later," he explained. "I'll never forget that day…"

From his stories, Marijana could picture Dave, a boy during the war with his mother and sister busy selling war bonds, his father installing cables on aircraft carriers in order to catch the planes as they landed, slowing them down to a complete stop so that they wouldn't flip into the ocean. Dave as he filled sandbags with his Boy Scout troop, so they would be ready for the Japanese incendiary balloon bombs that had started to float over the Pacific Northwest.

"Lana Turner, now she's what I remember most about the war," Dave said grinning.

"What? Did you see her?"

"Well," he said, knowing he had her full attention now, "she came to Tacoma to promote war bonds, and I just remember how glamorous she was."

"What was she wearing?" Marijana asked excitedly.

"She was standing next to the Roxy Theater, that's the fanciest movie theater we have in Tacoma, and she was wearing a white dress with black polka dots and a wide-brimmed black straw hat. It kept her face a little in the shadows. I'll always remember that."

Marijana nodded wistfully.

When Dave tried to turn the conversation to Marijana's own childhood, she was evasive. No brothers and sisters. "I'm an orphan," she said plainly, but not much else. He gathered that her parents had died when she was quite young, but he wasn't exactly sure how or why.

On another one of his visits, while Marijana was out of the room, Dave asked her Aunt Victoria what happened to Marijana's mother. She said quietly that Marijana's mother had died in a train accident. "Tragic, Marijana doesn't like to speak of it," Victoria explained. Too painful. The suddenness of Marijana's mother's death troubled him. He tried to imagine her a little girl, motherless, during wartime.

He noticed that Marijana often mentioned her grandmother. And perhaps those were the only moments where he heard rawness in her voice and could see the vulnerability in her eyes. She told him, "Sometimes I feel as if I've abandoned her, leaving her there all by herself with no one to look out for her."

"Do you write to her?" he asked.

"Yes, through a neighbor, we write. My grandmother needs help with writing, but she can read anything I send to her. I'm going to bring her to live with me, as soon as I can," she said determinedly. "My aunt thinks she's too old, but I don't think so. My grandmother needs me. She wants to see me. We promised each other."

He sat alone at a picnic table on a banana boat floating on the Escalante River. He held a pen with his right hand, and wrote the date: *11 de Diciembre, 1957.* Just before he left Caracas to work in the field for a month, he'd told Marijana, "*Voy a escribirte.*" He'd never written a letter in Spanish before. He worried what she would think of his spelling and grammar, so he asked the local crew to help him with certain words so that he could describe how the two-story boat often got stuck on a sandbar, when it couldn't negotiate the curves of the meandering river.

He glanced up from the blank page and stared at the swaying palm trees. In the distance he could see grass roofs and mud huts, and children running beside a scrappy-looking dog that barked from the banks of the river. He'd been living on the boat, on the river that emptied into the southern end of Lake Maracaibo. He set down his pen for a moment to gaze thoughtfully at the banana plantation.

The rumble of the engine brought his mind back to the letter. The air was heavy with moisture. He wiped his forehead, picked up his pen, took a deep breath, and began: *Dear Marijana,*

This is the first letter that I have written in Spanish to a girl… he paused for a moment struggling to find the right words… *and it's difficult not because it's for you, but because I have very little experience with the language. However, I believe that you will understand what I'm trying to say.* He continued to tell her about his journey to Santa Barbara, and how he had taken photographs of the clouds from the plane window since it was too hazy to see Lake Maracaibo. He told her how the hot weather made him think about the snow-covered mountains of his home state. He wrote in his rather straight handwriting: *We have a good cook and the life is good, but I like it better in Caracas.* He explained that he planned to go to Mérida for his one-week vacation so that he could ski, and how he wished she could go with him. *Receive this with all my affection, Dave.* He sealed the envelope and on the outside wrote *Marijana Kanjer* and the name of their office in Caracas.

That evening at dinner he found himself sitting beside Frank Klima, the pot-bellied Czech-American company manager, who had a Hitler-like moustache. There was always a pipe drooping from the side of his mouth. He grumbled when the single men who worked for him dated or married a city girl. "They'll never want to work out in the field now," he would mutter to himself.

Dave was talking with him about cables and explosives, when someone stood up and mentioned that he'd be returning to Caracas the next day, inquiring if anyone had mail. Dave pulled the letter from his pocket. He noticed Klima eyeing the name on the envelope suspiciously. Dave handed the envelope to a crewman. The next day he watched the plane, carrying his letter, glide across the water and lift off into the air. It disappeared into the morning haze.

During Christmas of 1957, he traveled to the white beaches of Trinidad instead of the rocky Andes of Mérida. He spent his first vacation sitting at the British Yacht Club, drinking rum and coca-cola with two of his co-workers, wondering what Marijana had thought when she opened his letter. He had never heard back from her. At the club he caught the tail end of a conversation, something about when Robert Mitchum had stayed at the hotel while he was filming a movie. Another man bragged that he'd gone on a date with Rita Hayworth. She'd gotten drunk, then hopped on a table and started dancing. Dave wished he could have seen Rita Hayworth shimmying her shoulders.

During his time in Trinidad, he befriended the telephone operator at his hotel. He'd stop at her desk and chat. June's dark skin was striking against her bright yellow blouse. He liked listening to her accent and the way she calmly asked if he would take a walk with her through the park. They strolled beside poinsettias and palms, and she invited him to go to church with her. The congregation welcomed him warmly even though he was the only white man there. The evening before he was about to leave for Caracas, she invited him to her parents' one-story house. June and Dave sat together on the porch. Vines climbed the outside walls of the house. They joked and laughed, and he felt completely at ease with her. The warm evening draped over them.

"What if we got married?" she asked suddenly, smiling, fixing her long flowered skirt with her hands. He looked at her surprised, then laughed nervously. He thought to himself, *It could happen, where one instant changes your entire life*. He cleared his throat, laughed again, and asked, "But what could I do here?"

She glanced at him thoughtfully. "Well, I could support you. You could just go to the beach."

"Just go to the beach?"

"Mmm-hmm."

"I don't know, June."

"Why?"

"Well, I think that a man should work."

"Even if a woman can instead?"

He nodded, raising his eyebrows helplessly.

"Maybe I'll come to Caracas on my next holiday," she said gracefully. They smiled at each other.

Marijana waited, but no letter appeared on her desk. Each time someone returned from the field, hope surged in her chest. Several times she even considered writing to him herself. Was he so busy that he couldn't write? Why did he promise her? Surely, she told herself, you don't even want a letter from a man who can't keep his word.

Still she longed to ask him to go see the Russian Ballet when he returned. She could see his kind, long face, his dark hair, small brown eyes, and his dimples. She worried that something had happened to him.

He probably didn't want to write, she eventually convinced herself. She was only some girl from the office. Maybe he was interested in someone else. A feeling of numbness enveloped her. There had been so much pain in her past, it was as if she couldn't bear anymore. As a child, when her parents had died and left her in this world by herself, she had barely survived.

She hadn't been able to control what happened to them; she hadn't been able to control her own illness, but for the time being, she could control who she loved.

After a couple weeks in Trinidad, Dave returned to Caracas. He'd spent several months out in the field. He returned on the very day the Venezuelan Air Force attacked Palacio de Miraflores, where the dictator General Pérez Jiménez was residing. The attempted coup failed, and the following day Dave went to the office as normal. His stomach fluttered; he couldn't wait to see Marijana again. When he saw her working at her drafting table, he tried to catch her eye, but she never looked up.

In the lunchroom, he casually walked over and said hello. She glanced at him coldly and quickly gathered her things and left. He stood there alone, stunned, staring through the open doorway. Was it the letter? Did she misunderstand something he'd written? Maybe he'd been too forward. He would look for her tomorrow.

For weeks, each time he passed Marijana in the lunchroom, he'd try to strike up a conversation, but she responded with silence. She averted her eyes. She wasn't exactly rude, but she clearly she wasn't speaking to him. Had he done something to upset her? He remained bewildered. Finally he decided that it was best not to push her; she would speak to him when she was ready.

One day he found himself listening to the endless sound of taxi horns blaring during a general strike, called to bring down the government. He began to feel a physical sadness. From his apartment window, he watched two young men across the street set a car on fire. He felt an aching deep within his chest; for two months, she hadn't spoken to him.

The government was overthrown, and he accepted that

his possible romance had vanished for some unknown reason the way the sky can suddenly darken. That year June came to visit him twice. But in the end, he decided not to see her anymore because he still hoped Marijana would come around. Spring, summer, autumn, and winter passed, and she hadn't uttered one word to him.

One morning, Marijana was startled to see the tattered envelope sitting on her desk. She remained standing as she tore open the envelope and gently pulled out the letter. She carefully held the onionskin paper. She sank in her chair. She didn't understand. The letter was from Dave, but it had been written one year ago.

She glanced at the envelope and double-checked the company name. Everything was in order. From the outside of the envelope, she could see that the letter had traveled all the way to Canada and eventually made its way south to her desk in Caracas. One year, she thought in shock. Her eyes watered.

Everything in her body raced. She needed to find him; she couldn't wait another instant. *Dave*, she said his name aloud. She couldn't work all morning; her mind traveled a thousand places.

As soon as she was certain he'd be there, she walked toward the lunchroom, clutching the letter in her hand. When she reached the door, she saw him there alone, flipping through the *Daily Journal*, the English-language newspaper.

"Dave," she said, taking a deep breath, and he turned to her. She was beaming. He was entranced by her presence.

"I got it," she said, half-laughing, holding up the letter and shaking it. "I got your letter."

"What letter?" he asked, puzzled.

"The letter you sent me from Lake Maracaibo," she said.

"What? I, I, thought you got that a long time ago. You never got it?"

"I got it today," she said. A few tears ran down her cheeks. She quickly wiped them away with the back of her hand.

"Today?" he asked as if he were standing on ice, trying to find his footing.

"Mmm-hmm," she nodded, biting her bottom lip for a moment.

"How? I mean, I sent it over a year ago. I don't understand."

"I don't understand either. Dave, I'm so sorry. It was wrong not to speak to you."

"That's why you weren't speaking to me?" he asked, blinking in astonishment.

She sighed, sliding into the chair beside him.

"I don't understand. Why you didn't get the letter? I mean, someone brought it from the field, someone brought it to the office by hand."

"It never came. I never got it. The envelope said it went to the Canadian office."

"The Canadian office? Why? That's strange."

"I know. Dave, I thought you didn't write to me. But you did. You wrote to me." She looked down at the folded letter in her hand, and unfolded it, smoothing it out on her lap. He recognized his own distinctive handwriting. They smiled at each other, realizing that it didn't matter what had happened to the letter because she was holding it in her hands right now. She reached out and touched his arm.

18

NEW YORK CITY

At the Zebra Bar in Caracas, they sat at a round table. The décor was black and white; waiters in black pants and white jackets moved gracefully, serving drinks to well-dressed Venezuelans. As they waited for their drinks to arrive, her mind wandered to the moment during a Louis Malle film when Dave had leaned over and kissed her. And then she thought of what Uncle Ivo had told her, "Now, Marijana, I think he's probably going to ask you to marry him soon. Please, whatever you do—don't say 'I don't know.' Just say *yes* or *no*. He's a good man, he deserves to know."

She admitted to herself that she did have strong feelings for Dave, but to decide to marry someone, she needed more time. She worried. At times an uncertainty seized her, a sadness would take hold of her; other times she felt courageous and ready for a great adventure.

Suddenly Dave took hold of her hands.

She stared shyly at the white tablecloth.

"Marijana, would you marry me?" There was such hopefulness in his voice. His eyes searched her face for an answer.

With all her heart, she wished she didn't have to do this, but there was no way around it, "Dave, we don't really know each other," she said.

"We don't?" he said confused.

"Not really. Really we've only been out a few times, and then we see each other at the office."

He sat back, wondering if he had misread their relationship. She picked up her wineglass and held it.

"Let's take some more time, okay?" she suggested cautiously.

"I feel as if I know you, really know you," he answered earnestly.

"I need more time," she said.

A few weeks later Marijana discovered that her boss hadn't turned in her overtime to payroll as he had for all the other men in the office. She was enraged as she began to calculate exactly how much overtime the company owed her for the past two years. If they didn't pay her, she would quit. If they did pay her, she would still quit. The next day, she stormed into her boss's office. He sat there dumbfounded as a whirlwind of words flew at him. She could be articulate when she lost her temper. "How did you think that you could get away with not paying me overtime like the rest of the men doing the same job as I do?"

Finally the company agreed to pay her all the money that they owed her, and then she quit. Her Aunt Victoria worried that she wouldn't be able to find another job so easily.

"I'm not worried," Marijana told her aunt and uncle. "I'm going to America."

"What? By yourself? Maybe you should save the money, for later," her aunt advised.

"I don't want to save the money. For what, for when I die?" Marijana said.

"Marijana! Sometimes you can be so willful," her aunt exclaimed.

"Now, Marijana," her uncle said, slipping into the conversation, "America's a big place. Where in America do you want to go?" He furrowed his brow inquisitively.

"There are only two places in America: Hollywood and New York. And I'm going to New York."

It was obvious to him that there would be no reasoning with his niece. She was going no matter what their feelings were on the subject.

She stared out the plane window and took a deep breath. New York City, she couldn't believe it. She rubbed the sides of her arms. Dave had called her in Caracas before her aunt and uncle had taken her to the airport. He wished her luck and made her promise to write. "More than one letter, just in case it doesn't arrive," he added, and they both laughed. Her aunt and uncle had arranged for her to stay at a residence for women, run by Catholic nuns, on East 72nd Street. Now she'd have at least two entire months without her aunt trying to run her life. She smiled and flipped a page of the *Vanidades* magazine in her lap.

From the airport, she made her way by taxi to the Catholic residence on the Upper East Side. One nun greeted her. After she showed Marijana to her room, she mentioned that the evening curfew was strictly enforced. Soon young women were visiting her room. Latin girls stuck working in the garment district, listening to the whirl of their sewing machines. American girls who were modeling or studying acting. And when they asked her what she was doing in New York, she answered, "So I learn to speak English better, and I'd like to take art classes."

She walked four blocks south to Hunter College to inquire about courses only to discover, much to her disappointment, she'd arrived too late; the semester had already started. She made the best of it and spent many winter afternoons at the Metropolitan Museum. Some days after pulling on her overcoat, she even walked all the way from Central Park to Greenwich Village, admiring shop windows and watching New Yorkers walk past her.

Her Aunt Klara and Uncle Louie ran a bar in Greenwich Village. She wasn't sure what she thought of them because when she'd been really sick, and her grandmother was trying to get her out of the country, they'd said they couldn't help. Her Uncle Louie was her grandmother's brother, and very old. Since he'd been living in New York for forty-five years, he could hardy remember his Croatian. Her Aunt Klara had emigrated from Germany. For some reason, she always wanted to cut Marijana's hair. She'd say in her New York-German accent that Marijana looked exactly like Brigitte Bardot and encouraged her to use blue eye shadow. Marijana didn't want her hair cut, but her Aunt Klara insisted, holding the scissors in her wavering right hand. Her Aunt Klara liked boozing, and whenever she had the chance, she drank. Sometimes she took Marijana to the bar with her. When the waiter would come to take their order, he'd first ask what the young lady wanted, and her Aunt Klara would answer for her in a raspy voice, "She doesn't drink. She's just a kid."

In the evenings, sometimes Marijana and her new friends from the Catholic residence smuggled in bottles of wine beneath their coats. They scrambled up the stairs muffling their giggles and gathered in her room in time for curfew. They had picnics on her bed.

During her first week in New York, Marijana also found time by herself to compose her first letter in the English language. So far, she had only spoken Spanish to Dave, but being in New York City gave her courage.

Dear Dave!

Today I decided to stay home because it is too cold, and me can't walk. The cold climate remembers me of my country. I forgot how cold it could be. It's like hell.

In the house where I live there are many girls of all nationalities. I became a good friend with two of them. One is American and the other is from Bogotá, Colombia. Very nice girls. We decided to skate one day when we have time. I came too late for my course, but I will look for another one just to learn the language. I think I will buy me a radio, a little one, and it will help something. In coffee shop they say that I speak a good English, but I don't think so, and you will not think so, when you read my letter. Otherwise it wouldn't be so many mistakes in it. Isn't that right? But please take in count that I don't use dictionary and this is an excuse, a little one.

The people here are very nice and kind. Many of them don't know me, but when they see me they always say: "Good morning miss" or "How do you do?" If they are younger they say: "Hello baby doll!" Everybody calls me: Honey, Sweetie, etc.

One girl asked me: "Are you from Ohio?" I said: "No, I am not from Ohio." And then she said: "I thought because of your accent." Then I had to laugh with all my heart. You see life can be very funny.

I have to buy me a coat. I saw one that I liked. It is a red coat. Short one, in Italy they call this Montgomery. Many teenagers dress like this and looks nice and practical.

I think I have to finish now. Dear Dave, write me as soon as you receive my letter, and I like your letters very much. The way you write is very sweet. Write me more than I did. I would like too, but wait, and when my English will be better then my letters will be longer. And now goodbye Sweetie! Marijana.

She felt happy when she posted the letter.

Less than a week later she received his answer. After a few months in New York, her English would be better than his, he wrote to her. He laughed when he read about the girl asking if she was from Ohio. He wrote:

You never mentioned it, but you must have landed at New York just about the time that the plane from Chicago crashed. Did you land before or after? I worried about you after you left and then when I first saw the headlines, I thought for a minute it might be your plane.

Marijana thought about the American Airlines plane from Chicago that had crashed into the East River. She read in the newspaper that sixty-five people had died. Only eleven survived, scrambling from the sinking plane. One man rescued an eight-year-old boy, who lost his entire family in the crash.

Marijana looked down again at Dave's letter. He let her know that a friend of theirs had broken off her engagement and was going to take Marijana's place at the office, inking cross-sections for them. At the end of the letter, he slipped in,

Don't call me "Sweetie," Marijana because I don't like the sound of it and usually girls say that to other girls. The correct thing is "Sweetheart," or "Honey," or "Darling," but that's just for couples who are engaged or married or going to be engaged. Please don't get mad because I said this Marijana! Since you say we don't "know" each other and may never see each other again, about all you can use is "Dear" which means only a friend and nothing special.

There I got carried away and wrote twice as much as I intended on the subject. Tell me more about you and New York!

As she read this part of the letter, her heart sank. She'd made a mistake. He misunderstood. How could he say that to her, when he knew that she was only teasing him? She was stunned. Before she left, she'd mentioned that maybe she'd stay in New York. But she hadn't told him, there was another part of her that wanted to return to Caracas and see him again. There was such distance between them now, and she felt frustrated that she couldn't find the words in English to express herself. He must be hurt because I said no to his proposal, she thought to herself. Of course, it was only natural that he was disappointed. Still, his words caused her great pain.

Three days later, she picked up her fountain pen and wrote back to him.

Dear Dave,

When I was reading your letter I was so sad. I was not mad at you, but it hurt me so much. It hurt me more because now I can see that you really do not know me. I am not the kind of girl you think. I ask me, what is the reason, and why do you want to make me so unhappy. I like you. I adore you and respect you more than any boy I have known. You sure have said to many girls "I like you", but I never did. Can you believe me? To say I like you means for me a great thing. It means more than a marriage. A marriage isn't the only thing that I want in my life. The most important thing to me is a true love.

I can tell you that with the word "Sweetie", I just wanted to say: "Here I am in the States, and the American girls speak like that. I wanted to say this in caricature. I don't like this kind of language and I will never use this even to my husband when I get married. Your American people use this. Your lovely people. I think you are different. Maybe you are more European than I am. You don't know me, but I can read your letter even behind your word. I would like that you do the same with mine. Let's talk of something else.

New York. Now I have seen more of the city. Metropolitan Museum in which you have the works of the most famous artists, from the most primitive art to Cubism (Picasso). Wonderful. I enjoyed looking at one whole mummy. I think I could spend months just looking. Didn't yet see The Empire State Building because I was waiting for a sunshine day because then I can see the city better. Now I know many streets by their names like Madison Ave., Lexington Ave. (I live near), Park Ave., 5th Ave., Broadway (this one I knew when I was ten years old). I have been to the cinema "Roxy" is the name, the movie was "The Hanging Tree" with Maria Shell and Gary Cooper (who I thought was pretty old for the lover). It was filmed in your state. Whole the movie remembered me your pictures.

I have found school for me. School of Design. They have courses in Advertising Design and Fashion Illustration. Yesterday I spoke to professor, he's a very nice old gentleman. He liked the work that I did in Argentina and brought here with me, and he thinks I will do good. I am afraid a little, because tomorrow is the first class for me. I suppose everything will be O.K. It always happens to me that I am afraid when I go for first time somewhere.

Dave, please forgive me if I wrote something wrong. I never wanted you to be angry with me because I like you too much. Dave, please send me your picture. I want to have it. Please write me if you have had any fun. How do you spend your weekends? Did you go to a dance? Write me everything about yourself. I think often of you, even if you are mad at me!

Marijana

P.S. Oh, Dave! I have a nice picture of Kim Novak if you want I can send it to you in the next letter.

As Dave read her letter, he felt flooded with relief. He could see that she did have strong feelings for him. Maybe she would change her mind about marrying him. He needed to be patient.

Letters flew back and forth between Caracas and New York City.

On February 25th, Dave wrote:

My Darling Marijana, When I call you darling it means I love you and I do love you Marijana. Do you love me? You say you like me, but in English that doesn't mean you love a person. I like Juan Carlos, but I don't love him.

It was my fault that I misunderstood your use of the word, "Sweetie", but I wasn't mad at you darling, I was just explaining how I felt about the word. I know you're not that kind of girl and that's why I love you. You're so honest and different than American girls. I've known you long enough and well enough to know what kind of character you have.

You say these things don't interest me, but they do. A true love is important to me too Marijana, but a true love that leads to a happy marriage. I want to spend the rest of my life working and living in the mountains, skiing in the winter, and hiking and mountain climbing in the summer. I want a wife who loves the mountains and forests as I do. That's why I would like to marry you darling. Maybe you don't want to or maybe you don't love me, but please tell me if you do.

I'd much rather have your picture than Kim Novak's. I don't like her anymore like I used to, especially since she ran around with a married man.

I get nervous too when I go somewhere for the first time. I was nervous the first time I took you out and that's why I waited so long to ask you. Anyway I don't think you'll have any trouble in your course. How long will it last? You know Marijana you have a very good command of the English language and your spelling is almost perfect. You spell better than many Americans and write better too. But Darling, if you ever think I'm saying something to hurt you in my letters, please ask me first to explain what I meant in case you misunderstood. I wouldn't intentionally hurt you for all the world Marijana so please have faith in me to always treat you right.

I'm getting sleepy darling so I'd better go to bed, but I'll think of you in my dreams. Goodnight!

All my love, Dave.

On March 10th she filled four pages:

Dear Dave,

Thank you for your picture. I like it very much your letter too. It was so nice and soft. I do love you very much, and I think I loved you long ago and did not know. I need you so much, and you are very important to me. Dave, I think it would be very nice to be married to you.

You must understand why I am so careful about marriage. When I marry somebody, this is for whole my life. I don't want to be divorced next year, and if I would, I would suffer all my life. Dave, are you sure you know me well enough? Do you think the same as I do about things? I do like the kind of life that you do. I would like to have a home. Small, but that I like it. That is important to me. When I was a little girl, I was always running home. It was so warm in it and so cold out. I wish I could write better and explain about a lot of things, but I cannot. I don't know the language that good. Dave, when I come back, I would like to stay always with you. We should go to dance, to the cinema, to the beach, whatever you like. Remember when I was mad at you, and we did not see each other. I was so unhappy. I wished to call you many times. When the Russian Ballet came to Caracas, I almost called you to take me to see it. There were many boys who could take me, and I did not like. Dave, please write me again how much you love me. Then I feel so strong and happy. I want to spend whole my free time with you when I come back. It will be in April. Three weeks more…

After Dave finished reading her letter, he was stunned. Then he reread the letter to be sure she was actually saying *Yes*. He kept rereading one line: *Dave, I think it would be nice to be married to you.*

She did want to marry him! He repeated it to himself so that it would sink in. He wanted to tell someone, but at the same time he wanted to keep it all to himself.

He spent the next two days composing his response:

My Dearest Darling, I love you! I love and I'll always love you Marijana. I want to make you happy as I am happy when I'm with you. I wasn't happy when you were mad at me, but I knew I had to leave you alone to find out for yourself that it is no good being angry and apart. I only ask, darling that when we are married and you get mad at me for something, please tell me what it is so we can talk about it and straighten it out.

Oh Marijana, I want you so much. Do you remember the first time I saw you, when you came downstairs and we shook hands. Your hands were so warm and I could smell the perfume you were wearing. Then that last night we were walking together and I picked a leaf from a tree and you took it from my hand and I grasped yours and held it. It felt so good to feel you close and with your hand in mine, so warm and alive. I could feel a tingle like an electric shock all through my body and I wanted to take you in my arms and kiss you and hold you close. April seems like years away until you come back my darling!

Two letters later, she boarded a plane for Caracas. Her Aunt Victoria had already started planning the wedding. And a month after she returned from New York, on the ninth of May, 1959, Marijana put on her wedding dress. It seemed as though she couldn't find one moment to herself. Her aunt followed her from room to room in the apartment, fixing this, adjusting that, telling her it was time for this, and telling her it was time for that.

"Go get dressed, you don't have much time," Marijana told her aunt, and then shut herself in the bathroom for a moment of peace. She looked in the mirror and touched her short light brown hair. The curls had turned out perfectly, *like Brigitte Bardot*, she smiled to herself, thinking of her Aunt Klara. She thought her lips were too thin, she wished they could be just a little fuller as she put on lipstick. She twirled around so she could see the back of her wedding dress. She pulled gently on her short sleeves, and smoothed the material on her chest. Her Italian friend and dressmaker had told her, "Marijana, not everyone has such a tiny waist! And not every woman looks so beautiful in her wedding dress."

Her uncle knocked at the door, and when she opened, she caught her breath. He looked distinguished in his dark suit and white tie. Ivo told her that the car was waiting outside. *It's time.* Her entire life was about to change. Her fingertips skimmed the white flowers at the top of her veil, which floated to the middle of her back.

She thought about how she had finally confided to Dave how difficult it was living with her aunt. Marijana wanted to live her own life, and make her own decisions, and her aunt couldn't understand that, she always wanted to interfere. Her aunt appeared outside. Her light gray dress had abstract, impressionistic black vertical stripes, and her V-neck collar folded over her shoulders. Marijana felt guilty. Her aunt had organized the entire wedding. The Catholic priest had tried to push up the price with so-called extras such as a red carpet. Once her aunt realized what he was doing, she said to Marijana in Croatian, "Who did he think he was dealing with? I'm not some stupid foreigner. No one is going to put something over on me!" She found the American church in Sabana Grande only charged one flat fee, half the amount that the Catholic priest tried to charge her. They switched churches.

What a character, Marijana thought fondly as she looked at her aunt's round face. Suddenly she wished her Baka could be there, making her drink tea and making her eat a bite of bread at the last minute. She could feel her grandmother's hand in her hand. Bakica would calm her down. "Marijana, your hair is so blond!" she could almost hear her saying.

She sat between her aunt and uncle in the car. Her aunt handed Marijana the long white gloves, and she slipped them on, one hand at a time. She wondered what her mother and father's village wedding had been like in Slavonia. She imagined her mother in a traditional costume, and music and dancing, and for a moment she remembered dancing with her mother when she was very small, whirling around in circles. Marijana felt lightheaded. Had she eaten? She must have. She wished that she had some water, her throat felt so dry. How would she say her wedding vows?

Her aunt and uncle stepped out of the ivory and sky-blue Plymouth sedan. Her aunt held up her dress, while her uncle took Marijana's hands and helped her out of the car. Marijana was hit with sudden panic. She wanted to run away.

"Auntie, I never told him about my TB. I never said anything. I haven't felt sick in a long time. But I don't know if I'm really well." She felt as if she were going to cry.

"Marijana, please, don't worry. Later, later, there's plenty of time for everything later. It's best you didn't tell him. Don't try to do everything at once. This all happened fast, which is good with love. Now look how much Dave loves you. You didn't speak to him for a year, and still he wanted to be with you." Her aunt clicked her tongue.

Marijana felt her chest tense up; she felt slightly breathless.

"Marijana, calm down. This is your wedding day. Don't think of anything else. Push all other thoughts from your mind," Uncle Ivo said firmly.

Finally, she noticed that they were standing outside the church's entrance, her uncle held out his elbow and she slipped her arm through his. Together they stepped into the church. Marijana turned to her aunt, and she helped lower the veil over her face. Marijana gripped the bouquet of white flowers.

Everyone turned around and stood up. The Croatian community and many close Caracas friends were there at her wedding. People caught their breaths; women sighed. She looked down the aisle at Dave, who was waiting for her.

19

CARACAS

I ran my hand over the polished wood of the church pew. It was empty inside the white-steepled church; the sounds of Caracas couldn't penetrate its thick walls. Sunlight drifted in through the oval stained-glass windows. I glanced at the empty rows toward my tall slender father, who stood beside the podium at the head of the church, speaking Spanish with a small woman. He explained why we were here. She responded in rapid-fire Venezuelan Spanish, one word falling over the next like a row of dominos. I wondered how could anyone understand why we had come all this way. When the woman left, he gazed down the center aisle. Over forty years ago, he had stood there in a black suit, white shirt and tie, waiting for my mother.

I gazed back at the entrance of the church, where my mom had once stood in her elegant wedding gown in 1959 on the ninth of May. She was twenty-three years old and wore long white gloves and a white-flowered head piece with an elbow-length veil, framing her radiant face and short curly hair. Her Italian friend had designed and hand-made the crinoline and short-sleeved gown that showed off my mom's hour-glass figure; the pleats added movement to the thick fabric, and four white roses cinched the center at the bottom of the gown, allowing her pointy, high-heeled shoes to peek out. Clutching a white bouquet with one hand, she slipped her slender arm through her Uncle Ivo's arm; everyone in the church rose to their feet. And then, she took her first steps toward her American husband, toward her American life.

The day after Christmas, my father and I had arrived at Maiquetía airport at 2:30 in the morning. We sped away from the Caribbean Sea toward the mountains that surrounded Caracas. Through the darkness, I fixed my eyes on the dots of light sprinkled over the hillside. A warm wind filled the car. I leaned back; my father leaned forward, peering out the open window.

Nine years had passed since my mother's death. My dad had retired from his last job in Houston and returned to the place where we had lived the longest, Colorado. Now he lived in a small apartment a few miles from my elementary school and my mom's grave.

That night, from the tiny cement balcony of our hotel room in Sabana Grande, I could see the skeleton of an empty high-rise, its circular balconies surging upward like the tower of Babel. While we were on this journey, my dad would turn seventy-two. He had cancer. He thought we should consider cancelling our trip. Maybe it was traveling at his age, maybe it was worrying about his health, or maybe it was traveling on our limited means that made him want to back out. I convinced him that we should go.

On our first day in Caracas we visited Edificio Sosa, the brick office building where they first met in 1956; Plaza

Candelaria, the square they had often walked across; Edificio Lourdes, an apartment building full of balconies with hanging plants, where my father had once lived. Eventually we returned to our hotel room to rest where my dad sat on his bed, flipping through the local phonebook, scouring the thin pages for familiar Croatian names, people he had known in the 1950s.

"Katie, guess what? I found names I recognize! Let's try to call some of them."

"Okay," I said cautiously. I wondered if anyone would remember them. I thought seeing the places that marked my parents' history was enough. One phone call later, we were summoned to lunch. A taxi dropped us off in the hills above the city, outside imposing iron gates. I stared up at the enormous apartment high-rise. Over the intercom a woman's voice said that she'd come right down to unlock the gate.

"Do you remember her? What she looks like?" I asked my dad.

"I think so," he said, scratching the top of his head for a moment. "I mean, well, she remembered Mama, and we once went to her house for a party." Anuša, I kept whispering her name, Anusha, practicing so that I could say it correctly. Over the phone, my father learned that she had been divorced for many years now, and had two grown children and two grandchildren. "Maybe when I see her in person, I'll remember which one she was," my dad added softly.

Anuša appeared at the apartment walkway, smiling, gliding toward us like a nun from *The Sound of Music*. Her long skirt flowed behind her. She was tall with a sense of purpose, and immediately I sensed she was a woman who would always be youthful. Her short blondish hair was curled. She wore white pearls. Before she unlocked the gate, she began to speak to us in British English, smiling broadly, exclaiming how happy she'd been to hear my father's voice. "My, it's been a long time," she said as she opened the gate wide.

"Who would have thought I'd be here forty years later?" my dad said, widening his eyes.

She looked up at him, her light-brown eyes narrowing slightly. "I was so sorry to hear about Marijana when you called."

At her apartment, Anuša had some Venezuelan friends over for a belated holiday lunch. In the corner of the living room, an elderly Croatian woman stood up. Anuša introduced her as Marija. She looked fragile until she spoke, demanding to know who I was. Anuša patiently explained, raising her voice slightly, who my great aunt and uncle were, "Ivo and Victoria," and then she added, "She's *Marijana's daughter*."

Marija's face flashed sudden recognition. In Spanish, she told me that she remembered my mom well, and that she had been to my parents' wedding.

Two people who knew my mom were in this room with me. It felt strange since in my New York City life, no one knew my mother, and they never would. They couldn't remember what she sounded like, they couldn't recall something she'd said, and they couldn't see the similarities between us.

Throughout the afternoon I tried to slow down time. I tried to catch anything that might have some connection to my mom. There was a flurry of conversations, questions and laughter. Anuša told us that this was the traditional Croatian meal for the 25th of December. *Sarma* was ground meat seasoned with spices and salt, mixed with rice, cooked in a cabbage leaf. "Didn't your mom make this for you?" Anuša asked, surprised.

"No," I answered, shaking my head.

The apartment felt typically Croatian: the lace tablecloth, the collections of silver spoons from different countries hanging on the wall, and colorful naïve paintings of peasants working in the field. Even the stack of *¡Hola!* magazines Anuša kept beside her couch brought instant memories of my mom, who somehow managed to get hold of that Spanish magazine even in '80s Colorado, so she could follow the lives of royalty and celebrities. The magazine was popular with European women, and certainly no one else in my Colorado neighborhood read it. Courtney, my friend who I'd met long after my mom died, mentioned that all of her Croatian aunts adored *¡Hola!*

I remembered how my mom and I had taken Flamenco classes when I was a teen. We stomped different rhythms onto the wooden floor, held onto the edges of our ruffled skirts and glared defiantly at ourselves in the mirror. My father and mother had lived in Venezuela and Spain before I was born, and somehow Spanish and South American culture was more evident in our house than any Croatian culture.

While my mom pushed a shopping cart at our local King Soopers grocery store, she would often break out into a *Sevillana*. "Mommm! Please," I'd plead with her; I was afraid that we'd see someone we knew. American moms didn't do that. They also didn't wear leather pants to go buy apples and tomatoes. My mom would look at me and laugh, and then a little while later, as we waited by the register, she'd stomp a rhythm in her high-heeled black boots. Although I found this maddening as an adolescent, I also found it endearing and wonderful.

After her death, during my second attempt at college, I went to Madrid for a month on a study abroad program, and I found it liberating to watch the young people gathered in the squares singing, clapping rhythms, playing the guitar, and dancing as part of their afternoon rituals. Unlike Americans who almost never broke out in song and dance on street corners with friends. My mom could dance when she felt like it. I wondered if some of the Spanish culture my mom passed onto me was born from the Spanish and Mexican films she had seen growing up in Zagreb. She loved traditional Mexican songs like *Las Mañanitas* and *Cielito Lindo*. We would croon together *Aye, yai, yai, canta y no llores*. Perhaps the South American and Spanish pieces of her history were easier to pass along since they were less painful than her Croatian past.

Anuša energetically served lunch, coffee, and dessert, somehow managing to give attention to each one of her guests. My dad listed off people's names from the 1950s, the time he'd been living in Caracas, and Anuša recounted what had happened to each of them: alive, dead, divorced, cancer, children live here, children in Miami, adopted her sister's children, waiting for a transplant…entire lives compressed into a few sentences. As they spoke, I realized that many Croatians had stayed in Venezuela, and she saw them often. Anuša asked about my mom, where my parents had traveled after they left Caracas. "We moved eight times the first year we were married," my dad said, shaking his head. "It was hard on Marijana."

And then she smiled at me and said, "I remember going to the beach with your mom." An old black-and-white photograph appeared in my mind; I had seen it many times: my mom as a young woman, standing barefoot on the sand between two friends. Small white waves splashed behind them. They wore fifties-style one-piece bathing suits that covered their upper thighs and had cinched, corset-like waists. There was a breeze; her friends were holding onto the edges of their broad straw hats. They laughed. My mom's short curly hair was exposed to the sun. She held her shoulders back and her chin up, smiling confidently.

The elderly woman, Marija, suddenly spoke in a commanding voice that broke into my daydream and halted all the different conversations. She said how pleased she was to have met Marijana's daughter. "Your mother was an intelligent, beautiful, and sincere woman."

Before we left, between two kisses on each cheek, Anuša pressed a phone number into my dad's hand. She told us, "Definitely, you must call Đurđa and Pero, two other Croatians who knew your mother, and aunt and uncle. They'll want to see you." I nodded, trying to grasp that other Croatians would want to see *me*. Anuša kissed me again on both cheeks and whispered into my ear how wonderful it had been to meet me. Still holding me by the shoulders, she stepped back and looked at me carefully.

On our third day in Caracas, we headed up into the hills. The taxi pulled up to a house behind a white wall; a sign by the gate said: *Quinta Croacia*, Croatian House. My dad laughed and said, "Well, I guess this is it!" My father told me that when Ivo and Victoria had retired in Spain they named their small house *Villa Marijana* after my mother.

Pero threw open the door. His white hair was combed away from his face, and he wore wire-rimmed glasses that gave him a gentle look. Đurđa soon joined us, her reddish-brown hair swept up into a neat ponytail, and she wore no make-up. They laughed with my dad, growing teary-eyed, reminiscing about how many years it had been. Pero and Đurđa only spoke Croatian and Spanish, so I used my limited college Spanish and my dad helped me.

They led us to their table, and Đurđa ladled soup into bowls for us. Pero listened intently while Đurđa asked how long had my mother been ill, did she know she was dying, had she suffered? "No, no," my father reassured her, "she seemed quite peaceful at the end. Not a lot of pain." My dad told them the story of my mother's death, what the last couple of months were like, little things he remembered, and along the way, Đurđa continued to ask him questions gently. It had been a long time since we had told the story of my mother's death. Here though, with this Croatian couple, who were almost strangers a few moments ago, it was easy to speak about my mom. As I listened to my dad, I also became aware that his memory had blended into my own because he had read the stories that I had written. My experience was now his experience.

Đurđa's eyes grew bright as my dad reached the end of the story, the Sunday morning my mom died. Pero removed his glasses for a moment and blinked, nodding slowly, as if he had taken in each word that my father said and was now absorbing their significance. For Đurđa and Pero, my mom had died only a few days ago, when they sat at Anuša's dining room table, overhearing a telephone conversation. Đurđa brushed away a tear with her fingers, and rubbed her cheek. Pero replaced his glasses. My dad stared at the table, his large hands clasped together.

"Katarina," Đurđa took a deep breath and turned to me, smiling, "I have something to show you." Pero grinned. She pulled out a white invitation and a black-and-white photograph and placed them in front of me. "It's your parents' wedding invitation, and here is a photo of us at the wedding." I held the invitation in my hands and stared at my parents' names. They had kept it all these years. In the photograph, Đurđa and Pero were both laughing; I recognized their younger faces. I pointed to Pero's dark moustache, and he laughed, taking his index fingers, brushing the place where his moustache had once been. I turned the photograph over and recognized my mom's exquisite handwriting, a small note in Croatian.

We spent the rest of the afternoon on their terrace, overlooking the valley of Caracas. Red poinsettias lined a half-brick wall. We sat on both sides of a long wooden table that had large colorful tiles running down the center. They explained to my father that when they met Marijana, they thought her aunt and uncle were her parents. "We always assumed that Marijana was related by blood to Ivo," Pero said. She seemed to be more like him. Really though, Victoria had been her grandmother's youngest sister, my dad explained now. Pero and Đurđa wanted to know what happened to my parents after they left Caracas. What had happened to my mom's Croatian relatives? As my father explained their history, once again, I learned new things about my mom.

In the summer of 1959, after my parents' Caracas wedding, it had been almost five years since my mom had seen her grandmother, who still lived in Zagreb. That summer she received a long letter from her grandmother's neighbor. Her Baka said to tell Marijana that she was alone and unhappy in that *big cursed house*. And that she'd decided not to rent out rooms anymore because she wanted to be *free within her own four walls*. Lastly, she told her neighbor to write her granddaughter: *It's my deepest wish to see her. I'm not afraid of traveling.*

Afterward, my parents moved to Lodi, California, where my father had a new job. My mother searched for ways to bring Baka from Communist Yugoslavia to America. She wired her money each month. Five months after my parents' wedding, in October of 1959, my mom wrote: *Draga Bakica, I will ask about the documents here. Please don't start anything over there until I write to you—otherwise things can go badly. Be patient. Everything will be fine. Don't worry that someone will double cross me. Dear Bakica, take care of yourself, and please don't start with anything until we ask what is best. Kisses, Marijana.*

The letter was returned to her, unopened. Her grandmother had died. My mom wept for weeks, inconsolable. She was alone, in a strange motel room, in a strange country, unable to drive, while my father worked.

Her Aunt Victoria wrote, trying to comfort her, *Draga Marijanica, I received your telegram and I was really shaken, and I started thinking and remembering Baka's life. You dear Marijana don't cry because you wrote to her that you will bring her over. So she lives in hope and she did not have any more worries about your life path. I told Uncle I am afraid that something happened to you, but only this happened. Don't cry Marijanica, you have us.*

In the same letter Ivo wrote, *Draga Marijana, try to be calm. If you just think a little rationally, you could expect that, because what else could happen if you are eighty years. We believe that before she died, she was happy, knowing that you are healthy, and happy, and content.*

Đurđa and Pero asked how my mother's health had been during the years after my parents left Caracas. They had never known that she was sick. My dad had only learned about her TB after they were married. He explained that while they were living in the Canary Islands, she began to cough blood again. Her TB resurfaced. So when they moved to Madrid, she underwent a special treatment developed by a Welsh doctor whose former patients were coal miners afflicted with TB. My dad explained that for three months she had to stay in a cast that went from her waist to her armpits, so that pleura could grow over the cavity, an enlarged air-and-fluid-filled space, in the upper lobe of her right lung. Her aunt and uncle were living in Spain and Marijana moved in with them. While my father was away working, they took care of her.

She was ordered by her doctor to stay in bed, with her legs raised, for three months. Afterward, she'd undergone surgery, the doctors cut off a piece of the lung; the cavity was removed successfully. My mom had told my dad how cruel the nuns had been during her recovery at the hospital in Madrid. She had awakened from major surgery in tremendous pain, but they refused to give her any painkillers. "The nuns believed it was good for patients to suffer and feel pain," my dad told them, then he added quietly, "After that, she never really had health problems again. That is, of course," then he sighed, raising his shoulders slightly, "until the cancer came."

Đurđa and Pero told me the little things that they knew about my mom, and her aunt and uncle. At times, each of us laughed or grew tearful. As my dad talked about Ivo and Victoria, my thoughts wandered to my childhood holidays in Torremolinos, Spain, where we had visited them a couple of times. There were afternoons in their lush garden when I was about four. I'd wear a yellow life vest and float in a tiny square pool while Ivo sat in a chair, watching me with his tired eyes. When Victoria sent us back to our hotel for a *siesta*, I curled up in my cot, across from my parents, holding the sleeve of my sweater against my nose. I inhaled and sighed contentedly; I loved the smell of Ivo's smoke. In the afternoons, we walked into town and sat together in outdoor cafes, the grown-ups drinking *café con leche* while I sipped bubbly orange Fanta and slid my spoon through a smooth *flan*.

By the time I was twelve, Uncle Ivo was dying of lung cancer. My mom left me in Colorado and flew to Spain to help take care of him during his final days. For many years Ivo had been deeply immersed in reading and writing political articles; he spent each night in his study. Once Ivo was called to the police station to help translate for a young Croatian man, a stowaway who escaped from Yugoslavia. He and Victoria let the young man stay with them. They fed him and helped him find work as a car mechanic. Each month they wrote letters to my mother and father, updating them on their daily lives, how they were looking for new shoes for Marijana, and describing their beloved mutt Cuki's latest misadventures. They always expressed their concern for my mom and dad's health.

They wrote to my father: *From your letter we learn Marijana's health is O.K., and from Marijana's letter that you are also very well. We are glad about that. To you there is no need to give you advices; we are sure you keep your exercises and follow medical treatment. We hope Marijana is taking care of her health too. Do not let her to go too thin. Better good health, than Hollywood look (stupid look).* Ivo signed off, *Well dear children, it is about all. Do write to us very soon. As ever, love to you both. Ivo*

After Ivo's death, my mom returned home to Colorado. She told my dad he had died in a great deal of pain, but she said nothing to me.

Several months after Uncle Ivo's death, a young man knocked down Aunt Victoria in the street when he stole her purse. She lay in a hospital bed, dazed. One day the doctor walked in, startled to find her lying in bed naked, her short round body atop the sheets. Her memory had been shaken, but she looked at the doctor and said, "This is the way I came into the world, this is the way I will leave it." She died the next day, and my mom lost her last Croatian relative.

Gradually we left my mom's history and ventured across Đurđa's and Pero's Croatian stories. At one point, I glanced at my watch and realized we had been there for eight hours; we had been lost in the whirlwind of memory. My head was spinning. I felt euphoric and exhausted. There was so much to process. We took photographs together. Đurđa grabbed my hand and held it strongly as if she wanted to give me something. We hugged and kissed beside their iron gate.

The next evening we were once again summoned to Đurđa and Pero's house, along with about twenty-five other Croatians, to celebrate New Year's Eve. There were Croatians who had married other Croatians with their grown children, some who spoke Croatian, some who only spoke Spanish.

There was a Spanish woman whose Croatian husband had recently died. Anuša smiled brightly, beckoning me to stand by her side. Everyone crowded around a table covered with food and softly began repeating the Lord's prayer in Croatian, then again in Spanish.

We ate outside on the terrace, overlooking the lights of Caracas. When midnight grew closer, everyone began counting grapes. Twelve, Anuša told me. "You have to eat twelve just before midnight." A Venezuelan tradition? A Croatian tradition? Before I had a chance to ask, Pero handed me a glass of champagne. He scurried around, making sure everyone had a glass. Đurđa's son held a transistor radio next to his ear, so that we would know the exact moment one year ended and another began.

Everyone stood up and looked toward the lights of Caracas. Đurđa's son shouted: "¡*Diez, nueve, ocho, siete*," and people joined in, clapping to the count. "*Seis, cinco, cuatro, tres, dos, uno*!" The Caracas night sky burst open with fireworks: red, blue, and yellow, fans of glimmering lights opening, again and again and again. Cracks and pops could be heard from every direction. Dogs barked. People shouted. I breathed in the sulfur and smoke, clouding the air. I stood beside my dad and we watched the lights together. A woman standing beside us explained that the fireworks lasted so long, people had to give their dogs sedatives. Đurđa, Pero, and Anuša came up to us saying, "¡*Feliz año*! ¡*Feliz año*! ¡*Feliz año*!" kissing us on each cheek. My father bent down so that they could reach him.

After the fireworks quieted, everyone crowded into the living room and pulled chairs into a circle around the coffee table. People were sitting, and standing, and wandering from the kitchen to the living room. I talked with Anuša, reciting aloud the few Croatian expressions that I knew. She was impressed by my accent and added that she had been talking with the others and they were amazed how Croatian I seemed. I blinked. She said, "You may not speak the language or know a lot about being Croatian, but you are so Croatian." I wondered if she meant the way I talked, or my expressions, or gestures, or the way I felt at ease with them. I grew up in a place where I only knew one Croatian: my mom.

Discovering Đurđa, Pero, and Anuša made me feel as if I were meeting long-lost relatives, ones that I'd most likely never see again. I wondered what my life would have been like if my parents had stayed in Caracas. I wondered would it have been easier to recover from my mom's death if I'd had more relatives? Here people called their friends' parents "uncle" and "aunt" even if they weren't related. They made you feel like you were part of a larger community.

Soon Croatian folk songs filled the room. People started to sing. Some argued about what region produced the best folk songs. Dalmatia won! Anuša told us that in the old days, Pero had organized a Croatian folk dancing group that performed all over Caracas. She rolled her eyes and laughed when she said she could still remember the time they stayed up all night, making the traditional costumes "from scratch." I remembered the four Croatian dolls in regional costumes that my mom had given me: dolls with braided hair, wearing white skirts, red aprons, and flat moccasin-like shoes.

Pero came around with a bottle of *šljivovica* and a tray of empty shot glasses. I knelt beside another Croatian woman who sat in a chair, while her grown daughter leaned against her, draping her arms over her mother's shoulders. I used to do the same. I longed for the way I would lean against my mom, or feel her hand in mine, or how when I was a girl, I would dance with her in the kitchen, my arms holding her waist, my small feet resting atop of hers, we swayed while she hummed the theme song from *Dr. Zhivago*.

Pero handed me an empty glass and filled it with the clear fiery liquid. I took a tiny sip and grimaced. My throat burned, the hair on my arms rose, and everyone laughed. "*Mira*," the Croatian mom said to me, and swallowed hers in one gulp. Quick. I raised my eyebrows and smiled. Đurđa demonstrated how it was done with her drink, and Anuša explained, "It's easier if you just drink it all at once. In one motion. Then it's smooth." Pero nodded his head in encouragement. I took a deep breath and held the glass up to my lips and swallowed it all at once. Smooth, with a kick at the end, and a slight burn. I put down the glass, and everyone cheered, clapping their hands loudly. I was taken off guard; I started to laugh. It felt as though someone lifted something off my shoulders, something I had been carrying for a long time.

Slatka Mala Marijana started playing on the record player. From across the room, my dad caught my eye. I heard him say urgently, "Katie, listen, Mama's song!" He pointed to the ceiling. I nodded. My mom's song. She used to sing this Dalmatian folk song. "One heavenly May night, a young man waits to meet Marijana, sweet little Marijana, for their first date. He waits while darkness falls all around him, while Marijana is sleeping alone and doesn't know that he's there. He waits until midnight passes, Marijana still doesn't come. He sits beneath a palm tree, his eyes closing, waiting for the day he's longing for."

A distinguished old man in a dark suit stood up and sang, harmonizing with the two old men sitting on each side of him. Their heads moved gently to the rhythm. They gestured with their hands, palms to the ceiling, while they sang. Women were swaying. Pero tossed his head back for the refrain. Everyone sang, even my dad, whose dark eyes grew shiny. I mouthed the words until I found my voice, and then I sang the chorus with them, *O Ma-ri-ja-na, slatka, mala, Ma-ri-ja-na, tebe ću čekat ja, dok svane dan...Oh Marijana, sweet, little Marijana, I'll be waiting for you until dawn comes...* My eyes wandered from face to face. Everything blurred in the soft light of the room.

When she died, I felt myself disappearing along with her. I needed her to exist, and so I searched for her. My mom used to say to me, "You're all that I have." And with those words she erased her past. I wondered if I carried her stories in my body. As I sang, I could hear her voice within my voice, and I was filled with the awareness of all the clues she had spread throughout my childhood, so that I could, someday, put them together. Something opened inside me, the realization that imagination connected us the most through life, and through death. I said to her, I come from the stories you never told me.

20 CROATIAN DAUGHTER

While I was stumbling through my research, I'd met Dr. Vedran Deletis, who by chance, worked at a hospital at the end of my street. And years later, it was Vedran who helped me plan my journey to Croatia. He helped me find a place to stay in Zagreb and insisted that I stop and visit his family on the island of Hvar.

In his village of Stari Grad, I'd walked over the red earth of the vineyard where Vedran hoped to make his own wine one day. I plucked tiny, sweet green grapes from the old vines. I sat on their shady terrace with Vedran's elderly father and his grown children, sipping Hvar wine, eating sweet yellow figs, crusty bread, *blitva*, fresh sardines that my mom would have loved, and the best cheese I'd ever tasted from the island of Pag.

In their two-hundred-year-old house, the green shutters of my third-story bedroom window opened out to the innermost portion of the port. Sailboats drifted in. Church bells rang. At dusk, swallows darted up and down under the eaves of the roof. Pensioners and tourists strolled beneath my window. Dogs roamed freely. No cars drove through the old part of town. The waterfront promenade was lined with a bakery, a butcher shop, an art gallery, and restaurants. People sat at outdoor cafes past midnight, while children chased each other over the ancient, polished white stones.

I wandered through the villages where Vedran and his wife Vinka had spent their childhoods. I watched tiny crabs crawling over the warm rocks. I hiked alongside the hills, stepping on dried pine needles that covered the trails. As I discovered hidden coves beside the translucent sea, I thought about what it must feel like to stay in the same house each summer where your family has lived for centuries.

The final week of my trip, Vedran and Vinka took me to see Anuša. From their house in Stari Grad, we drove across the island of Hvar, past charred trees from recent forest fires, through vineyards and isolated villages. We took the ferry to the mainland, and then drove through the winding roads along the Dalmatian Coast to Zaostrog, where Anuša was visiting her sister. It had been three years since I first met her in Caracas. Many Croatians who live abroad return to Croatia in the summertime. I had written Anuša in Caracas and asked if I could visit her during her summer holidays. She responded warmly, and we decided that I'd spend my final week with her.

From the car I saw her standing on the roadside. I leaned forward between the seats, and said, "That's Anuša!" to Vedran and Vinka. Anuša held an open umbrella; she leaned toward the roadway and squinted her eyes as she searched for us. Her summer dress blew in the Dalmatian wind. As soon as she caught sight of us in the car, she waved. I felt instant relief and sudden shyness. We were strangers in some way—we had only met a few times—yet we were linked together.

Outside the car, there were introductions, a rush of Croatian and laughter. We had gotten lost; Vedran had written down the wrong house number. I braced myself to say goodbye. I expected Vinka and Vedran to be on their way. They still had a long way to drive in order to visit their daughter in Dubrovnik, but we were all quickly ushered down the outdoor stairs to the side entrance of the house. Vinka and Vedran would stay for coffee; there was always time for coffee in Croatia. I sensed they also wanted to get to know Anuša, so that they knew I would be safe.

Anuša served coffee and pastries on a tray, and we sat in the living room with her dignified sister Dolores, who had an aura of gentleness. A slowness unfolded as it usually did when Croatians sat together, eating, drinking, and talking. A sense as if we had all the time in the world, a sensation I struggled to find in America. Dolores sat in the middle of the couch. She adjusted her large glasses and smiled as she spoke with Vinka and Vedran. I wondered if the portrait above her, a dignified man dressed in a suit and tie, was her husband. Vedran gazed at it too; he looked surprised. He recognized the man as one of his medical school professors in Sarajevo. It was Dolores's husband.

Dolores explained that during the war, Serbian soldiers came to take away her husband, but a neighbor, a good Serbian friend, talked them out of it. They knew it was a matter of time so they fled their house, leaving everything behind. "My rings, my pictures, everything," she said, her tired eyes gazing at us sadly. I spun my mother's white-gold wedding ring around my index finger, as Dolores continued to tell us what happened. The Serbian soldiers returned with a truck and took everything from their house. Then it was destroyed. Finally they escaped from the city. Not long afterward, her husband died. A heart attack. Dolores pressed her lips together. And we waited in the mournful silence.

I was thoughtful as I sat with them, only now was I learning about the Bosnian and Croatian wars for independence. Entire families had been trapped in the shattered city of Sarajevo. Those unable to escape were forced to improvise a life within the ruins. By day they dodged Serb sniper-fire and at night awoke to the thunder of artillery shelling, and mortar bombs that came from the surrounding hills and mountains. They walked by the dead left on the street and they shivered in the aching cold in unheated apartments. Each day, they waited in line for bread; they pushed wheelbarrows to collect firewood, books, cardboard, furniture, anything to heat their homes riddled with holes and blown-out windows. They washed clothes in basins of rainwater. They peered out apartment windows and saw flames and smoke curling into the sky; they walked by gutted cars, burnt-out houses, and scorched rooftops. They waited to fill their plastic jugs at the only tap for clean water. They stood outside, leaning against a wall, smoking a cigarette, hoping for some country to intervene. They buried their sons and daughters, mothers and fathers. Amid the sniper fire.

So many children who were forced to stay in Sarajevo were injured or killed. It happened as their stomachs growled with hunger, as they searched for fresh water with their brothers, as they hid in the cellar, as they curled up on the couch and took a nap, as they held their mother's hand and crossed a street, as they kicked a ball and played before bedtime.

The war seemed so far from this place by the sea, but there were echoes of it, even in this room.

We waved as Vinka and Vedran drove away. Anuša and I said goodbye to her sister and went back to her apartment in the seaside town of Makarska. For years she saved and worked extra teaching jobs in Caracas so that she could buy this place.

Now she came to Croatia every summer. In Makarska, she could be close to her sister and nieces, and she had a place for her children and grandchildren to visit, where they could rediscover the Croatian parts of themselves.

Anuša fled the former Yugoslavia at sixteen and had lived in Caracas ever since. I could see how she blended the Venezuelan and Croatian parts of herself, just as my mom had blended the American, South American, Spanish, and Croatian parts of herself. Anuša rolled her eyes dramatically when she told me the discussions that she had with the carpenter about modernizing the kitchen and bathrooms in her Makarska apartment. "He told me, 'But what do you need a bigger sink for? What do you need more cupboards for?' And I had to fight with him to put in my dishwasher!" My mom also appreciated the modern conveniences of America. "I can go to one store and buy all my groceries," she told me.

In Makarska, we spent our mornings on Anuša's balcony, overlooking the town, the red-tiled roofs, church steeples, the Adriatic sea, and the forested Sveti Petar Peninsula. A sailboat glided into the port, and Anuša pointed to it and joked, "My boyfriend is coming to pick me up."

I laughed. "Anuša, do you sit out here all the time?" I asked, standing up, leaning over the railing, looking back at the steep, craggy gray mountains looming behind us.

"Every morning, every afternoon," she said, contentedly. She showed me Biokovo Mountain, and I realized that it was the deep contrast between the sea and the mountains that made Makarska so breathtaking.

"Your mother," Anuša said to me softly, "was an extraordinary woman. I didn't know what she'd gone through until I read your manuscript." She shook her head sadly from side to side, pressing her lips together for a moment before she continued. "Now I feel as if I understand the woman

I knew in Caracas. You see, she wasn't open with us, she didn't tell us everything like the other Croatian girls. She was more..." Anuša motioned her hands inward, toward her chest..."reserved."

"She had to be that way, careful, because...because of everything she went through, everything that happened in her life." I felt protective of my mom and wanted Anuša to understand that my mom was open, in an unexpected sort of way.

"I see that now," she said with a steady gaze.

Before I'd left New York, through e-mail we'd agreed that I should send my manuscript to her, so that she could help me. In New York, Vedran had let me print out a copy at his office. I didn't own a printer. Then he'd driven me to Kinko's to get it bound. He parked on a side street and let me wait in his white Volkswagen. "It will be easier for her to read," he explained as he stepped out of the car. I looked up at him and said, "She will be the first Croatian woman to read it."

Out the window I watched cars inching forward on the side street. Klapa music filled the car, soft a capella music, men's voices harmonizing peacefully, taking me away from this crowded New York City street. I thought back to the day when I first met Vedran in his hospital office. He'd graciously cleared the papers from his round table and offered me a cappuccino. When we were both seated, I nervously attempted to describe my research. "I can't explain exactly what I'm looking for, but I'll know it when I find it, if that makes any sense." He scratched his short gray beard for a moment, and then peered at me through his small metal-rimmed glasses with great curiosity.

And so we began. In the evenings, he helped me translate letters, Croatian nursery rhymes, folk songs, Tito's slogans. He found old photographs for me, and began recounting some of his own childhood memories. He was born eleven years after my mother, but it was close enough; there were common memories, he knew his parents' stories, his wife's stories, and he found time to tell me things no one else had. He helped me travel into my mother's unreachable past. Many times during our conversations, he'd have a faraway gaze, then look at me and say, "Oh Katarina, you make me think of things I haven't thought about in a long time."

When my dad came across the only letter my mom had received from her grandmother, he quickly mailed a copy to me. It surprised both of us that the letter even existed; her grandmother had only a third-grade education. Usually a neighbor wrote for her. My mom never mentioned Baka's letter, yet she kept it all her life. The evening I opened my mailbox and found my dad's envelope, I ran to Vedran's office. I had waited my whole life to hear my great-grandmother's voice.

We sat by the round table and Vedran began translating. As was his custom, he went line by line, reading the Croatian first, then explaining what it meant in English. I scribbled it all down onto a yellow legal pad. It was a slow but exquisite process because it gave me a chance to absorb the emotion of the words. As he neared the end of the letter, I felt a ringing sensation throughout my whole body.

I stopped writing and wept. Vedran looked up, concerned. I bowed my head. When I could speak again, I asked hoarsely, "How could I know what she was like? I gave her the same words that she says in this letter."

Vedran leaned back in his chair, interlacing his fingers. He had spent his career mapping the brain. In a steady voice, he said that perhaps we are connected in ways that we can't even conceive of. Collective history, collective unconsciousness, collective memory… I had carried the legacy of my mother's losses even though she had never spoken a word of them to me.

At the Makarska Riviera, I swam in the sea, pausing every once in a while to tread water so that I could marvel at the view of the gray, rocky Biokovo Mountains rising up like a mirage. In the clear water, a school of tiny fish swam below my feet. I dipped downward gracefully, submerging myself in the water; my feet fluttering behind me, then I arched upward to surface, to the air, to the sky.

I climbed the iron ladder and crawled onto a warm slab of cement that covered the rocks. We reclined lazily on our beach towels. The sun quickly evaporated the water on my skin.

"Catherine, you don't seem American at all," Anuša said suddenly, grinning.

"Really?" I said, pleased. "What do you mean?"

"Oh, I don't know…I guess, you seem so open. You want to know and experience everything Croatian. Not everyone is like that."

As each day passed in Croatia, I felt myself changing. My voice grew softer, the rhythm of my words slowing, the tone rising, the accent leaning, as if I were absorbing the geography of memory. Vinka had said to me in the car on the way to Makarska, "I think you're ready to be 100 percent Croatian!" I laughed. I knew I would never feel completely Croatian, or American for that matter, but the more I had pieced together my mom's life, the more I felt as if I were striking a balance between the two.

I closed my eyes and felt the Makarska sun against my face. I didn't miss anything, I didn't long for anything. I had let go of everything to come here.

"*Gledaj*, Catherine. Look, over there," Anuša said, motioning toward the water. She raised her dark sunglasses. I looked over and watched a large white-haired man swimming breaststroke, his round chin dipping in and out of the water, his granddaughter paddling beside him, splashing. Anuša sighed contentedly. "You see why I love it here. See how an old man can swim and be happy? This is the life!"

Now I understood why it was so important for Anuša and Vedran to return home to Croatia each year. They had to restore a part of themselves, remember who they were when they were home. Where they would walk the same streets, visit the same friends, the same markets, the same graves, drink the same wine, bite into the same crusty bread. Repetition was home. Returning to the familiar and re-creating it makes us into who we are. This was something my mom didn't really have. She had lived in so many countries, the meaning of home had disintegrated. For her, returning to Croatia was walking through a minefield, her parents wasting away to tuberculosis, the violence of WWII, her own battle with TB, surviving and escaping communism, and her grandmother dying just before my mom could bring her to America. Perhaps that's why my mom didn't feel the pull homeward. But strangely I felt it for her.

Before I'd left Zagreb, I'd walked up the hill to Mirogoj cemetery. I stopped at one of the flower stands in front of the enormous walls, with copper domes powdered with verdigris that enclosed the cemetery. I bought flowers and one candle. The flower woman pressed a box of matches into my hand. "*Hvala*," I said, then followed the groups of families through the arching entrance and entered a serene forest of graves. I walked beside the avenues of trees, cypress and pine, chestnut and oak. I passed pavilions and mausoleums. Some graves had elaborate bronze statues: Jesus after the crucifixion, his thin body draped over Mary's knee, angels with their palms reaching skyward.

It was a place where you could easily get lost; it was enormous. I had only been there three times in my life, but I knew exactly where I was going. The last time, I had etched its location in my memory. As soon as I reached the towering golden cross, I turned right toward the trees, scanning the names on each gravestone until I came upon theirs, *Marija, Katica, Anton*—my grandparents and great-grandmother. I placed the flowers in the gray marble vase, struck the match, lit the candle, and sat beside them.

This was the first time I had ever visited their grave alone, and this was the first time that I could see them clearly. I could hear the things they had said. I told my grandparents and great-grandmother, "Yesterday, I walked through your house in Oriovac. I saw where my mom was born. I put my feet in the Sava River." I sat on their grave and talked to them. They were lying beneath me now—bone dust, no longer ghosts haunting my mother's sleep.

At the outdoor fruit market Anuša taught me that when bees were buzzing around the pale yellowish-green figs, they would taste good. She bought fresh fish, *trilja*, to grill for us. In the main square, she showed me the eighteenth century church, Sveti Marko, where she went to mass each week. Leisurely we walked through the square, pigeons flying up in the air. We walked through narrow streets, over the polished white stones. In the evening, we sat at a sidewalk café, spooning deliciously creamy *šumsko voće* (wild berry) ice cream into our mouths as we watched people stroll beside the port.

At home, in her apartment, I pulled out my little album, and we looked through the photographs that I carried all this way to show her. Anuša sighed, "Your mother was beautiful, like a movie star."

Anuša took me to the Internet café so that I could write

my dad and René. Since we couldn't afford to call each other, the three of us decided that we would communicate through email. For René, who was busy with teaching, writing, taking care of our dog, and who occasionally enjoyed facing an existential crisis of solitude, this wasn't so bad. Oftentimes he didn't even bother to answer my emails. But this was the first time I had gone so long without speaking to my father. Since my mother died, this was the first summer I hadn't visited him. Still, he had encouraged me to go to Croatia. "I think you should go, Katie. It will be good for you, good for your writing." We both understood that we would have to sacrifice our time together. In a recent email he'd written, *I miss our phone conversations very much and feel lost without them. When the phone rings, I think at first it might be you and then I remember where you are.*

One evening, Anuša handed me the phone. I looked at her surprised. "What's this for?" I asked.

"My gift. Tonight you will call your father."

Jugo, the warm southern wind, came. Anuša told me that *jugo* makes Dalmatians moody. It felt as if we were walking through a warm bath the entire day. It was a silly, slow, giddy feeling. In the evening, we stayed up late making strudel, chopping green apples, draining the juice, wrapping them in thin layers of dough, placing three long rolls, nestled together in the pan that we slipped into the oven. The entire apartment was warm and smelled of baking apples. With the back of her hand, Anuša pushed her short, blond-highlighted hair away from her forehead. She explained that we would bring the strudel to her sister's house tomorrow. Her eyes flashed and she added, "I bet Dave and René wish they were here to eat my good cooking!"

We sat on her sister Dolores's terrace overlooking the sea. We could see the tip of Hvar, ferries steadily traveling back and forth. Dolores's daughters, Alica and Ines, arrived. Ines, a pharmacist in Makarska, had Anuša's nose and lively brown eyes. Alica, a professor in Zagreb, had Dolores's cheeks and gentle demeanor. I noticed that all of us had strong arms and broad shoulders like my mom.

Ines and Alica were easy-going and friendly. Right away they wanted to know about my travels. All the women sat around the table, listening intently as I told them about my adventures, finding my mom's house, finding Brestovac, the TB sanatorium where my mom stayed as a teenager. They laughed, they sighed, their eyes watered. Afterward, Anuša shook her head. "Catherine, my goodness! I don't know how you did all those things by yourself. Going to the sanatorium, all on your own…it could have been dangerous." Her brow furrowed.

"I wasn't afraid," I told her calmly, and in my mind I said, I wasn't alone.

We spoke about Sarajevo, and Dolores's house there. She explained that she had never been back and she had no desire to return there. Alica and Ines told me that they did go back to Sarajevo once after the war. They went to the place where their house once stood. It was a pile of rubble. "Nothing left," Alica said, drawing a straight line with her palms flat to the table. "Yes," Ines said, "but, in the middle of the rubble, there was a small tree growing."

The next day I went down to the pebbly beach below the house with Alica and Ines. I found broken sea urchin shells. The round shells were thin and fragile. Beige dots spiraled out from the center in perfect lines. As I picked up broken, cracked sea-urchin shells, Ines offered to get me a live sea urchin from the sea. "There were so many at the beginning of the summer, but then we brought them to the shore so that no one would step on them," she explained. She could find one, then we could leave it outside to dry, pluck off all the spines, and then I would have a perfect one to take home. Waves splashed against the rocks. I stood with my feet barely in the water and watched as she looked beside the large rocks that barricaded this tiny cove. She carefully pulled one out and set him on a rock. His black spines wriggled in the air.

I had a sinking feeling. Quickly I said, "It's okay. I don't want him to die. I don't mind having a broken one." She nodded, and carefully dropped him back in the sea. She and Alica jumped back into the water.

I picked up a stone by my foot and held it in my hand. It was chalky and filled my palm. White with a tinge of orange, the stones change color when the waves sweep over them. I looked around and noticed each stone had a unique fossil-like design, lines, swirls, and holes. I placed the stone on a rock; it would be on my desk at home.

I walked out into the Adriatic, and swam, joining Alica and Ines. The three of us swam toward the village. The coast was lined with pine forests. On the hillside, there were olive groves and vineyards. As we swam, we ran into a little boy sitting on a raft, a neighbor Ines knew. The sisters joked around with him, playfully. In the summertime, Ines told me that each evening she swam to the village and back.

We turned, swimming in the opposite direction, away from the village. Seagulls flew overhead. The three of us stayed in the water for a long time, swimming, floating, treading water, talking. Tiny fish brushed my calves. Sometimes I dove underwater and listened; electrical sparks and buzzing, it sounded alive. When I came up for air, I tasted the salt on my tongue. I'd never been in the sea for so long.

Every once in a while, Ines and I treaded water. We chatted about different things. I began to laugh for no reason. Ines laughed with me. We felt the blissful drunkenness of swimming. I laughed so hard that I began to sink a little, my chin dipping down, swallowing a little water, choking, sputtering, until I flipped over and floated on my back, staring at the paintbrush clouds against the Adriatic sky.

On the terrace, I stretched out on the long stone bench. The stones were warm beneath my bare belly. Anuša appeared from the house with a camera and took my picture. Afterward, she said, "*Siesta*, sleep, take *siesta*," and disappeared back into the house. It was a relief that there was nowhere to go, nothing to do, no one waiting for me. I listened to the waves hitting the rocks and fell asleep. When I awoke, all the women were wandering around in their bathing suits, going to shower, changing, sitting outside with wet hair, smoking, planning what we would eat next. I am in a house full of Croatian women, I told myself in amazement.

Anuša asked if I wanted a *smokva*, a fig. Before this trip, I had never eaten a fig. She pointed to a tree beside the terrace. "Go pick some."

"It's okay?"

"Why not?"

I walked to the branches and held a yellow-skinned fig. I tugged once and it tumbled into my palm, as if it were meant to be there. From the tree into my mouth, I bit down into the tender skin and tasted its sweetness.

After I finished, I said, "Anuša…"

"Mmmm?"

"I'll never forget this. This was an incredible day!"

"I think you've had quite a few of them," she answered, smiling.

In the bathroom back at Anuša's apartment in Makarska, I felt a twinge of something as I looked at myself in the mirror. I'd just taken a hot shower, gotten dressed, and I was brushing my wet hair. I set the brush on the counter. I looked different. My face, my body, everything. My skin was suntanned, my brown eyes looked greener, my hair was sun streaked, my expression seemed lighter. I felt more of who I am, more relaxed, more the girlhood Catherine, more like my mother.

"Catherine," Anuša called up to me. She had made us dinner. As we ate, we could hear the wind outside. *Bura*, the cool northeasterly wind, descended from the mountains upon the town; summer was ending.

After dinner, I sat on the couch, and Anuša placed my manuscript on the coffee table before me. I smiled and picked it up. She sat down in a chair next to me.

"Oh Catherine, I *en*joyed reading this," she said, enunciating each word. "Each evening, I looked forward to reading more."

I felt vulnerable and glanced down at the polished wood floor; I placed my hands on top of my manuscript. I breathed in, raising my shoulder slightly. Anuša spoke, while I gently flipped through the pages, not reading, but feeling the words. With a gleam in her eye she said, "I didn't know that I have *blue* eyes."

I laughed because clearly her eyes were brown. She told me how my stories made her think of her own journey to South America. How, on the decks of the ship, she and her father met a priest who lent them his Spanish dictionary, and that was how they first began to learn the language. Something welled up in my chest.

"Catherine, I could never tell stories the way you do," Anuša said to me.

I waved my hand through the air and said, "That's not true. You've been telling me amazing stories ever since I got here. You just need to write them down." I admired Anuša's passion for life and most of all, the way she allowed people to see that passion.

"Would you read me the end?" Anuša said.

"What?" I looked at her, surprised.

"Would you read me the end of the last chapter?" she asked again.

"I don't know.... I don't know if I can," I said. I held my breath for a moment. I looked straight into her brown eyes. "Okay," I said, turning the pages. I read her the end of the last chapter, about all the Venezuelan Croatians singing *Slatka Mala Marijana* on that Caracas New Years' Eve, and when I got to the final lines, I stopped. "I'm sorry," I said, my voice wavering; my hands trembled with emotion. Her eyes watered. I looked back at the words on the page and said them aloud, my voice coming and going, half-crying, half-reading. I finished.

We sat in silence for a moment. I was suddenly aware that we had come to the end of my story together. Where there was nothing before, now there was something. It felt real and true. And Anuša made certain that I wasn't alone.

Anuša leaned forward and said, "Catherine, I have a surprise for you." Her voice was musical, her eyes sparkled with anticipation. She jumped up and went over to the stereo on the mantle. She pushed play. *Slatka Mala Marijana* filled the room. It was a slightly groovy '70s version of my mom's song; it made me smile.

"How did you?" I asked. It was an old song. Everyone knew it, but it was hard to find. I didn't even own a copy myself, and earlier in the week I'd mentioned that I was looking for it.

"Well," she said, "I had to go to several places and finally I found it!"

"I can't believe it!"

She smiled proudly. "It's for you," she said, her arms outstretched. "Come, come dance with me."

I laughed and went to her. She reached for my hands, and we swayed, our arms making a circle. I thought to myself, this was something my mom would have done. All at once, Anuša's face grew flushed. Her eyes were bright. She covered her face with one hand and sobbed. She took a little step back and said, "Your mother. She would have loved to be here, to see you now, to see everything you've done. Maybe…I'm here for her."

In bed that night, as my eyes closed, I felt the sensation of the waves again. It felt strong and real as if I were still in the Adriatic, swimming, my body rising and falling. I floated, letting myself be carried. It felt as if I were part of the sea, part of the water, we were one, endless, and whole.

House in Oriovac

Baka and Aunt Victoria

Katica

Victoria

Anton

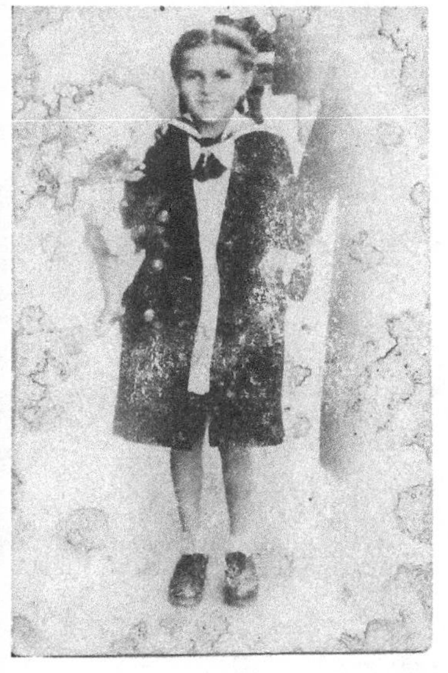

Little Marijana

Marijana and her parents

Baka

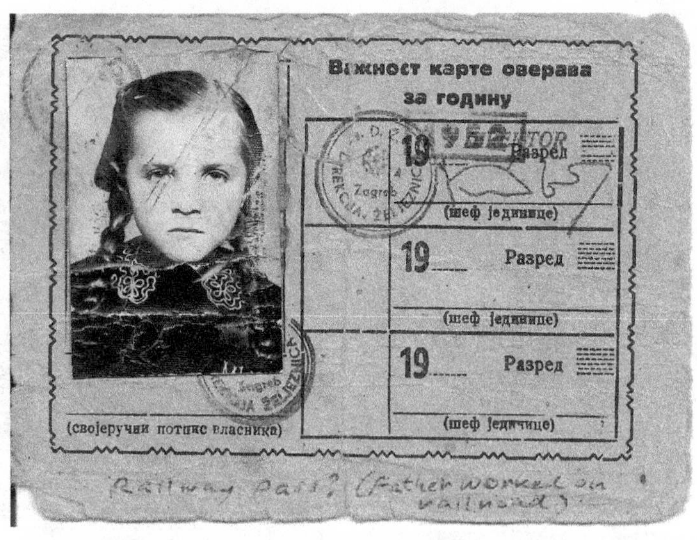

Важност карте оверава
за годину

19 Разред
(шеф јединице)

19____ Разред
(шеф јединице)

19____ Разред
(шеф јединице)

(својеручни потпис власника)

Zagreb

Railway pass? (Father worked on railroad.)

Marijana Railway Pass

Dave in the mountains

Dave in Venezeula

Marijana and Dave in Caracas

Marijana's Wedding

Dave and Marijana's Wedding

Marijana

Catherine in Hvar

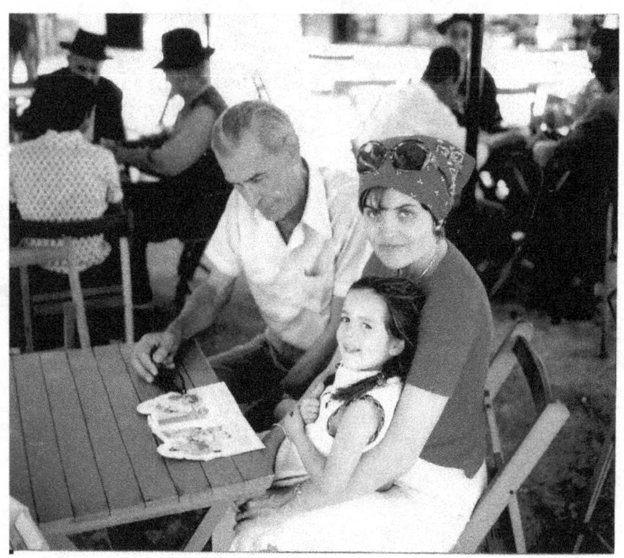

Uncle Ivo, Marijana and Catherine

Catherine in Torremolinos Spain

Milan Italy

ACKNOWLEDGMENTS

The road to writing this book has been long and hard, like running a never-ending marathon where there was lots of laughter and tears. There were years when I did not write at all, and there were years when I found my way back to my mother's story and was completely absorbed once again. Each time I began working, I was astonished how my mom's story kept giving me gifts. It pushed me to learn new things, gave me courage to talk to strangers, challenged me to dig into complex impossible-to-write-about history, revealed insights that I never considered, forced me to ask for help over and over again, and connected me with wonderful people, who so generously gave their time.

I am grateful to every single person who helped me on this journey. The following are only a few. A big thanks goes to Lis Harris and Richard Locke from Columbia University, who helped me claim my writing voice. Jennifer Poggiali, my determined librarian, lifted me out of research despair and helped me with the final wave. Janet Steen stepped in to help me with copyedits. Thanks to Kerry Ellis for her patience and beautiful design work. Thanks to my yoga family Jason Brown, Frances Taylor-Brown, Lynda Sing, Ruthie Lawyer, and Nikita Maxwell, who helped me get back on my feet after my dad's death, so I could find my way back to a writing life. Thanks to Heidi Frieze for helping me begin to understand the way my brain works. Thanks to Jeanie Snyder and Anna Peterson for their enthusiasm through the hard days of trying to finish the first draft. Thanks to Heloisa DeMelo who continues to champion all my artistic endeavors. Thank you to Maki Hirose for my author photo. Thank you to Veena Siddharth, Megan Franzen, Noemi Salinas, Emily Aita, and Penelope Katsaras for their steadfast friendship, and for giving me confidence. Thanks to my incredible Colorado childhood friends who have cheered me from the sidelines for years: Becky Holm, Terri Mairley, Kate Leahy Hein, Suzanne Leahy, and Teresa McFarlane. Thanks to Silvia, who helped me remember my Spanish and supported me in motherhood, so that I could write. Thanks to my mother-in-law Marie Vasicek who made sure her two favorite artists had a home.

A huge thanks to Maurizio Najt for all of his dedication and determination to help me get the Spanish right, and to his mother who happened to have actually traveled on the same ship (different years) as my mom did to Argentina. Thanks to my friends Barbara Parisi and Angela Wade for helping me summon the courage to continue on, and sorting out all the last-minute logistics. Thanks to my dear Croatian friends who made it their mission to improve my pronunciation of the Croatian for the recording of the book. Thanks to John Stefanac who helped me chase down the names and dates of my great-grandmother, Marija Jakovac's family. Thanks to Ivana Kordic Jelić and Zdravko who helped me navigate my mom's birth village. Thanks to Tončika and Ružica who loved my mom dearly and stepped into the past with me. A special thanks goes to Vinka Deletis and Katarina Deletis Tomaš who shared their home in Stari Grad with me and made me feel Croatian. Thanks to Đurđa and Pero Hrgetić who, in Caracas, threw open their doors and shared their memories. Thanks to Anuša Markov who did so much to help us find our way in Caracas and took care of me in Makarska. Her energy and resilience continue to inspire me.

Thanks to Brenda Lin and Elizabeth Seay for all their help developing this project by encouraging me to keep finding my way back to this manuscript when motherhood, caregiving, teaching, and life pulled me away. A heartfelt thanks to Jeanne Even for all her openness and getting me through the darkest of times.

Thanks especially to my cousin Ray Wampler and his wife Ann Romero, who never once wavered in their support and continue to advise and help me. An enormous thanks to Steve Wyckoff who encouraged me to keep trying to publish despite years of rejections and came to the rescue just in time for my final wave of edits.

I am eternally grateful to Dr. Vedran Deletis who made it possible to finally get a full draft completed. He made an enormous impact on my Croatian identity. A huge thanks to Courtney Angela Brkic, who inspired and advised me, and absolutely refused to let me give up. Long ago, in my very first creative writing class with Louise DeSalvo at Hunter College, I wrote one of the chapters for this book. Louise changed the course of my life and her writer's spirit still guides me.

Thanks to my wonderful boys, Rafa and Radek, who have taught me so much about seeing the world as a mother and as a child. At the end, they were my constant advisors and were so patient when they would wake up and find me writing. Through all the ups and downs, my husband René has always believed in this book even when I lost faith. Unbeknownst to me, he secretly sent out my manuscript during my "giving up" period. And after years of trying to get my book out there, he is the one who convinced me that I should send it out for one *final* manuscript contest: The Center for Fiction's Christopher Doheny Award.

I was floored when I won. I'm so grateful to The Center for Fiction, Audible.com, and the selection committee. Thanks especially to those who supported me through this final stretch: Kerry Donahue, Jennifer Bassuk, Diana Dapito, Beth Anderson, Mike Scalise, and Michelle Bailat-Jones. I am grateful to the late Christopher Doheny and to his family, and all those who supported this award for manuscripts dealing with serious illness.

An enormous thanks to my writing group: Nita Noveno, Nancy Agabian, and Cynthia Thompson. I cannot express how these writing sisters carried me through the Herculean effort it took to get to this point. I thank them for their love and laughter and daily texts. There is no one else in the world that I'd rather share my rejections with!

This book could not have been written without the full support of my dad, Dave Kapphahn. He answered years of questions, fact checked, proofread, and chased down medical records and other sources. During the final years of his life, his openness, honesty, and fact-based memory helped tremendously. In my mind, I'm handing him a copy of the book now.

Thanks to my mom who never knew me as a writer, but made me believe that I could do the impossible.

Catherine Kapphahn's *Immigrant Daughter: Stories You Never Told Me* received The Center for Fiction's Christopher Doheny Award. Her writing has received multiple grants from the Queens Council on the Arts. Her essays have appeared in *Astoria Magazine*, the Feminist Press Anthology *This is the Way We Say Goodbye*, *CURE Magazine*, and *SalonZine*. She has earned a B.A. from Hunter College and an M.F.A. in writing from Columbia University. Catherine is an adjunct lecturer at City University of New York at Lehman College in the Bronx, where her students' brave stories continue to inspire her. Catherine is also a yoga teacher. She grew up near the mountains in Colorado and now lives between two bridges in Queens, New York with her husband and two sons.